CAMBRIDGE LIBRARY COLLECTION

Books of endı

Travel an

The history of travel writing dates b
and the Crusaders, and its many th
recreation. Explorers from Columbus to Cook charted lands not previously visited by Western travellers, and were followed by merchants, missionaries, and colonists, who wrote accounts of their experiences. The development of steam power in the nineteenth century provided opportunities for increasing numbers of 'ordinary' people to travel further, more economically, and more safely, and resulted in great enthusiasm for travel writing among the reading public. Works included in this series range from first-hand descriptions of previously unrecorded places, to literary accounts of the strange habits of foreigners, to examples of the burgeoning numbers of guidebooks produced to satisfy the needs of a new kind of traveller - the tourist.

Personal Narrative of a Pilgrimage to El-Medinah and Meccah

The British explorer Sir Richard F. Burton (1821–90) was a colourful and often controversial character. A talented linguist and keen ethnologist, he worked in India during the 1840s as an interpreter and intelligence officer for General Sir Charles Napier, and published several books about his experiences in 1851–2. He first gained celebrity, however, for his adventurous 1853 trip to Mecca, disguised as a pilgrim, which is described in this lively three-volume publication (1855–6). Few Europeans had ever visited the Muslim holy places; one of them was John Lewis Burckhardt, whose 1829 account is also reissued in this series. Volume 1 of Burton's book describes his arrival in Egypt, the weeks he spent in Alexandria and Cairo polishing his linguistic and cultural skills, and how, at the end of Ramadan, he travelled to Suez by camel, and from there by boat to Yanbu al-Bahr.

Personal Narrative of a Pilgrimage to El-Medinah and Meccah

Volume 1: El-Misr

Richard Francis Burton

Cambridge University Press

CAMBRIDGE UNIVERSITY PRESS

Cambridge, New York, Melbourne, Madrid, Cape Town,
Singapore, São Paolo, Delhi, Tokyo, Mexico City

Published in the United States of America by Cambridge University Press, New York

www.cambridge.org
Information on this title: www.cambridge.org/9781108041980

This edition first published 1855
This digitally printed version 2012

ISBN 978-1-108-04198-0 Paperback

The original edition of this book contains a number of colour plates, which have been reproduced in black and white. Colour versions of these images can be found online at www.cambridge.org/9781108041980

R. BURTON DEL^{T} HANHART LITH.

VIEW OF EL MEDINAH.

TAKEN FROM THE HARRAH (OR RIDGE) WEST OF THE TOWN.

PERSONAL NARRATIVE

OF A

PILGRIMAGE TO EL-MEDINAH AND MECCAH.

BY RICHARD F. BURTON,

LIEUTENANT BOMBAY ARMY.

"Our notions of Mecca must be drawn from the Arabians; as no unbeliever is permitted to enter the city, our travellers are silent."—*Gibbon*, chap. 50.

IN THREE VOLUMES.

VOL. I.—EL-MISR.

LONDON:
LONGMAN, BROWN, GREEN, AND LONGMANS.
1855.

LONDON:
A. and G. A. SPOTTISWOODE,
New-street-Square.

أَللَّيْلُ وَالْخَيْلُ وَالْبَيْدَاءُ تَعْرِفُنِي

وَالسَّيْفُ وَالضَّيْفُ وَالْقِرْطَاسُ وَالْقَلَمِ

TO

COLONEL WILLIAM SYKES,

F. R. SOC., M. R. G. SOC., M. R. A. SOC.,

AND LORD RECTOR OF THE MARISCHAL COLLEGE,
ABERDEEN.

I DO not parade your name, my dear Colonel, in the van of this volume, after the manner of that acute tactician who stuck a Koran upon his lance in order to win a battle. Believe me it is not my object to use your orthodoxy as a cover to my heresies of sentiment and science, in politics, political economy and—what not?

But whatever I have done on this occasion,—if I have done any thing,—has been by the assistance of a host of friends, amongst whom you were ever the foremost. And the highest privilege I aim at is this opportunity of publicly acknowledging the multitude of obligations owed to you and to them. Accept, my dear Colonel, this humble return for your kindness, and ever believe me,

The sincerest of your well wishers,

RICHARD F. BURTON.

PREFACE.

The interest just now felt in everything that relates to the East would alone be sufficient to ensure to the author of "El Medinah and Meccah" the favourable consideration of the Reading Public. But when it is borne in mind that since the days of William Pitts of Exeter (A.D. 1678—1688) no European travellers, with the exception of Burckhardt* and Lieut. Burton†, have been able to send us back an account of their travels there, it cannot be doubted but that the present work will be hailed as a welcome addition to our knowledge of these hitherto mysterious *penetralia* of Mahommedan superstition. In fact, El Medinah may be considered

* In 1811.

† Captain Sadlier is not mentioned, as his Frankish dress prevented his entering the city.

almost a virgin theme; for as Burckhardt was prostrated by sickness throughout the period of his stay in the Northern Hejaz, he was not able to describe it as satisfactorily or minutely as he did the southern country,—he could not send a plan of the mosque, or correct the popular but erroneous ideas which prevail concerning it and the surrounding city.

The reader may question the propriety of introducing in a work of description, anecdotes which may appear open to the charge of triviality. The author's object, however, seems to be to illustrate the peculiarities of the people, — to dramatise, as it were, the dry journal of a journey, — and to preserve the tone of the adventures, together with that local colouring in which mainly consists "*l'education d'un voyage.*" For the same reason, the prayers of the "Visitation" ceremony have been translated at length, despite the danger of inducing tedium; they are an essential part of the subject, and cannot be omitted, nor be represented by "specimens."

The extent of the Appendix requires some explanation. Few but literati are aware of the existence of Lodovico Bartema's naïve recital, of the quaint narrative of Jos. Pitts, or of the wild journal of Giovanni Finati. Such extracts have been now made from these writers that the general reader can become acquainted with the adventures and opinions of the different travellers who have visited El Hejaz during a space of 350 years. Thus, with the second volume of Burckhardt's Travels in Arabia, the geographer, curious concerning this portion of the Moslem's Holy Land, possesses all that has as yet been written upon the subject.

The editor, to whom the author in his absence has intrusted his work, had hoped to have completed it by the simultaneous publication of the third volume, containing the pilgrimage to Meccah. The delay, however, in the arrival from India of this portion of the MS. has been such as to induce him at once to publish El Misr and El Medinah. The concluding volume on Meccah is now in the hands of the publisher, and will appear in the autumn of the present year. Meanwhile the Public will not lose sight of the subject of Arabia. Part of El Hejaz has lately been inspected by M. Charles Didier, an eminent name in French literature, and by the Abbé Hamilton,— persuaded, it is believed, by our author to visit Taif and Wady Laymun. Though entirely unconnected with the subjects of Meccah and El Medinah, the account of the Sherif's Court where these gentlemen were received with distinction, and of the almost unknown regions about Jebel Kora, will doubtless be welcomed by the Orientalists and Geographers of Europe.

Mr. Burton is already known by his "History of Sindh." And as if to mark their sense of the spirit of observation and daring evinced by him when in that country, and still more during his late journeyings in Arabia and East Africa, the Geographical Society, through their learned Secretary, Dr. Norton Shaw, have given valuable aid to this work in its progress through the press, supplying maps where necessary to complete the illustrations supplied by the author,—who, it will be perceived, is himself no mean draughtsman.

It was during a residence of many years in India that Mr. Burton had fitted himself for his late undertaking, by acquiring, through his peculiar aptitude for such studies, a thorough acquaintance with various dialects of Arabia and Persia; and, indeed, his Eastern cast of features (*vide* Frontispiece, Vol. II.) seemed already to point him out as the very person of all others best suited for an expedition like that described in the following pages.

It will be observed that in writing Arabic, Hindoostannee, Persian, or Turkish words, the author has generally adopted the system proposed by Sir William Jones and modified by later Orientalists. But when a word (like Fát-háh for Fatihah) has been "stamped" by general popular use, the conversational form has been preferred; and the same, too, may be said of the common corruptions, Cairo, Kadi, &c., which, in any other form, would appear to us pedantic and ridiculous. Still, in the absence of the author, it must be expected that some trifling errors and inaccuracies will have here and there crept in. In justice to others and himself, the Editor, however, feels bound to acknowledge, with much gratitude, that where such or even greater mistakes have been avoided, it has been mainly due to the continued kindness of an Eastern scholar of more than European reputation, — who has assisted in revising the sheets before finally consigning them to the printer.

Let us hope that the proofs now furnished of untiring energy and capacity for observation and research by our author, as well as his ability to bear fatigue and exposure to the most inclement climate, will induce the Governments of this country and of India to provide him with men and means (evidently all that is required for the purpose) to pursue his adventurous and useful career in other countries equally difficult of access, and, if possible, of still greater interest, than the eastern shores of the Red Sea.

T. L. W.

Hampton Court Palace,
June, 1855.

CONTENTS

OF

THE FIRST VOLUME.

CHAPTER VII.

CHAPTER VIII.

CHAPTER IX.

CHAPTER X.

CHAPTER XI.

CHAPTER XII.

CHAPTER XIII.

ERRATA IN THE FIRST VOLUME.

Page	*Line*	*For*	*Read*
65.	27.	harame	harami.
87.	1.	Abyssinian	Abyssinians.
111.	11.	Insak	Imsak.
117.	16.	Zumbak,	Tumbak,
123.	22.	El Hejar	El Hejaz.
"	"	Tazwid	Tajwid.
153.	25.	Nidu	Nidá.
156.	19.	Mautik	Mantik.
"	24.	Isaghuyi	Isaghuji.
159.	13.	Wazíship	Kaziship.
181.	12.	literal	literary.
185.	27.	Sinkee	Sinku.
188.	25.	110*l.*	110 dollars.
204.	14.	Sikandarijah	Sikandariyah.
208.	12.	Shayk	Shaykh.
213.	2.	Jehaymah	Jehaynah.
"	10.	Akbar	Ahbar.
223.	25.	Imaun	Imam.
226.	9.	Káta	Katá.
237.	6.	Rakl	Rakb.
239.	9.	Lamman	Samman.
250.	15.	Fazzeh	Farzeh.
251, 252.	12 and 22.	"	"
262.	21.	Jabarte	Jabarti.
267.	14.	Meyha	Megha.
277.	5 and 6.	Ton Toui	Toni.
"	23.	Toui	Toni.
281.	12.	ragged	rugged.
294.	8.	hill	hell.
296.	20.	Pirau	Piran.
301.	19.	Turikh	Tarikh.
302.	18.	Bandoleens	Bandoleers.
311.	22.	Hizbr	Hizb.
322.	15.	sand	land.
325.	11.	Maliar	Mahar.
326.	4.	Hutazmi	Hutaymi.
"	20.	Shamud	Thamud.
328.	22.	Shoa	Ohod.
329.	1.	He	We.
338.	16.	Ikran	Ikram.
339.	2.	Wuzúe	Wuzú.
342.	17.	Ishah	Isha.
349.	6.	Karaghi	Karashi.
"	"	Hindayli	Hudayli.
356.	3.	Wassat	Wassit.
358.	6.	Radhawh	Radhwah.
360.	16.	Musahlah	Musahhal.
379.	1.	Hanidah	Hamidah.

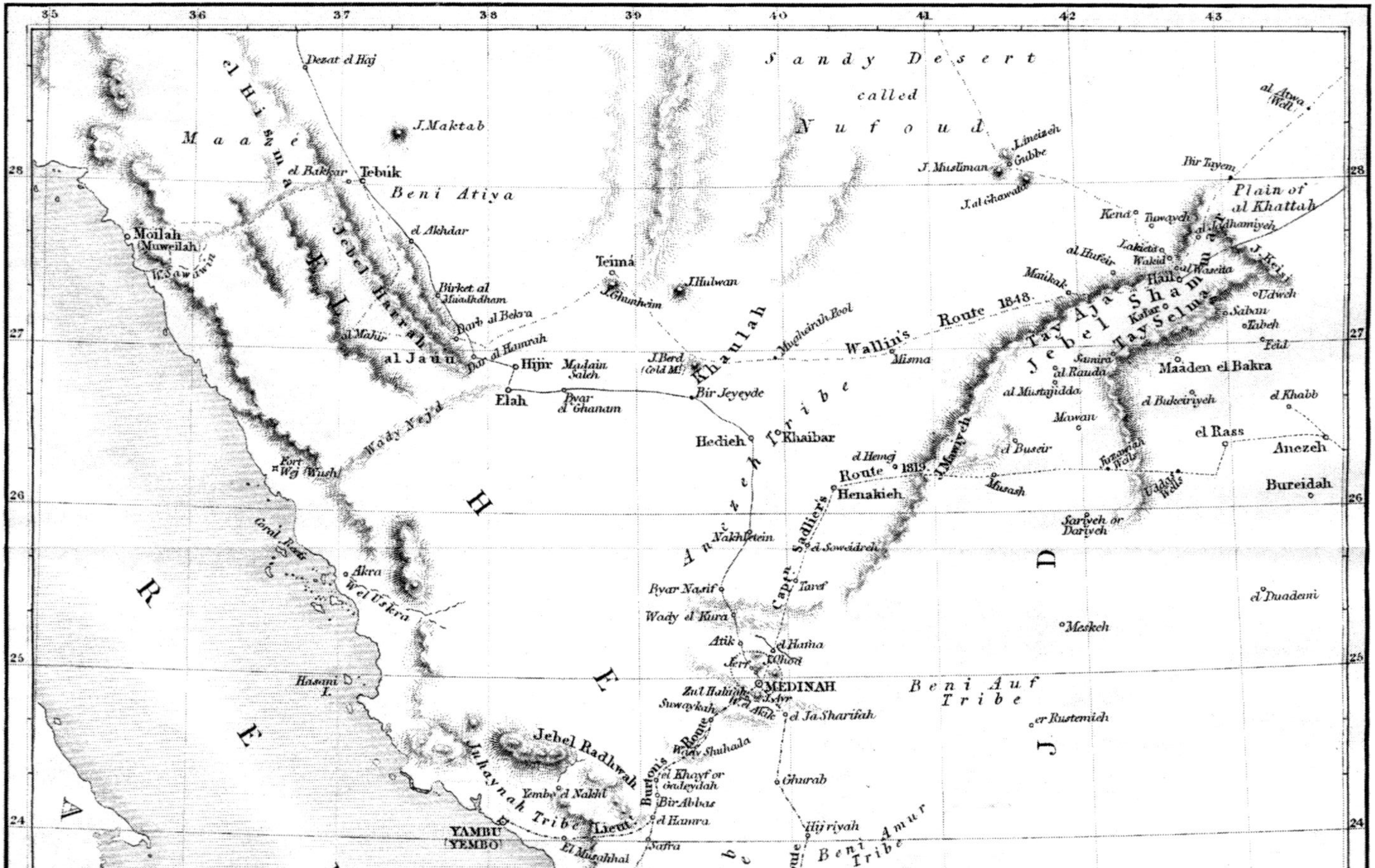
Sandy Desert
called
Nufoud
el Hisma
Maazé
J. Maktab
Tebuk
el Bakkar
Beni Atiya
Dezat el Haj
Moilah
(Muweilah)
Jebel Harrah
el Akhdar
Birket al Muadhdham
Darb al Bekra
al Mahir
al Jauu
Hijjr
Madain Saleh
Elah
Byar el Ghanam
Teima
J. Ghunheim
J. Hulwan
J. Berd (Cold Mt.)
Khaulah
Bir Jeyeyde
Mugheirah Pool
Wallin's Route 1848.
Misma
Hedieh
Khaibar
Wady Nejd
Fort Wej (Wush)
H
Coral Reefs
Akra
Wel Uskra
R
Hasani I.
E
A
J. Musliman
Lineizeh
Gubbe
J. al Ghawata
Bir Tayem
Plain of al Khattah
al Atwa (Well)
Kena
Tuwayeh
Lakieta
Wakid
al Hufeir
Mailkak
Hail
Jebel Tay Aja Shamar
Tay Selma
J. Keir
Udweh
Saban
Tabeh
Feid
Kafar
Samira
al Rauda
al Mustajidda
Maaden el Bakra
el Bukeiriyeh
el Khabb
Mawan
el Rass
Anezeh
Bureidah
el Buseir
Juzamah Wells
Uddai Wells
el Hemej
Route 1819.
Henakieh
J. Mawiyeh
Musash
Sariyeh or Dariyeh
D
el Duademi
Meskeh
Beni Auf Tribe
er Rustemieh
J
Anezeh Tribe
Nakhletein
Capt. Sadlier's
el Soweidreh
Taref
Byar Nasif
Wady el Kura
Atik
el Hafna
Ohod
MEDINAH
Zul Hulaifah
Suwaykah
el Ja Sharifah
Wady Shuhada
Burton's Route
Jebel Radhwah
Juhaynah Tribe
Yembo el Nakhl
el Khayf or Gadeydah
Bir Abbas
el Hamra
Ghurab
Hijriyah
Beni Amur Tribe
YAMBU (YEMBO)
El Musahhal
Safra
Lieut.

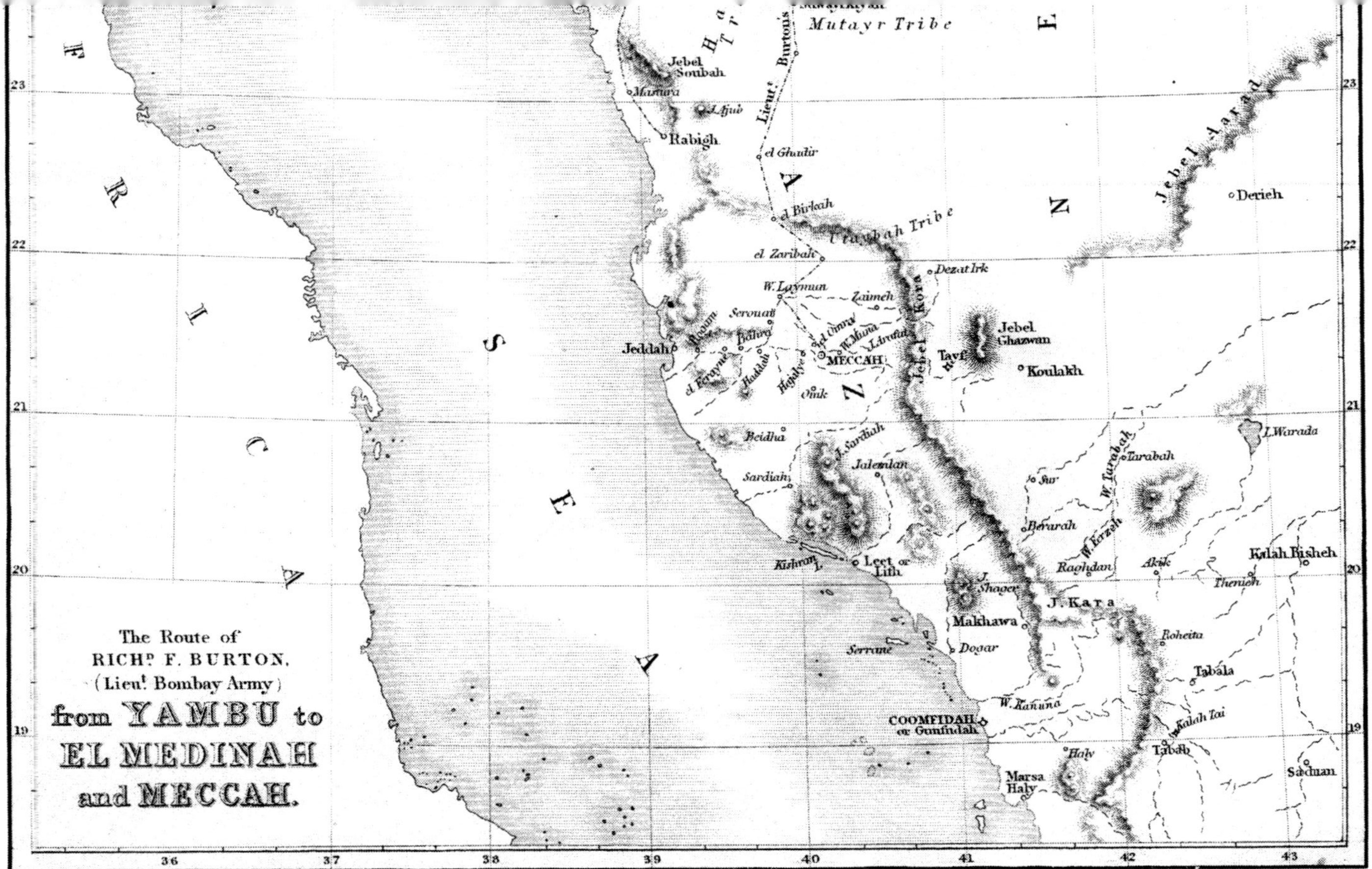

Drawn & Engraved by E. Weller, Duke Str. Bloomsbury.

London, Longman & Co.

A PILGRIMAGE

TO

EL MEDINAH AND MECCAH.

CHAPTER I.

TO ALEXANDRIA.

A FEW WORDS CONCERNING WHAT INDUCED ME TO A PILGRIMAGE.

In the autumn of 1852, through the medium of General Monteith, I offered my services to the Royal Geographical Society of London, for the purpose of removing that opprobrium to modern adventure, the huge white blot which in our maps still notes the eastern and the central regions of Arabia. Sir Roderick Murchison, Colonel P. Yorke and Dr. Shaw, a deputation from that distinguished body, with their usual zeal for discovery and readiness to encourage the discoverer, honoured me by warmly supporting, in a personal interview with the chairman of the Honourable the Court of Directors to the East India Company, my application for three years' leave of absence on special duty from India to Muscat. But they were unable to prevail upon Sir James Hogg, who, remembering the fatalities which of late years have befallen sundry soldier-travellers in the East, refused his sanction, alleging as a reason that the contemplated journey was of too dangerous a nature. In compensation, however, for the disappointment, I was graciously allowed by my honourable masters the additional furlough of a year, in order to pursue my Arabic studies in lands where the language is best learned.

What remained for me but to prove, by trial, that what might be perilous to other travellers is safe to me. The "experimentum crucis" was a visit to El Hejaz, at once the most difficult and the most dangerous point by which a European can enter Arabia. I had intended, had the period of leave originally applied for been granted, to land at Muscat — a favourable starting-place — and there to apply myself, slowly and surely, to the task of spanning the deserts. But now I was to hurry, in the midst of summer, after a four years' sojourn in Europe, during which many things Oriental had fallen away from my memory, and — after passing through the ordeal of Egypt, a country where the police is curious as in Rome or Milan—to begin with the Moslem's Holy Land, the jealously guarded and exclusive Haram. However, being liberally supplied with the means of travel by the Royal Geographical Society; thoroughly tired of "progress" and of "civilisation;" curious to see with my eyes what others are content to "hear with ears," namely, Moslem's inner life in a really Mohammedan country; and longing, if truth be told, to set foot on that mysterious spot which no tourist had yet described, measured, sketched and daguerreotyped, I resolved to resume my old character of a Persian wanderer*, and to make the attempt.

The principal object with which I started was this:—To cross the unknown Arabian Peninsula, in a direct line from either El Medinah to Muscat, or diagonally from Meccah to Makallah on the Indian Ocean. By what "circumstance the miscreator" my plans were defeated, the reader will discover in the course of these volumes. The secondary objects were numerous. I was desirous to find out if any market for horses could be

* The vagrant, the merchant, and the philosopher, amongst Orientals, are frequently united in the same person.

opened between Central Arabia and India, where the studs are beginning to excite general dissatisfaction; to obtain information concerning the Great Eastern wilderness, the vast expanse marked Ruba el Khali (the empty abode) in our maps; to inquire into the hydrography of the Hejaz, its water-shed, the disputed slope of the country, and the existence or non-existence of perennial streams; and finally, to try, by actual observation, the truth of a theory proposed by the learned Orientalist, Lieutenant-Colonel Sykes, namely, that if history speak truth, in the population of the vast Peninsula there must exist certain physiological differences sufficient to warrant our questioning the common origin of the Arab family. As regards the horses, I am satisfied that from the Eastern coast something might be done,—nothing on the Western, where the animals, though "thoroughbred," are mere "weeds," of a foolish price and procurable only by chance. Of the Ruba el Khali I have heard enough, from credible relators, to conclude that its horrid depths swarm with a large and half-starving population; that it abounds in wadys, valleys, gullies and ravines, partially fertilised by intermittent torrents; and therefore, that the land is open only to the adventurous traveller.

Moreover, I am satisfied, that in spite of all geographers, from Ptolemy to Jormard, Arabia, which abounds in *fiumaras**, possesses not a single perennial stream worthy the name of river†; and the testimony of the natives induces me to think, with Wallin, contrary to Ritter and others, that the Peninsula falls instead of rising towards the south. Finally, I have found proof, to be produced in a future part of this publication, for believing in three distinct races. 1. The aborigines of the country, driven, like the Bheels and other autochthonic Indians, into the eastern and south-eastern wilds bordering upon the ocean. 2. A Syrian or Mesopotamian stock, typified by Shem and Joktan, that drove the indigenæ from the choicest tracts of country; these invaders still enjoy their conquests, representing the great Arabian people. And 3. An impure Egypto-Arab clan — we personify it by

* In a communication made to the Royal Geographical Society, and published in the 24th vol. of the Journal, I have given my reasons for naturalising this word. It will be used in the following pages to express a "hill water-course, which rolls a torrent after rain, and is either partially or wholly dry during the drought season." It is in fact the Indian "Nullah."

† "In provinciis Arabum, ait Ibn Haukal, nullus dignoscitur fluvius, aut mare quod navigia ferat." This truth has been disputed, but now it is generally acknowledged.

Ishmael, his son Nebajoth and Edom (Esau, the son of Isaac) — that populated and still populates the Sinaitic Peninsula. And in most places, even in the heart of Meccah, I met with debris of heathenry, proscribed by Mohammed, yet still popular, though the ignorant observers of the old customs assign to them a modern and a rationalistic origin.

I have entitled this account of my summer's tour through El Hejaz, a personal narrative, and I have laboured to make its nature correspond with its name, simply because "it is the personal that interests mankind." Many may not follow my example*; but some perchance will be curious to see what measures I adopted, in order to appear sud-

* A French traveller, M. d'Escayrac-Lantune, was living at Cairo as a native of the East, and preparing for a pilgrimage when I was similarly engaged. Unfortunately he went to Damascus, where some disturbance compelled him to resume his nationality.

The only European I have met with who visited Meccah without apostatising, is M. Bertolucci, Swedish Consul at Cairo. This gentleman persuaded the Bedouin camel men who were accompanying him to Taif, to introduce him in disguise: he naïvely owns that his terror of discovery prevented his making any observations. Dr. George A. Wallin, of Finland, performed the Haj in 1845; but his "somewhat perilous position, and the filthy company of Persians," were effectual obstacles to his taking notes.

denly as an Eastern upon the stage of Oriental life; and as the recital may be found useful by future adventurers, I make no apology for the egotistical semblance of the narrative. Those who have felt the want of some " silent friend " to aid them with advice, when it must not be asked, will appreciate what may appear to the uninterested critic mere outpourings of a mind full of self.*

On the evening of April 3. 1853, I left London for Southampton. By the advice of a brother officer — little thought at that time the adviser or the advised how valuable was the suggestion — my Eastern dress was called into requisition before leaving town, and all my " impedimenta " were taught to look exceedingly Oriental. Early the next day a " Persian Prince " embarked

* No one felt the want of this " silent friend " more than myself; for though Eastern Arabia would not have been strange to me, the Western regions were a terra incognita.

Through Dr. Norton Shaw, Secretary to the Royal Geographical Society, I addressed a paper full of questions to Dr. Wallin, professor of Arabic at the University of Helsingfors. But that adventurous traveller and industrious Orientalist was then, as we afterwards heard with sorrow, no more; so the queries remained unanswered. In these pages I have been careful to solve all the little financial and domestic difficulties, so perplexing to the " Freshman," whom circumstances compel to conceal his freshness from the prying eyes of friends.

on board the Peninsular and Oriental Company's magnificent screw steamer "Bengal."

A fortnight was profitably spent in getting into the train of Oriental manners. For what polite Chesterfield says of the difference between a gentleman and his reverse,—namely, that both perform the same offices of life, but each in a several and widely different way—is notably as applicable to the manners of the Eastern as of the Western men. Look, for instance, at an Indian Moslem drinking a glass of water. With us the operation is simple enough, but his performance includes no less than five novelties. In the first place, he clutches his tumbler as though it were the throat of a foe; secondly, he ejaculates, "In the name of Allah the Compassionate, the Merciful!" before wetting his lips; thirdly, he imbibes the contents, swallowing them, not drinking, and ending with a satisfied grunt; fourthly, before setting down the cup, he sighs forth, "Praise be to Allah!"—of which you will understand the full meaning in the Desert; and, fifthly, he replies, "May Allah make it pleasant to thee!" in answer to his friend's polite "Pleasurably and health!" Also he is careful to avoid the irreligious action of drinking the pure element in a standing position, mindful, however, of the three recognised exceptions, the fluid of the Holy Well, Zem-zem, water distributed in charity, and that which remains after Wuzu, the lesser ablution. Moreover, in Europe one forgets the use of the right hand, the manipulation of the rosary, the abuse of the chair,—your genuine Oriental looks almost as comfortable in one as a sailor upon the back of a high-trotting horse—the rolling gait with the toes straight to the front, the grave look and the habit of pious ejaculations.

Our voyage over the "summer sea" was an eventless one In a steamer of two or three thousand tons one discovers the once dreaded, now contemptible, "stormy waters" only by the band—a standing nuisance be it remarked—performing

> "There we lay
> All the day,
> In the Bay of Biscay, O!"

The sight of the glorious Trafalgar* excites

* "Then came Trafalgar: would that Nelson had known the meaning of that name! it would have fixed a smile upon his dying lips!" so says the rider through the Nubian Desert, giving us in a foot note the curious information that "Trafalgar" is an Arabic word, which means the "*Cape of Laurels.*" Trafalgar is nothing but a corruption of Tarf el Gharb—the side or skirt of the West; it being the most occidental point then reached by Arab conquest.

none of the sentiments with which a tedious sail used to invest it. "Gib," the familiar name of Gibraltar, is, probably, better known to you, by Gautier and Warburton, than the regions about Cornhill; besides which, you anchor under the Rock exactly long enough to land and to breakfast. Malta, too, wears an old familiar face, which bids you order a dinner and superintend the icing of claret (beginning of Oriental barbarism), instead of galloping about on donkey-back through fiery air in memory of St. Paul and Red-Cross Knights. But though our journey was a monotonous one, there was nothing to complain of. The ship was in every way comfortable; the cook, strange to say, was good, and the voyage lasted long enough, and not too long. On the evening of the thirteenth day after our start, the big-trowsered pilot, so lovely in his deformities to western eyes, made his appearance, and the good screw "Bengal" found herself at anchor off the Headland of Figs.*

Having been invited to start from the house of a kind friend, John Larking, I disembarked with him, and rejoiced to see that by dint of a beard and a shaven head I had succeeded, like the Lord of

* In Arabic "Ras el Tin," the promontory upon which immortal Pharos once stood.

Geesh, in "misleading the inquisitive spirit of the populace." The mingled herd of spectators before whom we passed in review on the landing-place, hearing an audible "Alhamdulillah"* whispered "Moslem!" The infant population spared me the compliments usually addressed to hatted heads; and when a little boy, presuming that the occasion might possibly open the hand of generosity, looked in my face and exclaimed "Bakhshish,"† he obtained in reply "Mafish;"‡ which convinced the

* "Praise be to Allah, Lord of the (three) worlds!" a pious ejaculation, which leaves the lips of the True Believer on all occasions of concluding actions.

† "*Bakhshish,*" says a modern writer, "is a fee or present which the Arabs (he here means the Egyptians, who got the word from the Persians through the Turks,) claim on all occasions for services you render them, as well as for services they have rendered you. A doctor visits a patient gratis,—the patient or his servant will ask for a *bakhshish* (largesse); you employ, pay, clothe, and feed a child—the father will demand his *bakhshish;* you may save the life of an Arab, at the risk of your own, and he will certainly claim a *bakhshish.* This bakhshish, in fact, is a sort of alms or tribute, which the poor Arab believes himself entitled to claim from every respectable-looking person."

‡ Mafish, "there is none," equivalent to, "I have left my purse at home." Nothing takes the oriental mind so much as a retort alliterative or jingling. An officer in the Bombay army once saved himself from assault and battery by informing a furious band of natives, that under British rule "*harakat* na hiri, *barakat* hui," "*blessing* hath there been to you; *bane* there hath been none."

bystanders that the sheep-skin contained a real sheep. We then mounted a carriage, fought our way through the donkeys, and in half an hour found ourselves, chibouque in mouth and coffee-cup in hand, seated on divans in my friend's hospitable house.

Wonderful was the contrast between the steamer and that villa on the Mahmudiyah canal! Startling the sudden change from presto to adagio life! In thirteen days we had passed from the clammy grey fog, that atmosphere of industry which kept us at anchor off the Isle of Wight, through the liveliest air of the inland sea, whose sparkling blue and purple haze spread charms even on Africa's beldame features, and now we were sitting silent and still, listening to the monotonous melody of the East—the soft night-breeze wandering through starlit skies and tufted trees, with a voice of melancholy meaning.

And this is the Arab's *Kaif*. The savouring of animal existence; the passive enjoyment of mere sense; the pleasant languor, the dreamy tranquillity, the airy castle-building, which in Asia stand in lieu of the vigorous, intensive, passionate life of Europe. It is the result of a lively, impressible, excitable nature, and exquisite sensibility of nerve,

—a facility for voluptuousness unknown to northern regions; where happiness is placed in the exertion of mental and physical powers; where "Ernst ist das Leben;" where niggard earth commands ceaseless sweat of brow, and damp chill air demands perpetual excitement, exercise, or change, or adventure, or dissipation, for want of something better. In the East, man requires but rest and shade: upon the bank of a bubbling stream, or under the cool shelter of a perfumed tree, he is perfectly happy, smoking a pipe, or sipping a cup of coffee, or drinking a glass of sherbet, but above all things deranging body and mind as little as possible; the trouble of conversations, the displeasures of memory, and the vanity of thought being the most unpleasant interruptions to his *Kaif.* No wonder that Kaif is a word untranslatable in our mother-tongue! *

"Laudabunt alii claram Rhodon aut Mitylenem."

Let others describe this once famous capital of Egypt, the city of misnomers, whose dry docks are ever wet, and whose marble fountain is eternally

* In a coarser sense "kaif" is applied to all manner of intoxication. Sonnini is not wrong when he says, "the Arabs give the name of Kaif to the voluptuous relaxation, the delicious stupor, produced by the smoking of hemp."

dry, whose "Cleopatra's Needle"* is not Cleopatra's; whose "Pompey's Pillar" never had any earthly connection with Pompey; and whose Cleopatra's Baths are, according to veracious travellers, no baths at all. Yet is it a wonderful place, this "Libyan suburb" of our day, this outpost of civilisation planted upon the skirts of barbarism, Osiris seated side by side with Typho, his great old enemy. Still may be said of it, "it ever

* Cleopatra's Needle is called by the native Ciceroni "Masallat Firaun," Pharaoh's packing needle. What Solomon, and the genii and Sikandar zu'l karnain (Alexander of Macedon), are to other Moslem lands, such is Pharaoh to Egypt, the "Cæsar aut Diabolus" of the Nile. The ichneumon becomes "Pharaoh's cat,"—even the French were bitten and named it, le rat de Pharaon; the prickly pear, "Pharaoh's fig;" certain unapproachable sulphur springs, "Pharaoh's bath;" a mausoleum at Petra, "Pharaoh's place;" the mongrel race now inhabiting the valley of the Nile, is contemptuously named by Turks and Arabs "Jins Firaun," or "Pharaoh's Breed;" and a foul kind of vulture (vultur percnopterus, ak baba of the Turks, and ukab of Sindh), "Pharaoh's hen."

This abhorrence of Pharaoh is, however, confined to the vulgar and the religious. The philosophers and mystics of El Islam, in their admiration of his impious daring, make him equal, and even superior, to Moses. Sahil, a celebrated Sufi, declares that the secret of the soul (*i. e.* its emanation) was first revealed when Pharaoh declared himself a god. And El Ghazali sees in such temerity nothing but the most noble aspiration to the divine, innate in the human spirit. (Dabistan, vol. iii.)

beareth something new;"* and Alexandria, a threadbare subject in Bruce's time, is even yet, from its perpetual changes, "a fit field for modern description." †

The better to blind the inquisitive eyes of servants and visitors, my friend lodged me in an outhouse, where I could revel in the utmost freedom of life and manners. And although some Armenian Dragoman, a restless spy like all his race, occasionally remarked that "voilà un Persan diablement dégagé," none, except those who were entrusted with the secret, had any idea of the part I was playing. The domestics, devout Moslems, pronounced me to be an Ajemi ‡, a kind of Mohammedan, not a good one like themselves, but, still,

* *Αεί φερεί τι καίνον.* "Quid novi fert Africa?" said the Romans. "In the same season Fayoles, tetrarch of Numidia, sent from the land of Africa to Grangousier, the most hideously great mare that was ever seen; for you know well enough how it is said, that 'Africa always is productive of some new thing.'"

† Alexandria, moreover, is an interesting place to Moslems, on account of the prophecy that it will succeed to the honours of Meccah, when the holy city falls into the hands of the infidel. In its turn Alexandria will be followed by Kairawan (in the Regency of Tunis); and this by Rashid or Rosetta, which last endures to the end of time.

‡ A Persian opposed to an Arab.

better than nothing. I lost no time in securing the assistance of a Shaykh *, and plunged once more into the intricacies of the Faith, revived my recollections of religious ablution, read the Koran, and again became an adept in the art of prostration. My leisure hours were employed in visiting the baths and coffee-houses, in attending the bazaars, and in shopping,—an operation which hereabouts consists of sitting upon a chapman's counter, smoking, sipping coffee, and telling your beads the while, to show that you are not of the slaves for whom time is made; in fact, in pitting your patience against that of your adversary the shopman. I found time for a short excursion to a country village on the banks of the canal; nor was an opportunity of seeing "El-nahl" neglected, for it would be some months before my eyes might dwell on such pleasant spectacle again.

"Delicias videam, Nile jocosa, tuas!"

Careful of graver matters, I attended the mosque, and visited the venerable localities in which modern Alexandria abounds. Pilgrimaging Moslems are here shown the tomb of El-nabi Daniyal (Daniel the Prophet), discovered upon a spot where the

* A priest, elder, chieftain, language-master, &c. &c.

late Sultan Mahmud dreamed that he saw an ancient man at prayer.* Sikandar El-Rumi, a Moslem Alexander the Great, of course left his bones in the place bearing his name, or—as he ought to have done so—bones have been found for him. Alexandria also boasts of two celebrated Walis—holy men. One is Mahommed El-Busiri, the author of a poem called El-Burdah, universally read throughout the world of Islam, and locally recited at funerals, and on other solemn occasions. The other is Abu Abbas El-Andalusi, a sage and saint of the first water, at whose tomb prayer is never breathed in vain.

It is not to be supposed that the people of Alexandria could look upon my phials and pill-boxes, without a yearning for their contents. An Indian doctor, too, was a novelty to them; Franks they despised, but a man who had come so far from the West! Then there was something in-

* The Persians place the Prophet's tomb at Susan or Sus, described by Ibn Haukal (p. 76.).

The readers of Ibn Batutah may think it strange that the learned and pious traveller in his account of Alexandria (chap. 2.) makes no allusion to the present holy deceased that distinguish the city. All the saints are now clear forgotten. For it is the fate of saints, like distinguished sinners, to die twice.

finitely seducing in the character of a magician, doctor, and fakir, each admirable of itself, thus combined to make "great medicine." Men, women, and children besieged my door, by which means I could see the people face to face, and especially the fair sex, of which Europeans, generally speaking, know only the worst specimens. Even respectable natives, after witnessing a performance of "Mandal" and the Magic mirror*, opined that the stranger was a holy man, gifted with supernatural powers, and knowing everything. One old person sent to offer me his daughter in marriage; he said nothing about dowry, but on this occasion I thought proper to decline the honour. And a middle-aged lady proffered me the sum of 100 piastres, nearly one pound sterling, if I would stay at Alexandria, and superintend the restoration of her blind eye.

But the reader must not be led to suppose that

* The Mandal is that form of Oriental divination which owes its present celebrity in Europe to Mr. Lane. Both it and the magic mirror are hackneyed subjects, but I have been tempted to a few words concerning them in another part of these volumes. Meanwhile I request the reader not to set me down as a mere charlatan; medicine in the East is so essentially united with superstitious practices, that he who would pass for an expert practitioner, must necessarily represent himself an "adept."

I acted "Carabin," or "Sangrado" without any knowledge of my trade. From youth I have always been a dabbler in medical and mystical study. Moreover, the practice of physic is comparatively easy amongst dwellers in warm latitudes, uncivilised people, where there is not that complication of maladies which troubles more polished nations. And further, what simplifies extremely the treatment of the sick in these parts is, the undoubted periodicity of disease, reducing almost all to one type — ague.* Many of the complaints of tropical climates, as medical men well know, display palpably intermittent symptoms unknown to colder countries; and speaking from individual experience, I may safely assert that in all cases of suffering, from a wound to ophthalmia, this phenomenon has forced itself into my notice. So much by way of excuse. I therefore considered myself as well qualified for the work as if I had taken out a *buono per l'estero* diploma at Padua, and not more likely to do active harm than most of the regularly graduated young surgeons who start to "finish themselves" upon the frame of the British soldier.

* Hence the origin, I believe, of the chronothermal practice, a discovery which physic owes to Dr. Dickson.

After a month's hard work at Alexandria, I prepared to assume the character of a wandering Dervish, after reforming my title from "Mirza"* to "Shaykh" Abdullah.† A reverend man, whose name I do not care to quote, some time ago initiated me into his order, the Kadiriyah, under the high-sounding name of Bismillah-Shah ‡: and, after a due period of probation, he graciously elevated me to the proud position of a Murshid § in the mystic craft. I was therefore sufficiently well ac-

* The Persian "Mister." In future chapters the reader will see the uncomfortable consequences of my having appeared in Egypt as a Persian. Although I found out the mistake, and worked hard to correct it, the bad name stuck to me; bazaar reports fly quicker and hit harder than newspaper paragraphs.

† Arab Christians sometimes take the name of "Abdullah," servant of God—"which," as a modern traveller observes, "all sects and religions might be equally proud to adopt." The Moslem Prophet said, "the names most approved of God are, Abdullah, Abd-el-rahman (slave of the compassionate), and such like."

‡ "King in-the-name-of-Allah," a kind of Oriental "Praise-God-Barebones." When a man appears as a Fakir or Dervish, he casts off, in process of regeneration, together with other worldly sloughs, his laical name for some brilliant coat of nomenclature rich in religious promise.

§ A Murshid is one allowed to admit Murids or apprentices into the order. As the form of the diploma conferred upon this occasion may be new to many European Orientalists, I have translated it in Appendix I.

quainted with the tenets and practices of these Oriental Freemasons. No character in the Moslem world is so proper for disguise as that of the Dervish. It is assumed by all ranks, ages, and creeds; by the nobleman who has been disgraced at court, and by the peasant who is too idle to till the ground; by Dives, who is weary of life, and by Lazarus, who begs bread from door to door. Further, the Dervish is allowed to ignore ceremony and politeness, as one who ceases to appear upon the stage of life; he may pray or not, marry or remain single as he pleases, be respectable in cloth of frieze as in cloth of gold, and no one asks him — the chartered vagabond — Why he comes here? or Wherefore he goes there? He may wend his way on foot alone, or ride his Arab steed followed by a dozen servants; he is equally feared without weapons, as swaggering through the streets armed to the teeth. The more haughty and offensive he is to the people, the more they respect him; a decided advantage to the traveller of choleric temperament. In the hour of imminent danger, he has only to become a maniac, and he is safe; a madman in the East, like a notably eccentric character in the West, is allowed to say or do whatever the spirit directs. Add to this character a little knowledge of medicine, a "moderate skill in magic and a reputation for caring for nothing but study and books," together with capital sufficient to save you from the chance of starving, and you appear in the East to peculiar advantage. The only danger of the "Path"* is, that the Dervish's ragged coat not unfrequently covers the cut-throat, and, if seized in the society of such a "brother," you may reluctantly become his companion, under the stick or on the stake. For be it known, Dervishes are of two orders, the Sharai, or those who conform to religion, and the Be-Sharai, or Luti, whose practices are hinted at by their own tradition that "he we daurna name" once joined them for a week, but at the end of that time left them in dismay, and returned to whence he came.

* The Tarikat or path, which leads, or is supposed to lead, to Heaven.

CHAP. II.

I LEAVE ALEXANDRIA.

The thorough-bred wanderer's idiosyncrasy I presume to be a composition of what phrenologists call "inhabitiveness" and "locality" equally and largely developed. After a long and toilsome march, weary of the way, he drops into the nearest place of rest to become the most domestic of men. For a while he smokes the "pipe of permanence"* with an infinite zest; he delights in various siestas during the day, relishing withal a long sleep at night; he enjoys dining at a fixed dinner hour, and wonders at the demoralisation of the mind which cannot find means of excitement in chit-chat or small talk, in a novel or a newspaper. But soon the passive fit has passed away; again a paroxysm of ennui coming on by slow degrees, Viator loses appetite, he walks about his room all night, he yawns at conversations, and a book acts

* The long pipe which at home takes the place of the shorten chibouque used on the road.

upon him as a narcotic. The man wants to wander, and he must do so or he shall die.

After about a month most pleasantly spent at Alexandria, I perceived the approach of the enemy, and as nothing hampered my incomings and outgoings, I surrendered. The world was "all before me," and there was pleasant excitement in plunging single-handed into its chilling depths. My Alexandrian Shaykh, whose heart fell victim to a new "jubbeh," which I had given in exchange for his tattered zaabut * offered me, in consideration of a certain monthly stipend, the affections of a brother and religious refreshment, proposing to send his wife back to her papa, and to accompany me, in the capacity of private chaplain, to the other side of Kaf.† I politely accepted the "Bruderschaft," but many reasons induced me to decline his society and services. In the first place, he spoke the detestable Egyptian jargon. Secondly, it was

* The jubbeh is a long outer garment, generally of cloth, worn by learned and respectable men. The zaabut is a large bag-sleeved black or brown coloured robe, made of home-spun woollen, the garb of the peasant, the hedge-priest, and the dervish.

† The mountain which encircles the globe, according to the sacred geography of the Moslems. To "go to Kaf" is equivalent to our "go to Jericho," or — somewhere else.

but prudent to lose the "spoor" between Alexandria and Suez. And, thirdly, my "brother" had shifting eyes (symptoms of fickleness), close together (indices of cunning); a flat-crowned head, and large ill-fitting lips; signs which led me to think lightly of his honesty, firmness, and courage. Phrenology and physiognomy, be it observed, disappoint you often amongst civilised people, the proper action of whose brains and features is impeded by the external pressure of education, accident, example, habit, necessity, and what not. But they are tolerably safe guides when groping your way through the mind of man in his natural state, a being of impulse in that chrysalis stage of mental development which is rather instinct than reason. But before my departure there was much to be done.

The land of the Pharaohs is becoming civilised, and unpleasantly so: nothing can be more uncomfortable than its present middle-state, between barbarism and the reverse. The prohibition against carrying arms is rigid as in Italy; all "violence" is violently denounced, and beheading being deemed cruel, the most atrocious crimes, as well as those small political offences, which in the days of the Mamelukes would have led to a beyship or a bowstring, receive fourfold punishment by deportation to Faizoghli, the local Cayenne. If you order your peasant to be flogged, his friends gather in threatening hundreds at your gates; when you curse your boatman, he complains to your consul; the dragomans afflict you with strange wild notions about honesty; a government order prevents you from using vituperative language to the "natives" in general; and the very donkey boys are becoming cognisant of the right of man to remain unbastinadoed. Still the old leaven remains behind: here, as elsewhere in "morning-land," you cannot hold your own without employing your fists. The passport system, now dying out of Europe, has sprung up, or rather revived in Egypt, with peculiar vigour.* Its good effects claim for

* Sir G. Wilkinson, referring his readers to Strabo, remarks that the "troublesome system of passports seems to have been adopted by the Egyptians at a very early period." Its present rigours, which have lasted since the European troubles in 1848 and 1849, have a twofold object; in the first place, to act as a clog upon the dangerous emigrants which Germany and Italy have sent out into the world; and secondly, to confine the subjects of the present Pacha of Egypt to their fatherland and the habit of paying taxes. The enlightened ruler (this was written during the rule of Abbas Pacha) knows his own interests, and never willingly parts with a subject liable to cess, at times objecting even to their obeying the pilgrimage law. We, on the

it our respect; still we cannot but lament its inconvenience. *We*, I mean real Easterns. As strangers — even those whose beards have whitened in the land — know absolutely nothing of what unfortunate natives must endure, I am tempted to subjoin a short sketch of my adventures in search of a Tezkireh at Alexandria.*

Through ignorance which might have cost me dear but for my friend Larking's weight with the local authorities, I had neglected to provide myself with a passport in England, and it was not without difficulty, involving much unclean dressing and an unlimited expenditure of broken English, that I obtained from the consul at Alexandria, a certificate, declaring me to be an Indo-British subject named Abdullah, by profession a doctor, aged thirty, and not distinguished—at least so the frequent blanks seemed to denote—by any remarkable conformation of eyes, nose, or cheek. For this I disbursed a dollar. And here let me record the

other hand, in India, allow a freedom of emigration, in my humble opinion highly injurious to us. For not only does this exodus thin the population, and tend to impoverish the land, it also serves to bring our rule into disrepute in foreign lands. At another time I shall discuss this subject more fully.

* A passport in this country is called a Tezkireh.

indignation with which I did it. That mighty Britain—the mistress of the seas—the ruler of one-sixth of mankind—should charge five shillings to pay for the shadow of her protecting wing! That I cannot speak my modernised "*civis sum Romanus*" without putting my hand into my pocket, in order that these officers of the Great Queen may not take too ruinously from a revenue of 56 millions! O the meanness of our magnificence! the littleness of our greatness!

My new passport would not carry me without the Zabit or Police Magistrate's counter-signature, said the consul. Next day I went to the Zabit, who referred me to the Muhafiz (Governor) of Alexandria, at whose gate I had the honour of squatting at least three hours, till a more compassionate clerk vouchsafed the information that the proper place to apply to was the Diwan Kharijiyeh (the Foreign-Office). Thus a second day was utterly lost. On the morning of the third I started, as directed, for the palace, which crowns the Headland of Figs. It is a huge and couthless shell of building in parallelogrammic form containing all kinds of public offices in glorious confusion, looking with their glaring white-washed faces upon a central court, where a few leafless wind-wrung trees seem struggling for the breath of life in an eternal atmosphere of clay, dust, and sun-blaze.*

The first person I addressed was a Kawwas† or police officer, who, coiled comfortably up in a bit of shade fitting his person like a robe, was in full enjoyment of the Asiatic "Kaif." Having presented the consular certificate and briefly stated the nature of my business, I ventured to inquire what was the right course to pursue for a visá.

They have little respect for Dervishes, it appears, at Alexandria!

M'adri—"Don't know," growled the man of authority without moving any thing but the quantity of tongue necessary for articulation.

Now there are three ways of treating Asiatic officials, —by bribe, by bullying or by bothering them with a dogged perseverance into attending to you and your concerns. The latter is the peculiar

* The glare of Alexandria has become a matter of fable in the East. The stucco employed in overlaying its walls erected by Zulkarnain, was so exquisitely tempered and so beautifully polished, that the inhabitants, in order to protect themselves from blindness, were constrained to wear masks.

† The word literally means an "archer," reminding us of "les archers de la sainte Hermandade," in the most delicious of modern fictions. Some spell the word "Kawas!"

province of the poor; moreover, this time I resolved, for other reasons, to be patient. I repeated my question in almost the same words. Ruh! "Be off," was what I obtained for all reply. But this time the questioned went so far as to open his eyes. Still I stood twirling the paper in my hands, and looking very humble and very persevering, till a loud Ruh ya Kalb! "Go O dog!" converted into a responsive curse the little speech I was preparing about the brotherhood of El-Islam and the mutual duties obligatory on true believers. I then turned away slowly and fiercely, for the next thing might have been a cut with the Kurbaj*, and, by the hammer of Thor! British flesh and blood could never have stood that.

After which satisfactory scene,— for satisfactory it was in one sense, proving the complete fitness of the Dervish's dress,— I tried a dozen other promiscuous sources of information,—policemen, grooms, scribes, donkey boys, and idlers in general. At length, wearied of patience, I offered a soldier some pinches of tobacco, and promised him an oriental sixpence if he would manage the business for me. The man was interested by the tobacco and

* A whip of dried and twisted hippopotamus hide, the ferule, horsewhip, and "cat' o' nine tails" of Egypt.

the pence; he took my hand, and inquiring the while he went along, led me from place to place, till, mounting a grand staircase, I stood in the presence of Abbas Effendi, the governor's Naib or deputy.

It was a little, whey-faced, black-bearded Turk, coiled up in the usual conglomerate posture upon a calico-covered divan, at the end of a long bare large-windowed room. Without deigning even to nod the head, which hung over his shoulder with transcendent listlessness and affectation of pride in answer to my salams and benedictions, he eyed me with wicked eyes, and faintly ejaculated "Min ent?"* Then hearing that I was a Dervish and doctor—he must be an Osmanli Voltairian, that little Turk—the official snorted a contemptuous snort. He condescendingly added, however, that the proper source to seek was "Taht," which meaning simply "below," conveyed rather imperfect information in a topographical point of view to a stranger.

At length, however, my soldier guide found out that a room in the custom-house bore the honourable appellation of "Foreign Office." Accordingly

* For "man anta"? who art thou?

I went there, and, after sitting at least a couple of hours at the bolted door in the noon-day sun, was told, with a fury which made me think I had sinned, that the officer in whose charge the department was, had been presented with an olive branch in the morning, and consequently that business was not to be done that day. The angry-faced official communicated the intelligence to a large group of Anadolian, Caramanian, Boshniac, and Roumelian Turks,—sturdy, undersized, broad-shouldered, bare-legged, splay-footed, horny-fisted, dark-browed, honest-looking mountaineers, who were lounging about with long pistols and yataghans stuck in their broad sashes, head-gear composed of immense tarbooshes with proportionate turbans coiled round them, and two or three suits of substantial clothes, even at this season of the year, upon their shoulders.

Like myself they had waited some hours, but they were not patient under disappointment: they bluntly told the angry official that he and his master were a pair of idlers, and the curses that rumbled and gurgled in their hairy throats as they strode towards the door, sounded like the growling of wild beasts.

Thus was another day truly orientally lost. On the morrow, however, I obtained permission, in the character of Dr. Abdullah, to visit any part of Egypt I pleased, and to retain possession of my dagger and pistols.

And now I must explain what induced me to take so much trouble about a passport. The home reader naturally inquires, why not travel under your English name?

For this reason. In the generality of barbarous countries you must either proceed, like Bruce, preserving the "dignity of manhood," and carrying matters with a high hand, or you must worm your way by timidity and subservience; in fact, by becoming an animal too contemptible for man to let or injure. But to pass through the Holy Land, you must either be a born believer, or have become one; in the former case you may demean yourself as you please, in the latter a path is ready prepared for you. My spirit could not bend to own myself a Burma*, a renegade—to be pointed at and shunned and catechised, an object of suspicion to the many and of contempt to all. Moreover, it would have obstructed the aim of my wanderings. The convert is always watched with Argus eyes, and

* An opprobrious name given by the Turks to their Christian converts. The word is derived from Burmak, "to twist," "to turn."

men do not willingly give information to a "new Moslem," especially a Frank: they suspect his conversion to be a feigned or a forced one, look upon him as a spy, and let him see as little of life as possible. Firmly as was my heart set upon travelling in Arabia, by Heaven! I would have given up the dear project rather than purchase a doubtful and partial success at such a price. Consequently, I had no choice but to appear as a born believer, and part of my birthright in that respectable character was toil and trouble in obtaining a tezkirah.*

Then I had to provide myself with certain necessaries for the way. These were not numerous. The silver-mounted dressing-case is here supplied by a rag containing a miswak †, a bit of soap and a comb (wooden), for bone and tortoiseshell are not, religiously speaking, correct. Equally simple

* During my journey, and since my return, some Indian papers conducted by jocose editors made merry upon the occasion of an Englishman "turning Turk." Once for all, I beg leave to point above for the facts of the case; it must serve as a general answer to any pleasant little fictions which may hereafter appear.

† A stick of soft wood chewed at one end. It is generally used throughout the East, where brushes should be avoided, as the natives always suspect hogs' bristles.

was my wardrobe; a change or two of clothing.* The only article of canteen description was a zemzemiyah, a goat-skin water-bag, which communicates to its contents, especially when new, a ferruginous aspect and a wholesome, though hardly an attractive flavour of tanno-gelatine. This was a necessary; to drink out of a tumbler, possibly fresh from pig-eating lips, would have entailed a certain loss of reputation. For bedding and furniture I had a coarse Persian rug—which, besides being couch, acts as chair, table, and oratory—a cotton-stuffed chintz-covered pillow, a blanket in case of cold, and a sheet, which does duty for tent and mosquito curtains in nights of heat.† As shade is a convenience not always procurable, another necessary was a huge cotton umbrella of Eastern make, brightly yellow, suggesting the idea of an

* It is a great mistake to carry too few clothes, and those who travel as Orientals should always have at least one very grand suit for use on critical occasions. Throughout the East a badly dressed man is a pauper, and a pauper—unless he belongs to an order having a right to be poor—is a scoundrel.

† Almost all Easterns sleep under a sheet, which becomes a kind of respirator, defending them from the dews and mosquitoes by night and the flies by day. The "rough and ready" traveller will learn to follow the example, remembering that "nature is founder of customs in savage countries;" whereas, amongst the *soi-disant* civilised, nature has no deadlier enemy than custom.

overgrown marigold. I had also a substantial housewife, the gift of a kind friend; it was a roll of canvas, carefully soiled, and garnished with needles and thread, cobblers'-wax, buttons, and other such articles. These things were most useful in lands where tailors abound not; besides which, the sight of a man darning his coat or patching his slippers teems with pleasing ideas of humility. A dagger*, a brass inkstand and pen-holder stuck in the belt, and a mighty rosary, which on occasion might have been converted into a weapon of offence, completed my equipment. I must not omit to mention the proper method of carrying money, which in these lands should never be entrusted to box or bag. A common cotton purse secured in a breast pocket, (for Egypt now abounds in that civilised animal the pickpocket †,) contained silver pieces and small change.‡ My gold, of which I carried twenty-five

* It is strictly forbidden to carry arms in Egypt. This, however, does not prevent their being as necessary—especially in places like Alexandria, where Greek and Italian ruffians abound — as they ever were in Rome or Leghorn during the glorious times of Italian "liberty."

† In the Azhar Mosque, immediately after Friday service, a fellow once put his hand into my pocket, which fact alone is ample evidence of "progress."

‡ As a general rule, always produce, when travelling, the mi-

sovereigns, and papers, were committed to a substantial leathern belt of Maghrabi manufacture, made to be strapped round the waist under the dress. This is the Asiatic method of concealing valuables, and a more civilised one than ours in the last century, when Roderic Random and his companion, "sewed their money between the lining and the waistband of their breeches, except some loose silver for immediate expense on the road." The great inconvenience of the belt is its weight, especially where dollars must be carried, as in Arabia, causing chafes and inconvenience at

nutest bit of coin. At present, however, small change is dear in Egypt; the sayrafs, or money-changers, create the dearth in order to claim a high agio. The traveller must prepare himself for a most unpleasant task in learning the different varieties of currency, which appear all but endless, the result of deficiency in the national circulating medium. There are, however, few copper coins, the pieces of 10 or 5 foddthah (or parahs), whereas silver and gold abound. As regards the latter metal, strangers should mistrust all small pieces, Turkish as well as Egyptian. "The greater part are either cut or cracked, or perhaps both, and worn down to mere spangles: after taking them; it will not be possible to pass them without considerable loss."

Above all things, the traveller must be careful never to change gold except in large towns, where such a display of wealth would not arouse suspicion or cupidity; and on no occasion when travelling, even to pronounce the ill-omened word "kis" (purse). Many have lost their lives by neglecting these simple precautions.

night. Moreover, it can scarcely be called safe. In dangerous countries wary travellers will adopt surer precautions.*

A pair of common native khurjin or saddle-bags contained my wardrobe, the "bed," readily rolled up into a bundle, and for a medicine chest† I

* Some prefer a long chain of pure gold divided into links and covered with leather, so as to resemble the twisted girdle which the Arab fastens round his waist. It is a precaution well known to the wandering knights of old. Others, again, in very critical situations, open with a lancet the shoulder, or any other fleshy part of the body, and insert a precious stone, which does not show in its novel purse.

† Any "Companion to the Medicine Chest" will give, to those that require such information, the names of drugs and instruments necessary for a journey: but it must be borne in mind that hot countries require double quantities of tonics, and half the allowance of cathartics, necessary in cold climates. Sonnini, however, is right when he says of the Egyptian fellahs, that their stomachs, accustomed to digest bread badly baked, acrid and raw vegetables, and other green and unwholesome nourishment, require doses fit only for horses.

Advisable precautions are, in the first place, to avoid, if travelling as a native, any signs of European manufacture in knives, scissors, weights, scales and other such articles. Secondly, glass bottles are useless: the drugs should be stowed away in tin or wooden boxes, such as the natives of the country use, and when a phial is required, it must be fitted into an *étui* of some kind. By this means, ground glass stoppers and plentiful cotton stuffing, the most volatile essences may be carried about without great waste. After six months of the driest heat, bought a pea-green box with red and yellow flowers, capable of standing falls from a camel twice a day.

The next step was to find out when the local steamer would start for Cairo, and accordingly I betook myself to the Transit Office. No vessel was advertised; I was directed to call every evening till satisfied. At last the fortunate event took place: a "weekly departure," which, by the by, occurred once every fortnight or so, was in order for the next day. I hurried to the office, but did not reach it till past noon—the hour of idleness. A little, dark gentleman, so formed and dressed as exactly to resemble a liver-and-tan bull-terrier, who with his heels on the table was dosing, cigar in mouth, over the last "Galignani," positively refused, after a time,—for at first he would not speak at all,—to let me take my passage till three in the after-

in Egypt and Arabia, not more than about one-fourth of my Prussic acid and chloroform had evaporated. And, thirdly, if you travel in the East, a few bottles of tincture of cantharides —highly useful as a rubefacient, excitant, et cetera—must never be omitted.

I made the mistake of buying my drugs in England, and had the useless trouble of looking after them during the journey. Both at Alexandria and Cairo they are to be found in abundance, cheaper than in London, and good enough for practical purposes.

noon. I inquired when the boat started, upon which he referred me, as I had spoken bad Italian, to the advertisement. I pleaded inability to read or write, whereupon he testily cried "Alle nove! alle nove"! — at nine! at nine! Still appearing uncertain, I drove him out of his chair, when he rose with a curse and read 8 A. M. An unhappy Eastern, depending upon what he said, would have been precisely one hour too late.

Thus were we lapsing into the real good old Indian style of doing business. Thus Indicus orders his first clerk to execute some commission; the senior, having "work" upon his hands, sends a junior; the junior finds the sun hot, and passes on the word to a "peon;" the "peon" charges a porter with the errand, and the porter quietly sits or doses in his place, trusting that fate will bring him out of the scrape, but firmly resolved, though the shattered globe fall, not to stir an inch.

The reader, I must again express a hope, will pardon the egotism of these descriptions, — my object is to show him how business is carried on in these hot countries—business generally. For had I, instead of being Abdullah the Dervish, been a rich native merchant, it would have been the same. How many complaints of similar treatment have

I heard in different parts of the Eastern world! and how little can one realise them without having actually experienced the evil! For the future I shall never see a "nigger" squatting away half a dozen mortal hours in a broiling sun patiently waiting for something or for some one, without a lively remembrance of my own cooling of the *calces* at the custom-house of Alexandria.

At length, about the end of May all was ready. Not without a feeling of regret I left my little room among the white myrtle blossoms and the oleander flowers. I kissed with humble ostentation my kind host's hand in presence of his servants, bade adieu to my patients, who now amounted to about fifty, shaking hands with all meekly and with religious equality of attention, and, mounted in a "trap" which looked like a cross between a wheelbarrow and a dog-cart, drawn by a kicking, jibbing, and biting mule, I set out for the steamer.

CHAP. III.

THE NILE STEAM BOAT.

In the days of the Pitts we have invariably a "Relation" of Egyptian travellers who embark for a place called "Roseet" on the "River Nilus." Wanderers of the Brucian age were wont to record their impressions of voyage upon land subjects observed between Alexandria and Cairo. A little later we find every one inditing rhapsodies about, and descriptions of, his or her dahabiyeh (barge) on the canal. After this came the steamer. And after the steamer will come the railroad, which may disappoint the author tourist, but will be delightful to that sensible class of men who wish to get over the greatest extent of ground with the least inconvenience to themselves and others. Then shall the Mahmudiyah—ugliest and most wearisome of canals—be given up to cotton boats and grain barges, and then will note-books and the headings of chapters ignore its existence.

I saw the canal at its worst, when the water was low, and have not one syllable to say in its favour. Instead of thirty hours, we took three mortal days and nights to reach Cairo, and we grounded with painful regularity four or five times between sunrise and sunset. In the scenery on the banks sketchers and describers have left you nought to see. From Pompey's Pillar to the Maison Carrée, Kariom and its potteries, el Birkah * of the night birds, Bastarah with the alleys of trees, even unto Atfah, all things are perfectly familiar to us, and have been so years before the traveller actually sees them. The Nil El Mubarak itself—the Blessed Nile, as notably fails too at this season to arouse enthusiasm. You see nothing but muddy waters, dusty banks, a sand mist, a milky sky, and a glaring sun: you feel nothing but a breeze like the flues from a potter's furnace. You can only just distinguish through a veil of reeking vapours Shibr Katt from Kafr el Zayyat, and you steam too far from Wardan to enjoy the Timonic satisfaction of enraging its male population with "Haykal! ya"—sons of Hay-

* Villages notorious for the peculiar Egyptian revelry, an undoubted relic of the good old times, when "the most religious of men" revelled with an ardent piety in honour of Isis and Osiris.

kal!* You are nearly wrecked, as a matter of course, at the Barrage †; and as certainly dumbfoundered by the sight of its ugly little Gothic crenelles. The Pyramids of Cheops and Cephren, "rearing their majestic heads above the margin of the desert," only suggest the remark that they have

* "Haykal" was a pleasant fellow, who, having basely abused the confidence of the fair ones of Wardan, described their charms in sarcastic verse, and stuck his scroll upon the door of the village mosque, taking at the same time the wise precaution to change his lodgings without delay. The very mention of his name affronts the brave Wardanenses to the last extent, making them savage as Oxford bargees.

† The Barrage is a handsome bridge,—putting the style of architecture out of consideration,—the work of French engineers, originally projected by Napoleon the First. It was intended to act as a dam, raising the waters of the Nile and conducting them to Suez, the salt lakes, and a variety of other places, through a number of canals, which, however, have not yet been opened. Meanwhile, it acts upon the river's trunk as did the sea of old upon its embouchures, blocking it up and converting the land around it to the condition of a swamp. Moreover, it would have cleaned out the bed by means of sluice gates, forming an artificial increase of current to draw off the deposit; but the gates are wanting, so the piers, serving only to raise the soil by increasing the deposit of silt, collect and detain suspended matter, which otherwise would not settle. Briefly, by a trifling expenditure the Barrage might be made a blessing to Egypt; in its present state it is a calamity, an "enormous, cruel wonder," more crushing to the people than were the pyramids and sphinxes of old.

been remarkably well-sketched; and thus you proceed till with a real feeling of satisfaction you moor alongside of the tumble-down old suburb Bulak.

To me there was double dulness in the scenery: it seemed to be Sindh over again—the same morning mist and noon-tide glare; the same hot wind and heat clouds, and fiery sunset, and evening glow; the same pillars of dust and "devils" of sand sweeping like giants over the plain; the same turbid waters of a broad, shallow stream studded with sand-banks and silt-isles, with crashing earth slips and ruins nodding over a kind of cliff, whose base the stream gnaws with noisy tooth. On the banks, saline ground sparkled and glittered like hoar-frost in the sun; and here and there mud villages, solitary huts, pigeon towers, or watch turrets, whence little brown boys shouted and slung stones at the birds, peeped out from among bright green patches of palm-tree, tamarisk, and mimosa, maize, tobacco, and sugar-cane. Beyond the narrow tongue of land on the river banks lay the glaring, yellow desert, with its low hills and sand slopes bounded by innumerable pyramids of nature's architecture. The boats, with their sharp bows, preposterous sterns, and lateen sails, might have belonged to the Indus. So might the chocolate-skinned, blue-robed peasantry; the women carrying progeny on their hips, with the eternal waterpot on their heads; and the men sleeping in the shade, or following the plough, to which probably Osiris first put hand. The lower animals, like the higher, are the same gaunt, mange-stained camels, muddy buffaloes, donkeys, sneaking jackals and fox-like dogs. Even the feathered creatures were perfectly familiar to my eye—paddy birds, pelicans, giant cranes, kites and wild water-fowl.

I had taken a third-class or deck passage, whereby the evils of the journey were exasperated. A roasting sun pierced the canvas awning like hot water through a gauze veil, and by night the cold dews fell raw and thick as a Scotch mist. The cooking was abominable, and the dignity of Dervish-hood did not allow me to sit at meat with infidels or to eat the food they had polluted. So the Dervish squatted apart, smoking perpetually, with occasional interruptions to say his prayers and to tell his beads upon the mighty rosary, and he drank the muddy water of the canal out of a leathern bucket, and he munched his bread and garlic* with a desperate sanctimoniousness.

* Those skilled in simples, Eastern as well as Western, praise garlic highly, declaring that it "strengthens the body

The "Little Asthmatic," as the steamer is called, was crowded, and discipline not daring to mark out particular places, the scene on board of her was a motley one. There were two Indian officers, who naturally spoke to none but each other, drank bad tea, and smoked their cigars like Britons. A troop of the Kurd Kawwas*, escorting treasure, was surrounded by a group of noisy Greeks; these men's gross practical jokes sounding anything but pleasant to the solemn Moslems, whose saddle-bags and furniture were at every moment in danger of

prepares the constitution for fatigue, brightens the sight, and, by increasing the digestive power, obviates the ill effects arising from sudden change of air and water." The traveller inserts it into his dietary in some pleasant form, as "Provence-butter," because he observes that, wherever fever and ague abound, the people ignorant of cause, but observant of effect, make it a common article of food. The old Egyptians highly esteemed this vegetable, which, with onions and leeks, enters into the list of articles so much regretted by the Hebrews (Numbers, xi. 5.; Koran, chap. 2.). The modern people of the Nile, like the Spaniards, delight in onions, which, as they contain between 25 and 30 per cent. of gluten, are highly nutritive. In Arabia, however, the stranger must use this vegetable sparingly. The city people despise it as the food of a fellah — a boor. The Wahhabis have a prejudice against onions, leeks, and garlic, because the Prophet disliked their strong smell, and all strict Moslems refuse to eat them immediately before visiting the mosque or meeting for public prayer.

* A policeman; see Chap. I.

being defiled by abominable drinks and the ejected juices of tobacco. There was one pretty woman on board, a Spanish girl, who looked strangely misplaced—a rose in a field of thistles. Some silent Italians, with noisy interpreters, sat staidly upon the benches. It was soon found out, through the communicative dragoman, that their business was to buy horses for H. M. of Sardinia: they were exposed to a volley of questions delivered by a party of French tradesmen returning to Cairo, but they shielded themselves and fought shy with Machiavellian dexterity. Besides these was a German—a "beer-bottle in the morning and a bottle of beer in the evening," to borrow a simile from his own nation—a Syrian merchant, the richest and ugliest of Alexandria, and a few French house-painters going to decorate the Pacha's palace at Shoobra. These last were the happiest of our voyagers,—veritable children of Paris, Montagnards, Voltairiens, and thorough-bred Sans-Soucis. All day they sat upon deck chattering as only their lively nation can chatter, indulging in ultra-gallic maxims, such as "*on ne vieillit jamais à table;*" now playing écarté for love or nothing, then composing "*des ponches un peu chiques;*" now reciting adventures of the category "Mirabolant," then singing, then dancing, then sleeping and rising to play, to drink, talk, dance, and sing again. They being new comers, free from the western *morgue* so soon caught by Oriental Europeans, were particularly civil to me, even wishing to mix me a strong draught; but I was not so fortunate with all on board. A large shopkeeper threatened to "*briser*" my "figure" for putting my pipe near his pantaloons; but seeing me finger my dagger curiously, though I did not shift my pipe, he forgot to remember his threat. I had taken charge of a parcel for one M. P——, a student of Coptic, and remitted it to him on board; of this little service the only acknowledgment was a stare and a petulant inquiry why I had not given it to him before. And one of the Englishmen, half publicly, half privily, as though communing with himself, condemned my organs of vision because I happened to touch his elbow. He was a man in my own service; I pardoned him in consideration of the compliment paid to my disguise.

Two fellow-passengers were destined to play an important part in my comedy of Cairo. Just after we had started, a little event afforded us some amusement. On the bank appeared a short, fat, pursy kind of man, whose efforts to board the steamer were notably ridiculous. With attention divided between the vessel and a carpet-bag carried by his donkey boy, he ran along the sides of the canal, now stumbling into hollows, then climbing heights, then standing shouting upon the projections with the fierce sun upon his back, till every one thought his breath was completely gone. But no! game to the backbone, he would have perished miserably rather than lose his fare: "perseverance," say the copy-books, "accomplishes great things:" at last he was taken on board, and presently he lay down to sleep. His sooty complexion, lank black hair, features in which appeared *beaucoup de finesse*, that is to say, abundant rascality, an eternal smile and treacherous eyes, his gold* ring, dress of showy colours, fleshy stomach, fat legs, round back and a peculiar manner of frowning and fawning simultaneously, marked him an Indian. When he awoke he introduced himself to me as Miyan Khudabakhsh Namdar, a native of Lahore: he had carried on the trade of a shawl merchant in London and Paris, where he lived two years, and after a pilgrimage intended to purge away the sins of civilised lands, had settled at Cairo.

* The stricter sort of Moslems, such as the Arabs, will not wear gold ornaments, which are forbidden by their law.

My second friend, Haji Wali, I will introduce to the reader in a future chapter.

Long conversations in Persian and Hindostani abridged the tediousness of the voyage, and when we arrived at Bulak, the polite Khudabakhsh insisted upon my making his house my home. I was unwilling to accept the man's civility, disliking his looks, but he advanced cogent reasons for changing my mind. His servants cleared my luggage through the custom house, and a few minutes after our arrival I found myself in his abode near the Ezbekiyah Gardens, sitting in a cool mashrabiyah* that gracefully projected over a garden, and sipping the favourite glass of pomegranate syrup.

As the wakálahs or caravanserais were at that time full of pilgrims, I remained with Khudabakhsh ten days or a fortnight. But at the end of that time, my patience was thoroughly exhausted. My host had become a civilised man, who sat on chairs, ate with a fork, talked European politics, and had learned to admire, if not to understand liberty—liberal ideas! and was I not flying from

* The projecting latticed window, made of wood richly carved, for which Cairo was once so famous. But they are growing out of fashion with young Egypt, disappearing before glass and unsightly green blinds.

such things? Besides which, we English have a peculiar national quality, which the Indians, with their characteristic acuteness, soon perceived, and described by an opprobrious name. Observing our solitary habits, that we could not, and would not, sit and talk and sip sherbet and smoke with them, they called us "Jungli"—wild men, fresh caught in the jungle and sent to rule over the land of Hind.* Certainly nothing suits us less than perpetual society, an utter want of solitude, when one cannot retire into oneself an instant without being asked some puerile question by a friend, or look into a book without a servant peering over one's shoulder; when from the hour you rise to the time you rest, you must ever be talking or listening, you must converse yourself to sleep in a public dormitory, and give ear to your companions' snores and mutterings at midnight.†

* Caste in India arises from the peculiarly sociable nature of the native mind, for which reason "it is found existing among sects whose creeds are as different and as opposite as those of the Hindoo and the Christian." (B. A. Irving's Prize Essay on the Theory and Practice of Caste.) Hence, nothing can be more terrible to a man than expulsion from caste; the excommunication of our feudal times was not a more dreadful form of living death.

† With us, every man's house is his castle. But caste di-

The very essence of Oriental hospitality, however, is this family style of reception, which costs your host neither coin nor trouble. You make one more at his eating tray, and an additional mattress appears in the sleeping room. When you depart, you leave if you like a little present, merely for a memorial, with your entertainer; he would be offended if you offered it him openly as a remuneration *, and you give some trifling sums to the servants. Thus you will be welcome wherever you go. If perchance you are detained perforce in such a situation,—which may easily happen to you, medical man,—you have only to make yourself as disagreeable as possible, by calling for all manner of impossible things. Shame is a passion with Eastern nations. Your host would blush to point out to you the indecorum of your conduct; and the laws of hospitality oblige him to supply

vides a people into huge families, each member of which has a right to know every thing about his "caste-brother," because a whole body might be polluted and degraded by the act of an individual. Hence, there is no such thing as domestic privacy, and no system of espionnage devised by rulers could be so complete as that self-imposed by the Hindoos.

* I speak of the rare tracts in which the old barbarous hospitality still lingers.

the every want of a guest, even though he be a *détenu.*

But of all orientals, the most antipathetical companion to an Englishman is, I believe, an Indian. Like the fox in the fable fulsomely flattering at first, he gradually becomes easily friendly, disagreeably familiar, offensively rude, which ends by rousing the "spirit of the British lion." Nothing delights the Indian so much as an opportunity of safely venting the spleen with which he regards his victors.* He will sit in the

* The Calcutta Review (No. 41.), noticing "L'Inde sous la domination Anglaise," by the Baron Barchou de Penhoën, delivers the following sentiment: "Whoever states, as the Baron B. de P. states and repeats, again and again, that the natives generally entertain a bad opinion of the Europeans generally, states what is decidedly untrue."

The reader will observe that I differ as decidedly from the Reviewer's opinion.

Popular feeling towards the English in India was "at first one of fear, afterwards of horror: Hindoos and Moslems considered the strangers a set of cow-eaters and fire-drinkers, tetræ belluæ ac molossis suis ferociores, who would fight like Eblis, cheat their own fathers, and exchange with the same readiness a broadside of shots and thrusts of boarding-pikes, or a bale of goods and a bag of rupees." (The English in Western India.) We have risen in a degree above such low standard of estimation; still, incredible as it may appear to the Frank himself, it is no less true, that the Frank everywhere in the East is considered a contemptible being, and dangerous presence of a magistrate, or an officer, the very picture of cringing submissiveness. But after leaving the room, he is as different from his former self as a counsel in court from a counsel at a concert, a sea captain at a hunt dinner from a sea captain on his quarter deck. Then he will discover that the English are not brave, nor clever, nor generous, nor civilised, nor anything but surpassing rogues; that every official takes bribes, that their manners are utterly offensive, and that they are rank infidels. Then he will descant complacently upon the probability of a general Bartholomew's day in the East, and look forward to the hour when enlightened Young India will arise and drive the "foul invader" from the land. Then he will submit his political opinions nakedly, that India should be wrested from the Company and given to the Queen, or taken from the Queen

withal. As regards Indian opinion concerning our government, my belief is, that in and immediately about the three presidencies, where the people owe every thing to and hold every thing by our rule, it is most popular. At the same time I am convinced that in other places the people would most willingly hail any change; and how can we hope it to be otherwise,—we, a nation of strangers, aliens to the country's customs and creed, who, even while resident in India, act the part which absentees do in other lands? Where, in the history of the world, do we read that such foreign dominion ever made itself popular?

and given to the French. If the Indian has been a European traveller, so much the worse for you. He has blushed to own,—explaining, however, conquest by bribery,—that 50,000 Englishmen hold 150,000,000 of his compatriots in thrall, and for aught you know, republicanism may have become his idol. He has lost all fear of the white face, and having been accustomed to unburden his mind in

> "The land where, girt by friend or foe,
> A man may speak the thing he will,"—

he pursues the same course in other lands where it is exceedingly misplaced. His doctrines of liberty and inequality he applies to you personally and practically, by not rising when you enter or leave the room,—at first you could scarcely induce him to sit down,—by not offering you his pipe, by turning away when you address him,—in fact, by a variety of similar small affronts which none know better to manage skilfully and with almost impalpable gradations. If,—and how he prays for it!—an opportunity of refusing you any thing presents itself, he does it with an air.

> "In rice strength,
> In an Indian manliness," *

* In the Arabic "Murruwwat," generosity, the noble part of human nature, the qualities which make a man.

say the Arabs. And the Persians apply the following pithy tale to their neighbours. "Brother," said the leopard to the jackal, "I crave a few of thy cast-off hairs; I want them for medicine*; where can I find them?" "Wallah!" replied the jackal, "I don't exactly know—I seldom change my coat—I wander about the hills. Allah is bounteous† brother! hairs are not so easily shed."

Woe to the unhappy Englishman, Pacha, or private soldier, who must serve an Eastern lord! Worst of all, if the master be an Indian who, hating all Europeans‡, adds an especial spite to oriental coarseness, treachery, and tyranny. Even the experiment of associating with them is almost

* "For medicine," means for an especial purpose, an urgent occasion.

† "Allah Karim!" said to a beggar when you do not intend to be bountiful.

‡ Read an account of Tippoo Sahib's treatment of his French employés. If Runjeet Singh behaved better to his European officers, it was only on account of his paramount fear and hatred of the British. The Panjabi story of the old lion's death is amusing enough, contrasted with that Anglomania of which so much has been said and written. When the Sikh king, they declare, heard of our success in Afghanistan—he had allowed us a passage through his dominions, as ingress into a deadly trap—his spirits (metaphorically and literally) failed him; he had not the heart to drink, he sickened and died.

too hard to bear. But a useful deduction may be drawn from such observations; and as few have had greater experience than myself, I venture to express my opinion with confidence, however unpopular or unfashionable it may be.

I am convinced that the natives of India cannot respect a European who mixes with them familiarly, or especially who imitates their customs, manners, and dress. The tight pantaloons, the authoritative voice, the pococurante manner, and the broken Hindostani impose upon them—have a weight which learning and honesty, which wit and courage, have not. This is to them the master's attitude: they bend to it like those Scythian slaves that faced the sword but fled from the horsewhip. Such would never be the case amongst a brave people, the Afghan for instance. And for the same reason it is not so, we read, with the North American tribes. "The free trapper combines in the eye of an Indian (American) girl, all that is dashing and heroic, in a warrior of her own race, whose gait and garb and bravery he emulates, with all that is gallant and glorious in the white man." There is but one cause for this phenomenon; the "imbelles Indi" are still, with few exceptions*, a cowardly and

* The Rajputs, for instance, "whose land has ever been the focus of Indian chivalry, and the home of Indian heroes."

slavish people, who would raise themselves by depreciating those superior to them in the scale of the creation. The Afghans and American aborigines, being chivalrous races, rather exaggerate the valour of their foes, because by so doing they exalt their own.*

* As my support against the possible, or rather the probable, imputation of "extreme opinions," I hold up the honoured name of the late Sir Henry Elliot (Preface to the Biographical Index to the Historians of Mohammedan India).

"These idle vapourers (bombastic Baboos, and other such political ranters), would learn that the sacred spark of patriotism is exotic here, and can never fall on a mine that can explode; for history will show them that certain peculiarities of physical, as well as moral organisation, neither to be strengthened by diet nor improved by education, have hitherto prevented their ever attempting a national independence; which will continue to exist to them but as a name, and as an off-scouring of college declamations."

CHAP. IV.

LIFE IN THE WAKÁLAH.

THE "wakálah," as the caravanserai or khan is called in Egypt, combines the offices of hotel, lodging house, and store. It is at Cairo, as at Constantinople, a massive pile of buildings surrounding a quadrangular "hosh" or court-yard. On the ground-floor are rooms like caverns for merchandise, and shops of different kinds—tailors, cobblers, bakers, tobacconists, fruiterers, and others. A roofless gallery or a covered verandah, into which all the apartments open, runs round the first and sometimes the second story: the latter, however, is usually exposed to the sun and wind. The accommodations consist of sets of two or three rooms, generally an inner one and an outer; this contains a hearth for cooking, a bathing place, and similar necessaries. The staircases are high, narrow, and exceedingly dirty, dark at night and often in bad repair; a goat or donkey is tethered upon the different landings; here and there a fresh skin is stretched in process of tanning, and the smell reminds the veteran traveller of those closets in the old French inns where cats used to be prepared for playing the part of jugged hare. The interior is unfurnished; even the pegs upon which clothes are hung have been pulled down for fire-wood: the walls are bare but for stains, thick cobwebs depend in festoons from the blackened rafters of the ceiling, and the stone floor would disgrace a civilised prison: the windows are huge apertures carefully barred with wood or iron, and in rare places show remains of glass or paper pasted over the framework. In the court-yard the poorer sort of travellers consort with tethered beasts of burden, beggars howl, and the slaves lie basking and scratching themselves upon mountainous heaps of cotton bales and other merchandise.

This is not a tempting picture, yet is the wakálah a most amusing place, presenting a succession of scenes which would delight lovers of the Dutch school—a rich exemplification of the grotesque, and what is called by our artists the "dirty picturesque."

I could find no room in the Wakálah Khan Khalil, (the Long's, or Meurice's, of native Cairo,) I was therefore obliged to put up with the Jemaliyah, the Greek quarter, a place swarming with drunken Christians, and therefore about as fashionable as Oxford Street or Covent Garden. Even for this I had to wait a week. The pilgrims were flocking to Cairo, and to none other would the prudent hotel keepers open their doors, for the following sufficient reasons. When you enter a wakálah the first thing you have to do is to pay a small sum, varying from two to five shillings, for the 'miftah (the key). This is generally equivalent to a month's rent, so the sooner you leave the house the better for it. I was obliged to call myself a Turkish pilgrim in order to get possession of two most comfortless rooms, which I afterwards learned were celebrated for making travellers ill, and I had to pay eighteen piastres for the key and eighteen ditto per mensem for rent, besides five piastres to the man who swept and washed the place. So that for this month my house hire amounted to nearly four pence a day.

But I was fortunate enough in choosing the Jemaliyah Wakálah, for I found a friend there. On board the steamer a fellow voyager, seeing me sitting alone and therefore as he conceived in discomfort, placed himself by my side and opened a hot fire of kind inquiries. He was a man about forty-five, of middle size, with a large round head closely shaven, a bull-neck, limbs sturdy as a Saxon's, a thin red beard, and handsome features beaming with benevolence. A curious dry humour he had, delighting in "quizzing," but in so quiet, solemn, and quaint a way that before you knew him you could scarcely divine his drift.

"Thank Allah we carry a doctor!" said my friend more than once, with apparent fervour of gratitude, after he had discovered my profession. I was fairly taken by the pious ejaculation, and some days elapsed before the drift of his remark became apparent.

"You doctors," he explained when we were more intimate, "what do you do? a man goes to you for ophthalmia. It is a purge, a blister, and a drop on the eye! Is it for fever? well! a purge and kinakina (quinine). For dysentery? a purge and extract of opium. Wallah! I am as good a physician as the best of you," he would add with a broad grin, "if I only knew the Dirham-birhams *, and a few break-jaw Arabic names of diseases."

* The second is an imitative word, called in Arabic grammar Tabi, as "Zayd Bayd," "Zayd and others"; so used, it denotes contempt for drachms and similar parts of drug-craft.

Haji Wali * therefore emphatically advised me to make bread by honestly teaching languages. "We are doctor-ridden," said he, and I found it was the case.

When we lived under the same roof, the Haji and I became fast friends. During the day we called on each other frequently, we dined together, and passed the evening in a mosque, or some other place of public pastime. Coyly at first, but less guardedly as we grew bolder, we smoked the forbidden weed "hashish †," conversing lengthily the while about that world of which I had seen so much. Originally from Russia he also had been a traveller, and in his wanderings had cast off most of the prejudices of his people. "I believe in

* The familiar abbreviation of Wali el din: this was the name assumed by the enterprising traveller Dr. Wallin.

† By the Indians called Bhang, the Persians Bang, and the natives of Barbary, I believe, Fasukh. The Hottentots use it, and even the Siberians, we are told, intoxicate themselves by the vapour of this seed thrown upon red-hot stones. Egypt surpasses all other nations in the variety of compounds into which this fascinating drug enters, and will one day probably supply the Western world with "Indian hemp," when its solid merits are duly appreciated. At present in Europe it is chiefly confined, as cognac and opium used to be, to the apothecary's shelves. Some adventurous individuals at Paris, after the perusal of Monte Christo, attempted an "orgie" in one of the cafés, but with poor success.

Allah and his Prophet, and in nothing else" was his sturdy creed; he rejected alchemy, genii and magicians, and truly he had a most unoriental distaste for tales of wonder. When I entered the wakálah, he constituted himself my Cicerone, and especially guarded me against the cheating of tradesmen. By his advice I laid aside the Dervish's gown, the large blue pantaloons, and the short shirt, in fact all connection with Persia and the Persians. "If you persist in being an Ajemi," said the Haji, "you will get yourself into trouble; in Egypt you will be cursed, in Arabia you will be beaten because you are a heretic, you will pay the treble of what other travellers do, and if you fall sick you may die by the roadside." After long deliberation about the choice of nations I became a Pathan.* Born in India of Afghan parents, who had settled in the country, educated at Rangoon, and sent out to wander, as men of that race fre-

* The Indian name of an Afghan, supposed to be a corruption of the Arabic Fathan (a conqueror), or a derivation from the Hindostani *paithna*, to penetrate (into the hostile ranks). It is an honourable term in Arabia, where "Khurasani" (a native of Khorassan), leads men to suspect a Persian, and the other generic appellation of the Afghan tribes. Sulaymani, a descendant from Solomon, reminds the people of their proverb, "Sulaymani harame"! "the Afghans are ruffians!"

quently are, from early youth, I was well guarded against the danger of detection by a fellow-countryman. To support the character requires a knowledge of Persian, Hindostani and Arabic, all of which I knew sufficiently well to pass muster; any trifling inaccurary was charged upon my long residence at Rangoon. This was an important step: the first question at the shop, on the camel, and in the mosque, is "What is thy name?" the second "Whence comest thou?" This is not generally impertinent, or intended to be annoying; if, however, you see any evil intention in the questioner, you may rather roughly ask him, "What may be his maternal parent's name" — equivalent to enquiring, *Anglicè*, in what church his mother was married — and escape your difficulties under cover of a storm. But this is rarely necessary. I assumed the polite pliant manners of an Indian physician, and the dress of a small Effendi*, still, however, representing myself to be a Dervish, and frequenting the places where Dervishes congregate. "What business," asked the Haji, "have those reverend men with politics or statistics, or any of the information which you are collecting? Call

* Gentleman.

yourself a religious wanderer if you like, and let those who ask the object of your peregrinations know that you are under a vow to visit all the holy places in Islam. Thus you will persuade them that you are a man of rank under a cloud, and you will receive much more civility than perhaps you deserve," concluded my friend with a dry laugh. The remark proved his sagacity, and after ample experience I had not to repent having been guided by his advice.

Haji Wali, by profession a merchant at Alexandria, had accompanied Khudabakhsh the Indian, to Cairo on law-business. He soon explained his affairs to me, and as his case brought out certain oriental peculiarities in a striking light, with his permission I offer a few of its details.

My friend was defendant in a suit instituted against him in our Consular court by one Mohammed Shafia, a scoundrel of the first water. This man lived, and lived well, by setting up in business at places where his name was not known; he enticed the unwary by artful displays of capital, and after succeeding in getting credit, he changed residence, carrying off all he could lay hands upon. But swindling is a profession of personal danger in uncivilised countries, where law punishes pauper debtors by a short imprisonment; and the cheated parties prefer to gratify their revenge by the staff or the knife. So Mohammed Shafia, after a few narrow escapes, hit upon a prime expedient. Though known to be a native of Bokhara — he actually signed himself so in his letters — and his appearance at once bespoke his origin, he determined to protect himself by a British passport. Our officials are sometimes careless enough in distributing these documents, and by so doing, they expose themselves to a certain loss of reputation at Eastern courts *; still Mohammed Shafia found some difficulties in effecting his fraud. To recount

* For the simple reason that no Eastern power confers such an obligation except for value received. In old times, when official honour was not so rigorous as it is now, the creditors of Eastern powers and principalities would present high sums to British Residents and others for the privilege of being enrolled in the list of their subjects or servants. This they made profitable; for their claims, however exorbitant, when backed by a name of fear, were certain to be admitted, unless the Resident's conscience would allow of his being persuaded by weightier arguments of a similar nature to abandon his protégé.

It is almost needless to remark that nothing of the kind can occur in the present day, and at the same time that throughout the Eastern world it is firmly believed that such things are of daily occurrence. The fame descends to distant generations, whilst good deeds, if they blossom, as we are told, in the dust, are at least as short lived as they are sweet.

all his Reynardisms would weary the reader; suffice it to say that by proper management of the subalterns in the consulate, he succeeded without ruining himself. Armed with this new defence, he started boldly for Jeddah on the Arabian coast. Having entered into partnership with Haji Wali, whose confidence he had won by prayers, fastings and pilgrimages, he openly trafficked in slaves, sending them to Alexandria for sale, and writing with matchless impudence to his correspondent that he would dispose of them in person, but for fear of losing his passport.

Presently an unlucky adventure embroiled this worthy British subject with Faraj Yusuf, the principal merchant of Jeddah, and also an English protégé. Fearing so powerful an adversary, Mohammed Shafia packed up his spoils and departed for Egypt. Presently he quarrels with his former partner, thinking him a soft man, and claims from him a debt of 165*l.* He supports his pretensions by a document and four witnesses, who are ready to swear that the receipt in question was "signed, sealed, and delivered" by Haji Wali. The latter adduces his books to show that accounts have been settled, and can prove that the witnesses in question are paupers, therefore, not legal, and moreover, that each has received from the plaintiff two dollars, the price of perjury.

Now had such a suit been carried into a Turkish court of justice, it would very sensibly have been settled by the bastinado, for Haji Wali was a respectable merchant, and Mohammed Shafia a notorious swindler. But the latter was a British subject, which notably influenced the question. The more to annoy his adversary, he went up to Cairo, and began proceedings there, hoping by this acute step to receive part payment of his demand.

Arrived at Cairo Mohammed Shafia applied himself stoutly to the task of bribing all who could be useful to him, distributing shawls and piastres with great generosity. He secured the services of an efficient lawyer, and, determining to enlist heaven itself in his cause, he passed the Ramadhan ostentatiously, he fasted, and he slaughtered sheep to feed the poor.

Meanwhile Haji Wali, a simple truth-telling man, who could never master the rudiments of that art, which teaches man to blow hot and to blow cold with the same breath, had been persuaded to visit Cairo by Khudabakhsh, the wily Indian, who promised to introduce him to influential persons, and to receive him in his house till he could provide himself with a lodging at the Wakâlah. But

Mohammed Shafia, who had once been in partnership with the Indian, and possibly knew more than was fit to meet the public ear, found this out, and, partly by begging, partly by bullying, persuaded Khudabakhsh to transfer the influential introductions to himself. Then the Hakim Abdullah—your humble servant — appears upon the scene: he has travelled in Feringistan, he has seen many men and their cities, he becomes an intimate and an adviser of the Haji, and he finds out evil passages in Mohammed Shafia's life. Upon which Khudabakhsh ashamed, or rather afraid of his duplicity, collects his Indian friends. The Hakim Abdullah draws up a petition addressed to Mr. Walne, the British consul, by the Indian merchants and others resident at Cairo, informing him of Mohammed Shafia's birth, character, and occupation as a vendor of slaves, offering proof of all assertions, and praying him for the sake of their good name to take away his passport. And all the Indians affix their seals to this paper. Then Mohammed Shafia threatens to waylay and to beat the Haji. The Haji, not loud or hectoringly, but with a composed smile, advises his friends to hold him off.

One would suppose that such a document would have elicited some inquiry.

But Haji Wali was a Persian protégé, and proceedings between the consulates had commenced before the petition was presented. The pseudo-British subject, having been acknowledged as a real one, must be supported. Consuls, like kings, may err, but must not own to error. No notice was taken of the Indian petition; worse still, no inquiry into the slave-affair was set on foot*, and it was discovered that the passport having been granted by a consul-general could not with official etiquette be resumed by a consul.†

* It may be as well to remark that our slave laws require reform throughout the East, their severity, like Draco's Code, defeating their purpose. In Egypt, for instance, they require modification. Constitute the offence a misdemeanour, not a felony, inflict a fine (say 100*l.*), half of which should be given to the informer, and make the imprisonment either a short one, or what would be better still, let it be done away with, except in cases of non-payment; and finally, let the consul or some other magistrate residing at the place have power to inflict the penalty of the law, instead of being obliged, as at present, to transmit offenders to Malta for trial.

As the law now stands, our officials are unwilling to carry its rigours into effect; they therefore easily lend an ear to the standard excuse—ignorance—in order to have an opportunity of decently dismissing a man, with a warning not to do it again.

† Yet at the time there was at Alexandria an acting consul-general, to whom the case could with strict propriety have been referred.

Thus matters were destined to proceed as they began. Mohammed Shafia had offered 5,000 piastres to the Persian consul's interpreter; this of course was refused, but still some how or other all the Haji's affairs seemed to go wrong. His statements were mistranslated, his accounts were misunderstood, and the suit was allowed to drag on to a suspicious length. When I left Cairo in July Haji Wali had been kept away nearly two months from his business and family, though both parties —for the plaintiff's purse was rapidly thinning— appeared eager to settle the difference by arbitration; when I returned from Arabia in October matters were almost *in statu quo antè*, and when I started for India in January, the proceedings had not closed.

Such is a brief history, but too common, of a case in which the subject of an Eastern state has to contend against British influence. It is doubtless a point of honour to defend our protégés from injustice, but the higher principle should rest upon the base of common honesty. The worst part of such a case is, that the injured party has no redress.

"Fiat *in*justitia, ruat cœlum,"

is the motto of his "natural protectors," who would

violate every law to gratify the false pride of a petty English official. And, saving the rare exceptions where rank or wealth command consideration, with what face, to use the native phrase, would a hapless Turk appeal to the higher powers, our ministers or our Parliament?

After lodging myself in the Wakálah, my first object was to make a certain stir in the world. In Europe your travelling doctor advertises the loss of a diamond ring, the gift of a Russian autocrat, or he monopolises a whole column in a newspaper, feeing perhaps a title for the use of a signature; the large brass plate, the gold-headed cane, the rattling chariot, and the summons from the sermon complete the work. Here, there is no such royal road to medical fame. You must begin by sitting with the porter, who is sure to have blear eyes, into which you drop a little nitrate of silver, whilst you instil into his ear the pleasing intelligence that you never take a fee from the poor. He recovers; his report of you spreads far and wide, crowding your doors with paupers. They come to you as though you were their servant, and when cured, turn their backs upon you for ever. Hence it is that European doctors generally complain of ingratitude on the part of their Oriental patients. It is true that if you save a man's life, he naturally asks you for the means of preserving it. Moreover, in none of the Eastern languages with which I am acquainted, is there a single term conveying the meaning of our "gratitude," and none but the Germans * have ideas unexplainable by words. But you must not condemn this absence of a virtue without considering the cause. An Oriental deems that he has a right to your surplus. "Daily bread is divided" (by heaven), he asserts, and eating yours, he considers it his own. Thus it is with other things. He is thankful to Allah for the gifts of the Creator, but he has a claim to the good offices of a fellow creature. In rendering him a service you have but done your duty, and he would not pay you so poor a compliment as to praise you for the act. He leaves you, his benefactor, with a short prayer for the length of your days. "Thank you," being expressed by "Allah increase thy weal!" or the selfish wish that your

* Johann Gottlieb Fichte expressly declares that the scope of his system has never been explained by words, and that it even admits not of being so explained. To make his opinions intelligible, he would express them by a system of figures each of which must have a known and positive value.

shadow (with which you protect him and his fellows) may never be less. And this is probably the last you hear of him.

There is a discomfort in such proceedings, a reasonable, a metaphysical coldness, uglily contrasting in theory with the genial warmth which a little more heart would infuse into them. In theory, I say, not in practice. What can be more troublesome than, when you have obliged a man, to run the gauntlet of his and his family's thanksgivings. "To find yourself become a master from being a friend," a great man where you were an equal; not to be contradicted, where shortly before every one gave his opinion freely. You must be unamiable if these considerations deter you from benefiting your friend, yet, I humbly opine, you still may fear his gratefulness.

To resume. When the mob has raised you to fame, patients of a better class will slowly appear on the scene. After some coquetting about "etiquette," whether you are to visit them, or they are to call upon you, they make up their minds to see you, and to judge with their eyes whether you are to be trusted or not; whilst you, on your side, set out with the determination that they shall at once cross the Rubicon,—in less classical phrase, swallow your drug. If you visit the house, you insist upon the patient's servants attending you; he must also provide and pay an ass for your conveyance, no matter if it be only to the other side of the street. Your confidential man accompanies you, primed for replies to the "fifty searching questions" of the "servants' hall." You are lifted off the saddle tenderly, as nurses dismount their charges, when you arrive at the gate, and you waddle up stairs with dignity. Arrived at the sick room, you salute those present with a general "peace be upon you!" to which they respond, "and upon you be the peace and the mercy of Allah, and his blessing!" To the invalid you say, "There is nothing the matter, please Allah, except the health;" to which the proper answer—for here every sign of ceremony has its countersign * —is, "may Allah give thee health!" You then sit down, and acknowledge the presence of the company by raising your right hand to your lips and forehead, bowing the while circularly; each individual returns the civility by a similar gesture. Then inquiry about the state of your health ensues. Then you are asked what refreshment you will

* M. C. de Perceval (Arabic Grammar), and Lane (Mod. Egyptians, Chapter 8. *et passim*) give specimens.

take: you studiously mention something not likely to be in the house, but at last you rough it with a pipe and a cup of coffee. Then you proceed to the patient, who extends his wrist, and asks you what his complaint is. Then you examine his tongue, you feel his pulse, you look learned, and — he is talking all the time — after hearing a detailed list of all his ailments, you gravely discover them, taking for the same as much praise to yourself as does the practising phrenologist, for a similar simple exercise of the reasoning faculties. The disease, to be respectable, must invariably be connected with one of the four temperaments, or the four elements, or the "humours of Hippocrates." Cure is easy, but it will take time, and you, the doctor, require attention; any little rudeness it is in your power to punish by an alteration in the pill, or the powder, and, so unknown is professional honour, that none will brave your displeasure. If you would pass for a native practitioner, you must then proceed to a most uncomfortable part of your visit, bargaining for fees. Nothing more effectually arouses suspicion than disinterestedness in a doctor. I once cured a rich Hazramaut merchant of rheumatism, and neglected to make him pay for treatment; he carried off one of my coffee cups, and was unceasingly wondering where I came from. So I made him produce five piastres, a shilling, which he threw upon the carpet, cursing Indian avarice. "You will bring on another illness," said my friend, the Haji, when he heard of it. Properly speaking, the fee for a visit to a respectable man is 20 piastres, but with the rich patient you begin by making a bargain. He complains, for instance, of dysentery and sciatica. You demand 10*l.* for the dysentery, and 20*l.* for the sciatica. But you will rarely get it. The Eastern pays a doctor's bill as an Irishman does his "rint," making a grievance of it. Your patients will show indisputable signs of convalescence: he will laugh and jest half the day; but the moment you appear, groans and a lengthened visage, and pretended complaints welcome you. Then your way is to throw out some such hint as

"The world is a carcass, and they who seek it are dogs."

And you refuse to treat the second disorder, which conduct may bring the refractory one to his senses. "Dat Galenus opes," however, is a Western apothegm: the utmost "Jalinus" can do for you here is to provide you with the necessaries and the comforts of life. Whatever you prescribe must be solid and material, and if you accompany it with something painful, such as rubbing unto scarification with a horse brush, so much the better. Easterns, as our peasants in Europe, like the doctor to "give them the value of their money." Besides which rough measures act beneficially upon their imagination. So the Hakim of the King of Persia cured fevers by the bastinado; patients are beneficially baked in a bread-oven at Bagdad; and an Egyptian at Alexandria, whose quartan resisted the strongest appliances of European physic, was effectually healed by the actual cautery, which a certain Arab Shaykh applied to the crown of his head. When you administer with your own hand the remedy — half-a-dozen huge bread pills, dipped in a solution of aloes or cinnamon water, flavoured with assa-fœtida, which in the case of the dyspeptic rich often suffice, if they will but diet themselves — you are careful to say, "In the name of Allah, the compassionate, the merciful." And after the patient has been dosed, "Praise be to Allah, the curer, the healer;" you then call for pen, ink, and paper, and write some such prescription as this: —

"A *

"In the name of Allah, the compassionate, the merciful, and blessings and peace be upon our Lord the Prophet, and his family, and his companions one and all! But afterwards let him take bees-honey and cinnamon and album græcum, of each half a part, and of ginger a whole part, which let him pound and mix with the honey, and form boluses, each bolus the weight of a miskal, and of it let him use every day a miskal on the saliva.† Verily its effects are wonderful. And let him abstain from flesh, fish, vegetables, sweetmeats, flatulent food, acids of all descriptions, as well as the major ablution, and live in perfect quiet. So shall he be cured by the help of the King the Healer.‡ And the peace." §

The diet, I need scarcely say, should be rigorous; nothing has tended more to bring the European system of medicine into contempt among orientals than our inattention to this branch of the therapeutic art. When an Indian takes cathartic medicine, he prepares himself for it by diet and rest two or three days before its adhibition, and as gradually after the dose, he relapses into his usual habits; if he break through the régime it is concluded that fatal results

* A monogram generally placed at the head of writings. It is the initial letter of "Allah," and the first of the alphabet, used from time immemorial to denote the origin of creation. "I am Alpha and Omega, the first and the last."

† "Al' ar-rik," that is to say, fasting — the first thing in the morning.

‡ The Almighty. § Was'-salam, *i. e.* adieu.

must ensue. The ancient Egyptians we learn from Herodotus devoted a certain number of days in each month to the use of alteratives, and the period was consecutive, doubtless in order to graduate the strength of the medicine. The Persians, when under salivation, shut themselves up in a warm room, never undress, and so carefully guard against cold that they even drink tepid water. When the Afghan princes find it necessary to employ Chob-Chini, (the Jinseng,* or China root so

* From M. Huc we learn that Jin-seng is the most considerable article of Manchurian commerce, and that throughout China, there is no chemist's shop unprovided with more or less of it. He adds, "the Chinese report marvels of the Jin-seng, and no doubt it is for Chinese organisation a tonic of very great effect for old and weak persons; but its nature is too heating, the Chinese physicians admit, for the European temperament, already in their opinion too hot. The price is enormous, and doubtless its dearness contributes with a people like the Chinese to raise its celebrity so high. The rich and the Mandarins probably use it only because it is above the reach of other people, and out of pure ostentation."

It is the principal tonic used throughout Central Asia, and was well known in Europe when Sarsaparilla arose to dispute with it the palm of popularity. In India, Persia, and Afghanistan, it is called chob-chini,—the "Chinese-wood." The preparations are in two forms, 1. Sufuf, or powder; 2. Kahwah, or decoction. The former is compound of Radix China Orient. with gum mastich and sugar-candy, equal parts; about a dram of this compound is taken once a day, early in the morning.

celebrated as a purifier, tonic, and aphrodisiac) they choose the spring season; they remove to a garden, where flowers and trees and bubbling streams soothe their senses; they carefully avoid fatigue and trouble of all kinds, and will not even hear a letter read, lest it should contain bad news.

When the prescription is written out, you affix an impression of your ring seal to the beginning and the end of it, that no one may be able to add

For the decoction one ounce of fine parings is boiled for a quarter of an hour in a quart of water. When the liquid assumes a red colour it is taken off the fire and left to cool.

Furthermore there are two methods of adhibiting the chobchini: 1. Band; 2. Khola. The first is when the patient confines himself to a garden, listening to music, enjoying the breeze, the song of birds, and the bubbling of a flowing stream. He avoids every thing likely to trouble and annoy him; he will not even open a letter, and the doctor forbids any one to contradict him. Some grandees in central Asia will go through a course of forty days every second year: it reminds one of Epicurus' style of treatment,—the downy bed, the garlands of flowers, the good wine, and the beautiful singing girl, and is doubtless at least as efficacious in curing, as the sweet relaxation of Grafenberg or Malvern. So says Socrates, according to the Anatomist of Melancholy,

"Oculum non curabis sine toto capite,
Nec caput sine toto corpore,
Nec totum corpus sine animo."

The "Khola" signifies that you take the tonic without other precautions than the avoiding acids, salt, and pepper, and choosing summer time, as cold is supposed to induce rheumatism.

to, or to take from its contents. And when you send medicine to a patient of rank, who is sure to have enemies, you adopt some similar precaution against the box or the bottle being opened. One of the Pashas whom I attended,— a brave soldier who had been a favourite with Mohammed Ali, and therefore was degraded by his successor,— kept an impression of my ring in wax, to compare with that upon the phials. Men have not forgotten how frequently, in former times, those who became obnoxious to the state were seized with sudden and fatal cramps in the stomach. In the case of the doctor it is common prudence to adopt these precautions, as all evil consequences would be charged upon him, and he would be exposed to the family's revenge.

Cairo, though abounding in medical practitioners, can still support more; but they must be Indians, or Chinese, or Maghrabis to thrive. The Egyptians are thoroughly disgusted with European treatment, which is here about as efficacious as in India — that is to say, not at all. But they are ignorant of the medicine of Hind, and therefore great is its name; deservedly perhaps, for skill in simples and dietetics. Besides which the Indian may deal in charms and spells,—things to which the latitude gives such force that even Europeans learn to put faith in them. The traveller who, on the banks of the Seine, scoffs at Sights and Sounds, Table-turning and Spirit-rapping, in the wilds of Tartary and Thibet sees a something supernatural and diabolical in the bungling *Sie-fa* of the *Bokte.** Some sensible men, who pass for philosophers among their friends, have been caught by the incantations of the turbaned and bearded Cairo magician. In our West African colonies the phrase "growing black," was applied to colonists, who, after a term of residence, became thoroughly imbued with the superstitions of the land. And there are not wanting old English Indians, intelligent men, that place firm trust in tales and tenets too puerile even for the Hindus to believe. As "Hindi" I could use animal magnetism, taking care, however, to give the science a specious super-

* Certain Lamas who, we learn from M. Huc, perform famous Sie-fa, or supernaturalisms, such as cutting open the abdomen, licking red-hot irons, making incisions in various parts of the body, which an instant afterwards leave no trace behind, &c. &c. The devil may "have a great deal to do with the matter" in Tartary, for all I know; but I can assure M. Huc, that the Rufia Dervishes in India and the Saadiyah at Cairo perform exactly the same feats. Their jugglery, seen through the smoke of incense, and amidst the enthusiasm of a crowd, is tolerably dexterous, and no more.

natural appearance. Haji Wali, who, professing positive scepticism, showed the greatest interest in the subject, as a curiosity, advised me not to practise pure mesmerism; otherwise, that I should infallibly become a "Companion of Devils." "You must call this an Indian secret," said my friend, "for it is clear that you are no Mashaikh *, and people will ask, where are your drugs, and what business have you with charms?" It is useless to say that I followed his counsel; yet patients would consider themselves my Murids, and delighted in kissing the hand of the Sahib Nafas † or minor saint.

The Haji repaid me for my docility by vaunting me everywhere as the very phœnix of physicians. My first successes were in the Wakálah: opposite to me there lived an Arab slave dealer, whose

* A holy man. The word has a singular signification in a plural form, "*honoris causâ.*"

† A title literally meaning the "master of breath," one who can cure ailments, physical as well as spiritual, by breathing upon them—a practice well known to mesmerists. The reader will allow me to observe, (in self-defence, otherwise he might look suspiciously upon so credulous a narrator), that when speaking of animal magnetism, as a thing established, I allude to the lower phenomena, rejecting the discussion of all disputed points, as the existence of a magnetic aura, and of all its unintelligibilities—Prevision, Introvision, and other divisions of Clairvoyance.

Abyssinian constantly fell sick. A tender race, they suffer when first transported to Egypt from many complaints, especially consumption, dysentery and varicose veins. I succeeded in curing one girl. As she was worth at least fifteen pounds, the gratitude of her owner was great, and I had to dose half a dozen others in order to cure them of the pernicious and price-lowering habit of snoring. Living in rooms opposite these slave girls, and seeing them at all hours of the day and night, I had frequent opportunities of studying them. They were average specimens of the steatopygous Abyssinian breed, broad-shouldered, thin-flanked, fine-limbed, and with haunches of a prodigious size. None of them had handsome features, but the short curly hair that stands on end being concealed under a kerchief, there was something pretty in the brow, eyes and upper part of the nose, coarse and sensual in the pendent lips, large jowl and projecting mouth, whilst the whole had a combination of piquancy with sweetness. Their style of flirtation was peculiar.

"How beautiful thou art, O Maryam!—what eyes! — what —"

"Then why,"—would respond the lady — "don't you buy me ?"

"We are of one faith—of one creed—formed to form each other's happiness."

"Then why don't you buy me?"

"Conceive, O Maryam, the blessing of two hearts—"

"Then why don't you buy me?"

and so on. Most effectual gag to Cupid's eloquence! Yet was not the plain-spoken Maryam's reply without its moral. How often is it our fate in the West, as in the East, to see in bright eyes and to hear from rosy lips an implied, if not an expressed, "Why don't you buy me?" or, worse still, "Why can't you buy me?"

All I required in return for my services from the slave dealer, whose brutal countenance and manners were truly repugnant, was to take me about the town, and explain to me certain mysteries in his craft, which knowledge might be useful in time to come. Little did he suspect who his interrogator was, and freely in his unsuspiciousness he entered upon the subject of slave hunting in the Somali country, and Zanzibar, of all things the most interesting to me. I have nothing new to report concerning the present state of bondsmen in Egypt. England has already learned that slaves are not necessarily the most wretched and degraded of men.

Some have been bold enough to tell the British public, that, in the generality of Oriental countries*, the serf fares far better than the servant, or indeed than the poorer orders of freemen. "The laws of Mahomet enjoin his followers to treat slaves with the greatest mildness, and the Moslems are in general scrupulous observers of the Prophet's recommendation. Slaves are considered members of the family, and in houses where free servants are kept besides, they seldom do any other work than filling the pipes, presenting the coffee, accompanying their master when going out, rubbing his feet when he takes his nap in the afternoon, and driving away the flies from him. When a slave is not satisfied, he can legally compel his master to sell him. He has no care for food, lodging, clothes and washing, and has no taxes to pay; he is exempt from military service and soccage, and

* In the generality, not in all. Nothing, for instance, can be more disgraceful to human nature than the state of prœdial slavery, or serfs attached to the glebe, when Malabar was under the dominion of the "mild Hindu." And as a rule in the East it is only the domestic slaves who taste the sweets of slavery. Yet there is truth in Sonnini's terrible remark: "The severe treatment under which the slaves languish in the West Indies is the shameful prerogative of civilisation, and is unknown to those nations among whom barbarism is reported to hold sway." (Travels in Upper and Lower Egypt, vol. ii.)

in spite of his bondage is freer than the freest Fellah in Egypt." * This is, I believe, a true statement, but of course it in nowise affects the question of slavery in the abstract. A certain amount of reputation was the consequence of curing the Abyssinian girls: my friend Haji Wali carefully told the news to all the town, and before fifteen days were over, I found myself obliged to decline extending a practice which threatened me with fame.

Servants are most troublesome things to all Englishmen in Egypt, but especially to one travelling as a respectable native, and therefore expected to have slaves. After much deliberation, I resolved to take a Berberi †, and accordingly sum-

* The author has forgotten to mention one of the principal advantages of slaves, namely, the prospect of arriving at the highest rank of the empire. The Pacha of the Syrian caravan with which I travelled to Damascus, had been the slave of a slave, and he is but a solitary instance of cases perpetually occurring in all Moslem lands. "*C'est un homme de bonne famille,*" said a Turkish officer in Egypt, "*il a été acheté.*"

† A "Barbarian" from Upper Egypt. Some authorities, Mr. Lane for instance, attribute the good reputation of these people to their superior cunning. Sonnini says, "they are intelligent and handy servants, but knaves." Others believe in them. As far as I could find out, they were generally esteemed more honest than the Egyptians, and they certainly possess a

moned a Shaykh — there is a Shaykh for every thing down to thieves in Asia — and made known my want. The list of *sine quâ nons* was necessarily rather an extensive one,—good health and a readiness to travel anywhere, a little skill in cooking, sewing and washing, willingness to fight, and a habit of regular prayers. After a day's delay the Shaykh brought me a specimen of his choosing, a broad-shouldered, bandy-legged fellow, with the usual bull-dog expression of the Berberis, in his case rendered still more expressive by the drooping of an eyelid—an accident brought about with acrid juice in order to avoid conscription. He responded sturdily to all my questions. Some Egyptian donkey boys and men were making a noise in the room at the time, and the calm ferocity with which he ejected them commanded my approval. When a needle, thread, and an unhemmed napkin were handed to him, he sat down, held the edge of the cloth between his big toe and its neighbour, and finished the work in

certain sense of honour, unknown to their northern brethren. "Berberi" is a term of respect; "Masri," (corrupted from Misri,) in the mouth of a Bedouin or an Arab of Arabia, is a reproach. "He shall be called an Egyptian," means "he shall belong to a degraded race."

quite a superior style. Walking out he armed himself with a Kurbaj, which he used, now lightly, then heavily, upon all laden animals, biped and quadruped, that came in the way. His conduct proving equally satisfactory in the kitchen, after getting security from him, and having his name registered by the Shaykh *, I closed with him for eighty piastres a month. But Ali the Berberi and I were destined to part. Before a fortnight he stabbed his fellow servant — a Surat lad, who wishing to return home forced his services upon me, and for this trick he received, with his dismissal, 400 blows on the feet by order of the Zabit, or police magistrate. After this I tried a number

* Who becomes responsible, and must pay for any theft his protégé may commit. Berberis being generally, as "les Suisses," of respectable establishments are expected to be honest. But I can assert from experience, that, as a native, you will never recover the value of a stolen article, without having recourse to the police. For his valuable security, the Shaykh demands a small fee (7 or 8 piastres), which, despite the urgent remonstrances of protector and protégé, you deduct from the latter's wages. The question of pay is a momentous one; too much always spoils a good servant, too little leaves you without one. An Egyptian of the middle class would pay his Berberi about 40 piastres a month, besides board, lodging, some small perquisites, and presents on certain occasions. This, however, will not induce a man to travel, especially to cross the sea.

of servants, Egyptians, Saidi *, and clean and unclean eating † Berberis. Recommended by different Shaykhs all had some fatal defect — one cheated recklessly, another robbed me, a third drank, a fourth was always in scrapes for infringing the Julian edict, and the last, a long-legged Nubian, after remaining two days in the house, dismissed me for expressing a determination to travel by sea from Suez to Yambu. I kept one

* A man from the Said or Upper Egypt.

† A favourite way of annoying the Berberis is to repeat the saying, "we have eaten the clean, we have eaten the unclean,"—meaning, that they are by no means cunning in the difference between right and wrong, pure and impure. I will relate the origin of the saying, as I heard it differently, from Mansfield Parkyns, (Life in Abyssinia, chap. 31.).

A Berberi, said my informant, had been carefully fattening a fine sheep for a feast, when his cottage was burned by an accident. In the ashes he found roasted meat, which looked tempting to a hungry man: he called his neighbours, and all sat down to make merry over the mishap; presently they came to the head, which proved to be that of a dog, some enemy having doubtless stolen the sheep and put the impure animal in its place. Whereupon, sadly perplexed, all the Berberis went to their priest, and dolefully related the circumstance, expecting absolution, as the offence was involuntary. "You have eaten filth," said the man of Allah. "Well," replied the Berberis, falling upon him with their fists, "filth or not, we have eaten it." The Berberi, I must remark, is the "Paddy" of this part of the world, celebrated for bulls and blunders.

man; he complained that he was worked to death: two—they did nothing but fight; and three—they left me, as Mr. Elwes said of old, to serve myself. At last, thoroughly tired of Egyptian domestics, and one servant being really sufficient for comfort, as well as suitable to my assumed rank, I determined to keep only the Indian boy. He had all the defects of his nation; a brave at Cairo, he was an arrant coward at el Medinah: the Bedouins despised him heartily for his effeminacy in making his camel kneel to dismount, and he could not keep his hands from picking and stealing. But the choice had its advantages: his swarthy skin and chubby features made the Arabs always call him an Abyssinian slave, which, as it favoured my disguise, I did not care to contradict; he served well, was amenable to discipline, and, being completely dependant upon me, was therefore less likely to watch and especially to prate about my proceedings. As master and man we performed the pilgrimage together; but, on my return to Egypt after the pilgrimage, Shaykh Nur, finding me to be a Sahib *, changed for the worse. He would not work, and reserved all his energy

* The generic name given by Indians to English officials.

for the purpose of pilfering, which he practised so audaciously upon my friends, as well as upon myself, that he could not be kept in the house.

Perhaps the reader may be curious to see the necessary expenses of a bachelor residing at Cairo. He must observe, however, in the following list that I was not a strict economist, and, besides that, I was a stranger in the country: inhabitants and old settlers would live as well for little more than two-thirds the sum.

		Piastres.	Foddthah.
House rent at 18 piastres per mensem		0	24
Servant at 80 piastres per do.		2	26
Breakfast for self and servant.	10 eggs	0	5
	Coffee	0	10
	Water melon	1	0
	Two rolls of bread	0	10
Dinner.	2 lbs. of meat	2	20
	Two rolls of bread	0	10
	Vegetables	0	20
	Rice	0	5
	Oil and clarified butter	1	0
Sundries.	A skin of Nile water	0	0
	Tobacco*	1	0
	Hammam, (hot bath)	3	20
	Total	13	30

equal to about two shillings and ninepence.

* There are four kinds of tobacco smoked in Egypt. The first and best is the well-known Latakia, generally called

In these days who at Cairo without a Shaykh? I thought it right to conform to popular custom,

"Jebeli," either from a small seaport town about three hours' journey south of Latakia, or more probably because grown on the hills near the ancient Laodicea. Pure, it is known by its blackish colour, fine shredding, absence of stalk, and an undescribable odour, to me resembling that of creosote; the leaf, too, is small, so that when made into cigars it must be covered over with a slip of the yellow Turkish tobacco called Bafrah. Except at the highest houses unadulterated Latakia is not to be had in Cairo. Yet, mixed as it is, no other growth exceeds it in flavour and fragrance. Miss Martineau smoked it, we are told, without inconvenience, and it differs from our Shag, Bird's-eye, and Returns, in degree, as does Château Margeau from a bottle of cheap strong Spanish wine. To bring out its flavour, the connoisseur smokes it in long pipes of cherry, jasmine, maple, or rose-wood, and these require a servant skilled in the arts of cleaning and filling them. The best Jebeli at Cairo costs about seven piastres the pound; after which a small sum must be paid to the Farram, or chopper, who prepares it for use.

2nd. Suri (Syrian), or Shami, or Suryani, grown in Syria, an inferior growth, of a lighter colour than Latakia, and with a greenish tinge; when cut, its value is about three piastres per pound. Some smokers mix this leaf with Jebeli, which, to my taste, spoils the flavour of the latter without improving the former. The strongest kind, called Korani or Jebayl, is generally used for cigarettes; it costs, when of first-rate quality, about five piastres per pound.

3rd. Tumbak, or Persian tobacco, called Hejazi, because imported from the Hejaz, where everybody smokes it, and supposed to come from Shiraz, Kazerun, and other celebrated places in Persia. It is all but impossible to buy this article unadulterated, except from the caravans returning after the and accordingly, after having secured a servant, my efforts were directed to finding a teacher—the pretext being that as an Indian doctor I wanted to read Arabic works on medicine, as well as to perfect myself in divinity and pronunciation.* My theological studies were in the Shafei school for two reasons: in the first place, it is the least

pilgrimage. The Egyptians mix it with native growths, which ruins its flavour, and gives it an acridity that "catches the throat," whereas good tumbak never yet made a man cough. Yet the taste of this tobacco, even when second-rate, is so fascinating to some smokers that they will use no other. To be used it should be wetted and squeezed, and it is invariably inhaled through water into the lungs: almost every town has its favourite description of pipe, and these are of all kinds, from the pauper's rough cocoa-nut mounted with two reeds, to the prince's golden bowl set with the finest stones. Tumbak is cheap, costing about four piastres a pound, but large quantities of it are used.

4th. Hummi, as the word signifies, a "hot" variety of the tumbak, grown in Yemen and other countries. It is placed in the tile on the Buri or cocoa-nut pipe, unwetted, and has a very acrid flavour. Being supposed to produce intoxication, or rather a swimming in the head, hummi gives its votaries a bad name: respectable men would answer "no" with rage if asked whether they are smoking it, and when a fellow tells you that he has seen better days, but that now he smokes hummi in a Buri, you understand him that his misfortunes have affected either his brain or his morality. Hence it is that this tobacco is never put into pipes intended for smoking the other kinds. The price of hummi is about five piastres per pound.

* A study essential to the learned, as in some particular portions of the Koran, a mispronunciation becomes a sin.

rigorous one of the four orthodox, and, secondly, it most resembles the Shiah heresy, with which long intercourse with Persians had made me familiar.* My choice of doctrine, however, confirmed those around me in their conviction that I was a rank heretic, for the Ajemi, taught by his religion to conceal offensive tenets † in lands where the open expression would be dangerous, always represents himself to be a Shafei. This, together with the original mistake of appearing publicly at Alexandria as a Mirza in a Persian dress, caused me infinite small annoyance at Cairo, in spite of all precautions and contrivances. And throughout my journey, even in Arabia, though I drew my knife every time an offensive hint was thrown out, the ill fame clung to me like the shirt of Nessus.

It was not long before I happened to hit upon a proper teacher, in the person of Shaykh Mo-

* The Shafei, to quote but one point of similarity, abuse Yezid, the Syrian tyrant who caused the death of the Imam Husayn: this expression of indignation is forbidden by the Hanafi doctors, who rigidly order their disciples to "judge not."

† A systematic concealment of doctrine and profession of popular tenets, technically called by the Shiahs "Takiyyah:' the literal meaning of the word is "fear," or "caution."

hammed el Attar, or the druggist. He had known prosperity, having once been a Khatib (preacher) in one of Mohammed Ali's mosques. But his Highness the late Pacha had dismissed him, which disastrous event, with its subsequent train of misfortunes, he dates from the melancholy day when he took to himself a wife. He talks of her abroad as a stern and rigid master dealing with a naughty slave, though, by the look that accompanies his rhodomontade, I am convinced that at home he is the very model of "managed men." His dismissal was the reason that compelled him to fall back upon the trade of a druggist, the refuge for the once wealthy, though now destitute, sages of Egypt.

His little shop in the Jemeliyah Quarter is a perfect gem of Nilotic queerness. A hole pierced in the wall of some house, about five feet long and six deep, it is divided into two compartments separated by a thin partition of wood, and communicating by a kind of arch cut in the boards. The inner box, germ of a back parlour, acts store-house, as the pile of empty old baskets tossed in dusty confusion upon the dirty floor shows. In the front is displayed the stock in trade, a matting full of Persian tobacco and pipe bowls of red clay, a palm-leaf bag containing vile coffee and large lumps of coarse, whity-brown sugar wrapped up in browner paper. On the shelves and ledges are rows of well-thumbed wooden boxes, labelled with the greatest carelessness, pepper for rhubarb, arsenic for tafl, or wash-clay, and sulphate of iron where sal ammoniac should be. There is also a square case containing, under lock and key, small change and some choice articles of commerce, damaged perfumes, bad antimony for the eyes, and pernicious rouge. And dangling close above it is a rusty pair of scales, ill poised enough for Egyptian justice herself to use. To hooks over the shop-front are suspended reeds for pipes, tallow candles, dirty wax tapers and cigarette paper; instead of plate-glass windows and brass-handled doors, a ragged net keeps away the flies when the master is in, and the thieves when he goes out to recite in the Hasanayn mosque his daily "Ya Sin."* A wooden shutter which closes down at night-time, and by day two palm-stick stools intensely dirty and full of fleas, occupying the place of the Mastabah †,

* One of the most esteemed chapters of the Koran, frequently recited as a Wazifah or daily task by religious Moslems in Egypt.

† The Mastabah here is a long earthern bench plastered over with clay, and raised about 2 feet from the ground, so as to

which accommodated purchasers, complete the furniture of my preceptor's establishment.

There he sits or rather lies, (for verily I believe he sleeps through three fourths of the day), a thin old man about fifty-eight *, with features once handsome and regular, a sallow face, shaven head, deeply wrinkled cheeks, eyes hopelessly bleared, and a rough grey beard ignorant of oil and comb. His turban, though large, is brown with wear, his coat and small clothes display many a hole, and though his face and hands must be frequently washed preparatory to devotion, still they have the quality of always looking unclean. It is wonderful how fierce and gruff he is to the little boys and girls who flock to him grasping farthings for pepper and sugar. On such occasions I sit admiring to see him, when forced to exertion, wheel about on his place, making a pivot of that portion of our organi-

bring the purchaser's head to a level with the shop. Mohammed Ali ordered the people to remove them, as they narrowed the streets: their place is now supplied by "Kafas," cages or stools of wicker-work.

* A great age in Lower Egypt, where but few reach the 12th lustre. Even the ancients observed that the old Egyptians, despite their attention to diet and physic, were the most short-lived, and the Britons, despite their barbarism, the longest lived of men.

sation which mainly distinguishes our species from the other families of the Simiadæ, to reach some distant drawer, or to pull down a case from its accustomed shelf. How does he manage to say his prayers, to kneel and to prostrate himself upon that two feet of ragged rug, scarcely sufficient for a British infant to lie upon? He hopelessly owns that he knows nothing of his craft, and the seats before his shop are seldom occupied. His great pleasure appears to be when the Haji and I sit by him a few minutes in the evening, bringing with us pipes, which he assists us to smoke, and ordering coffee, which he insists upon sweetening with a lump of sugar from his little store. There we make him talk and laugh, and occasionally quote a few lines strongly savouring of the jovial: we provoke him to long stories about the love borne him in his student days by the great and holy Shaykh Abdul Rahman, and the antipathy with which he was regarded by the equally great and holy Shaykh Nasr el Din, his memorable single imprisonment for contumacy*, and the temperate but effective lecture, beginning with "O almost entirely destitute of shame!" delivered on that occasion in

* This is the "imposition" of Oxford and Cambridge.

presence of other under-graduates by the Right Reverend principal of his college. Then we consult him upon matters of doctrine, and quiz him tenderly about his powers of dormition, and flatter him, or rather his age, with such phrases as, "the water from thy hand is of the waters of Zemzem," or, "we have sought thee to deserve the blessings of the wise upon our undertakings." Sometimes, with interested motives it must be owned, we induce him to accompany us to the Hammam *, where

* The Hammam, or hot bath, being a kind of religious establishment, is one of the class of things—so uncomfortably numerous in Eastern countries—left *ala jud'ak*, "to thy generosity." Consequently, you are pretty sure to have something disagreeable there, which you would vainly attempt to avoid by liberality. The best way to deal with all such extortioners, with the Lawingi (undresser) of a Cairo Hammam, or the "jarvey" of a London Hansom, is to find out the fare, and never to go beyond it—never to be generous.

The Hammam has been too often noticed to bear another description: one point, however, connected with it I must be allowed to notice. Mr. Lane (Modern Egyptians) asserts that a Moslem should not pray nor recite the Koran in it, as the bath is believed to be a favourite resort of Ginn (or genii). On the contrary it is the custom of some sects to recite a Rukatain (two prostration) prayer immediately after religious ablution in the hot cistern. This, however, is *makruh*, or improper without being sinful, to the followers of Abu Hanifah. As a general rule, throughout Islam, the *Farz* (obligatory) prayers may be recited everywhere, no matter how impure the place may be: but he insists upon paying the smallest sum, quarrelling with every thing and every body, and giving the greatest trouble. We are generally his only visitors; acquaintances he appears to have few, and no friends; he must have had them once, for he was rich, but is not so now, so they have fallen away from the poor old man.

When the Shaykh Mohammed sits with me or I climb up into his little shop for the purpose of receiving a lesson from him, he is quite at his ease, reading when he likes, or making me read, and generally beginning each lecture with some such preamble as this *: —

"*Aywa! aywa! aywa!*" † even so, even so,

those belonging to the classes *sunnat* (traditionary) and *nafilah* (supererogatory) are *makruh*, though not actually unlawful, in certain localities.

I venture this remark on account of the extreme accuracy of the work referred to. A wonderful contrast to the generality of Oriental books, it amply deserves a revision in the rare places requiring care.

* Europeans so seldom see the regular old Shaykh, whose place is now taken by polite young men educated in England or France, that this scene may be new even to those who have studied of late years on the banks of the Nile.

† This word is often used to signify simply "yes." It is corrupted from Ay' w'allah, "yes, by Allah." In pure Arabic "ay" or "I" is synonymous with our "yes" or "ay"; and "Allah" in these countries enters somehow into every other phrase.

even so! "we take refuge with Allah from the stoned fiend! In the name of Allah, the compassionate, the merciful, and the blessings of Allah upon our lord Mahommed, and his family, and his companions one and all! Thus saith the author, may Almighty Allah have mercy upon him! 'Section I, of chapter two, upon the orders of prayer,' &c."

He becomes fiercely sarcastic when I differ with him in opinion, especially upon a point of the grammar, or the theology over which his beard has grown grey.

"Subhan' Allah! Allah be glorified!* What words are these? If thou be right, enlarge thy turban †, and throw away thy drugs, for verily it is better to quicken men's souls than to destroy their bodies, O Abdullah!"

Oriental like he revels in giving good counsel.

"Thou art always writing, O my brave! ‡" (this is said on the few occasions when I venture to

* This is of course ironical: "Allah be praised for creating such a prodigy of learning as thou art!"

† The larger the turban, the greater are the individual's pretensions to religious knowledge and respectability of demeanour. This is the custom in Egypt, Turkey, Persia, and many other parts of the Moslem world.

‡ *Ya gadda*, as the Egyptians pronounce it, is used exactly like the "mon brave" of France, and our "my good man."

make a note in my book,) "what evil habit is this? Surely thou hast learned it in the lands of the Frank. Repent!"

He loathes my giving medical advice gratis.

"Thou hast two servants to feed, O my son! The doctors of Egypt never write A, B, without a reward. Wherefore art thou ashamed? Better go and sit upon the mountain * at once, and say thy prayers day and night!"

And finally he is prodigal of preaching upon the subject of household expenses.

"Thy servant did write down 2 lbs. of flesh yesterday! What words are those, O he?† Dost thou never say, 'Guard us, Allah, from the sin of extravagance?'"

He delights also in abruptly interrupting a serious subject when it begins to weigh upon his spirits. For instance,

"Now the waters of ablution being of seven dif-

* The "mountain" in Egypt and Arabia is what the "jungle" is in India. When informed that "you come from the mountain," you understand that you are considered a mere clod-hopper: when asserting that you will "sit upon the mountain," you hint to your hearers an intention of turning anchorite or magician.

† *Ya hu*, a common interpellative, not, perhaps, of the politest description.

ferent kinds, it results that —— hast thou a wife? No? Then verily thou must buy thee a female slave, O youth! This conduct is not right, and men will say of thee——Repentance: I take refuge with Allah *—— 'of a truth his mouth watereth for the spouses of other Moslems.'"

But sometimes he nods over a difficult passage under my very eyes, or he reads it over a dozen times in the wantonness of idleness, or he takes what school-boys call a long "shot" most shamelessly at the signification. When this happens I lose my temper, and raise my voice, and shout, "Verily there is no power nor might save in Allah, the High, the Great!' Then he looks at me, and with passing meekness whispers—

"Fear Allah, O man!"

* A religious formula used when compelled to mention any thing abominable or polluting to the lips of a pious man.

CHAP. V.

THE RAMAZAN.

THIS year the Ramazan befel in June, and a fearful infliction was that "blessed month." For the space of sixteen consecutive hours and a quarter, we were forbidden to eat, drink, smoke, snuff, and even to swallow our saliva designedly. I say forbidden, for although the highest orders of Turks* may break the ordinance in strict privacy, popular opinion would condemn any open infraction of it with uncommon severity. In this, as in most human things, how many are there who hold that

> "Pecher en secret n'est pas pecher,
> Ce n'est que l'éclat qui fait le crime."

The middle and lower ranks observe the duties of the season, however arduous, with exceeding zeal: of the many who suffered severely from such total abstinence, I found but one patient who would eat even to save his life. And among the

* This class is popularly described as

"Turco fino
Mangia porco è beve vino."

vulgar, sinners who habitually drink when they should pray, will fast and perform their devotions through the Ramazan.

Like the Italian and Greek fasts, the chief effect of the "blessed month" upon true believers is to darken their tempers into positive gloom. Their voices, never of the softest, acquire, especially after noon, a terribly harsh and creaking tone. The men curse one another * and beat the women. The women slap and abuse the children, and these in their turn cruelly entreat and use harsh language to the dogs and cats. You can scarcely spend ten minutes in any populous part of the city without hearing some violent dispute. The "Karakun," or station-houses, are filled with lords who have administered an undue dose of chastisement to their ladies, and with ladies who have scratched, bitten, and otherwise injured the bodies of their lords. The Mosques are crowded with a sulky,

* Of course all quarrelling, abuse, and evil words are strictly forbidden to the Moslem during Ramazan. If one believer insult another, the latter should repeat "I am fasting" three times before venturing himself to reply. Such is the wise law. But human nature in Egypt, as elsewhere, is always ready to sacrifice the spirit to the letter, rigidly to obey the physical part of an ordinance, and to cast away the moral, as if it were the husk and not the kernel.

grumbling population, making themselves offensive to one another on earth, whilst working their way to heaven; and in the shade, under the outer walls, the little boys who have been expelled the church attempt to forget their miseries in spiritless play. In the bazars and streets, pale long-drawn faces, looking for the most part intolerably cross, catch your eye, and at this season a stranger will sometimes meet with positive incivility. A shopkeeper, for instance, usually says when he rejects an insufficient offer, "yaftah Allah," "Allah opens": in the Ramazan, he will grumble about the bore of Ghashim (" Johnny raws"), and gruffly tell you not to stand there wasting his time. But as a rule the shops are either shut or destitute of shopmen, merchants will not purchase, and students will not study. In fine, the Ramazan, for many classes, is one twelfth of the year wantonly thrown away.

The following is the routine of a fast day. About half an hour after midnight, the gun sounds its warning to faithful men that it is time to prepare for the "Sahur," or morning meal. My servant then wakes me, if I have slept, brings water

* Allah opens (the door of daily bread) is a polite way of informing a man that you and he are not likely to do business; in other words, that you are not in want of his money.

for ablution, spreads the Sufrah *, and places before me certain remnants of the evening's meal. It is some time before the stomach becomes accustomed to such early hours, but in matters of appetite, habit is everything, and for health's sake one should strive to eat as plentifully as possible. Then sounds the Salam, or Blessings on the Prophet †, an introduction to the call of morning prayer. Smoking sundry pipes with tenderness, as if taking leave of a friend, and until the second gun, fired at about half past two A.M., gives the Insak †,— the order to abstain from food,— I wait the Azan ‡, which in this month is called somewhat earlier than usual. Then, after a ceremony termed the Niyat § of fasting, I say my prayers, and prepare

* The Sufrah is a piece of leather well tanned, and generally of a yellow colour, bordered with black. It is circular, has a few small pouches for knives or spoons, and, by means of a thong run through rings in the periphery, can be readily converted into a bag for carrying provisions on a journey. Figuratively it is used for the meal itself. "Sufrah hazir" means that dinner is upon the table.

† The Salam at this hour of the morning is confined to the devotions of Ramazan. The curious reader may consult Lane's Modern Egyptians, chap. 25., for a long and accurate interpretation of these words.

‡ The summons to prayer.

§ In the Mohammedan church every act of devotion must be preceded by what is called its Niyat or purpose. This Niyat for repose.* At 7 A.M. the labours of the day begin for the working classes of society; the rich spend the night in revelling, and rest from dawn to noon.

The first thing on rising is to perform the Wuzu, or lesser ablution, which invariably follows sleep in a reclining position; without this it would be improper to pray, to enter the mosques, to approach a religious man, or to touch the Koran. A few pauper patients usually visit me at this hour, report the phenomena of their complaints,—which they do, by the by, with unpleasant minuteness of detail,—and receive fresh instructions. At 9 A.M. Shaykh Mohammed enters, with "lecture" written upon his wrinkled brow, or I pick him up on the way, and proceed straight to the

must be either mentally conceived, or, as the more general rule is, audibly expressed. For instance, the worshipper will begin with "I purpose to pray the four prostrations of mid-day prayer to Allah the Almighty," and then he will proceed to the act of worship. Moslems of the Shafei faith must perform the Niyat of fasting every night for the ensuing day; the Málikés, on the other hand, "purpose" abstinence but once for the thirty days of Ramazan.

* Many go to sleep immediately after the Imsak, or about a quarter of an hour before the dawn prayer, and do not perform their morning devotions till they awake. But this is not, strictly speaking, correct.

Mosque El Azhar. After three hours' hard reading with little interruption from by-standers — this is long vacation — comes the call to mid-day prayer. The founder of Islam ordained but few devotions for the morning, which is the business part of the Eastern day, but during the afternoon and evening they succeed one another rapidly, and their length increases. It is then time to visit my rich patients, and afterwards, in order to accustom myself to the sun, to wander through the bookshops for an hour or two, or simply to idle in the street. At 3 P. M. I return home, recite the afternoon prayers, and re-apply myself to study.

This is the worst part of the day. In Egypt the summer nights and mornings are, generally speaking, pleasant, but the forenoons are sultry, and the afternoons serious. A wind wafting the fine dust and furnace heat of the desert blows over the city, the ground returns with interest the showers of caloric from above, and not a cloud or a vapour breaks the dreary expanse of splendour on high. There being no such comforts as Indian tatties, and few but the wealthiest houses boasting glass windows, the interior of your room is somewhat more fiery than the street. Weakened with fasting, the body feels the heat trebly, and the disordered stomach almost affects the brain. Every minute is counted with morbid fixity of idea as it passes on towards the blessed sunset, especially by those whose terrible lot is manual labour at such a season. A few try to forget their afternoon miseries in slumber, but most people take the Kailulah, or Siesta, shortly after the meridian, holding it unwholesome to sleep late in the day.

As the Maghrib, the sunset hour, approaches — and how slowly it comes! — the town seems to recover from a trance. People flock to the windows and balconies, in order to watch the moment of their release. Some pray, others tell their beads, while others, gathering together in groups or paying visits, exert themselves to while away the lagging time.

O gladness! at length it sounds, the gun from the citadel. Simultaneously rises the sweet cry of the Muezzin, calling men to prayer, and the second cannon booms from the Abbasiyah Palace *,

* When the late Pacha of Egypt (His Highness Abbas Hilmi) came to power, he built a large pile of palace close outside the walls of Cairo, on the direction of Suez, and induced his courtiers to follow his example. This was done readily enough, for Asiatics, like Europeans, enjoy the fine air of the desert after the rank atmosphere of towns and cities. If the successor of His Highness does not follow the usual Oriental method of wiping away all vestiges of the predecessor, except

—"Al fitar! al fitar!" fast-breaking! fast-breaking! shout the people, and a hum of joy rises from the silent city. Your acute ears waste not a moment in conveying the delightful intelligence to your parched tongue, empty stomach, and languid limbs. You exhaust a pot full of water, no matter its size. You clap hurried hands * for a pipe, you order coffee, and, provided with these comforts, you sit down, and calmly contemplate the coming pleasures of the evening.

Poor men eat heartily at once. The rich break their fast with a light meal,—a little bread and

his grave, there will be, at no distant period, a second Cairo on the site of the Abbasiyah.

* One of our wants is a history of the bell and its succedania. Strict Moslems have an aversion to all modifications of this instrument, striking clocks, gongs, &c., because they were considered by the Prophet peculiar to the devotions of Christians. He, therefore, instituted the Azan, or call to prayer, and his followers still clap their hands when we should ring for a servant.

"The symbolical meaning of the bell, as shown in the sistrum of Isis, seems to be the movement and mixture of the elements, which is denoted by clattering noise." "Hence," observes a learned antiquary, "the ringing of bells and clattering of plates of metal were used in all lustrations, sacrifices, &c." We find them amongst the Jews, worn by the high priest; the Greeks attached them to images of Priapus, and the Buddhists of Thibet still use them in their worship, as do the Catholics of Rome when elevating the Host.

fruit, fresh or dry, especially water-melon, sweet-meats, or such digestible dishes as "Muhallabah" — a thin jelly of milk, starch, and rice-flower. They then smoke a pipe, drink a cup of coffee or a glass of sherbet, and recite the evening prayers; for the devotions of this hour are delicate things, and while smoking a first pipe after sixteen hours' abstinence, time easily slips away. Then they sit down to the Fatúr (breakfast), *the* meal of the twenty-four hours, and eat plentifully, if they would avoid an illness.

There are many ways of spending a Ramazan evening. The Egyptians have a proverb, like ours of the Salernian school.

> "After El-Ghada rest, if it be but for two moments:
> After El-asha * walk, if it be but two steps."

The streets are now crowded with a good-humoured throng of strollers, the many bent on pleasure, the few wending their way to mosque, where the Imam recites "Tarawih" prayers.† They saunter about, the accustomed pipe in hand,

* El-Ghada is the early dinner: El-asha, the supper, eaten shortly after sunset. See Lane's Modern Egyptians, Chap. 5.

† Extra prayers repeated in the month of Ramazan, (Lane, Chap. 25., "Taraweeh"). They take about an hour, consisting of 23 prostrations, with the Salam (or blessing on the Prophet) after every second prostration.

shopping, for the stalls are open till a late hour, or they sit in crowds at the coffee-house entrance, smoking Shishas *, chatting, and listening to story-tellers, singers and itinerant preachers. Here a bare-footed girl trills and quavers, accompanied by a noisy tambourine and a "scrannel pipe" of abominable discordance, in honour of a perverse saint whose corpse insisted upon being buried inside some respectable man's dwelling-house.† The scene reminds you strongly of the "Sonneurs" of Brittany and the Zampognari from the Abruzzian Highlands bag-piping before the Madonna. There a tall gaunt Maghrabi displays upon a square yard of dirty

* The Shisha, or Egyptian water-pipe, is too well known to require any description. It is filled with a kind of tobacco called Zumbak, for which see Chap. 4. of this Volume.

† Strangers often wonder to see a kind of cemetery let into a dwelling-house, in a crowded street. The reason is, that some obstinate saint has insisted upon being buried there, by the simple process of weighing so heavily in his bier, that the bearers have been obliged to place him upon the pavement. Of course, no good Moslem would object to have his ground-floor occupied by the corpse of a holy man.

The reader will not forget, that in Europe statues have the whims which dead bodies exhibit in Egypt. So, according to the Abbé Marche, the little statue of Our Lady, lately found in the forest of Pennacom, "became, notwithstanding her small size, heavy as a mountain, and would not consent to be removed by any one but the chaplain of the chateau."

paper certain lines and blots, supposed to represent the venerable Kaabah, and collects coppers to defray the expenses of his pilgrimage. A steady stream of loungers sets through the principal thoroughfares towards the Ezbekiyah, which skirts the Frank quarter, where they sit in the moonlight, listening to Greek and Turkish bands, or making merry with cakes, toasted grains, coffee, sugared-drinks, and the broad pleasantries of Kara Gyuz.* Here the scene is less thoroughly oriental than within the city, but the appearance of Frank dress amongst the varieties of Eastern costume, the moon-lit sky, and the light mist hanging over the deep shade of the acacia trees — whose rich scented yellow white blossoms are popularly compared to the old Pacha's beard † — make it passingly picturesque. And the traveller from the far East remarks with wonder the presence

* Europeans compare "Kara Gyuz" to our Chinese shadows. He is the Turkish "Punch," and his pleasantries may remind the traveller of what he has read concerning the Mimes and Fescennine performances of the Romans. On more than one occasion, Kara Gyuz has been reported to the police for scandalously jibing and deriding consuls, Frank merchants, and even Turkish dignitaries.

† Mohammed Ali drained and planted the Ezbekiyah, which, before his day, was covered with water and mud long after the inundation had ceased. The Egyptians extract a perfume, which they call "Fitneh," from this kind of acacia.

of certain ladies, whose only mark of modesty is the Burka, or face veil: upon this laxity the police looks with lenient eyes, inasmuch as, until very lately, it paid a respectable tax to the state.*

Returning to the Moslem quarter, you are bewildered by its variety of sounds. Everyone talks, and talking here is always in extremes, either in a whisper, or in a scream; gesticulation excites the lungs, and strangers cannot persuade themselves that men so converse without being or becoming furious. All the street cries, too, are in the soprano key. "In thy protection! in thy protection!" shouts a Fellah to a sentinel, who is flogging him towards the station-house, followed by a tail of women, screaming, "O my calamity! O my shame!" The boys have elected a pacha, whom they are conducting in procession, with wisps of straw for Mashals, or Cressets, and outrunners, all huzzaing with ten-schoolboy power. "O thy right! O thy left! O thy face! O thy heel! O thy back, thy

* All "Agapemones" are at this time suppressed, by order of His Highness (Abbas Pacha), whose august mother occasionally insists upon banishing whole colleges of Ambubaiæ to Upper Egypt. As might be expected, this proceeding has a most injurious effect upon the morals of society. I was once at Cairo during the ruler's absence on a tour up to the Nile; his departure was the signal for the general celebration of cotyttia.

back!" cries the panting footman, who, huge torch on shoulder, runs before the grandee's carriage; "bless the Prophet, and get out of the way!" "O Allah bless him!" respond the good Moslems, some shrinking up to the walls to avoid the stick, others rushing across the road, so as to give themselves every chance of being knocked down. The donkey boy beats his ass with a heavy palm-cudgel; he fears no treadmill here, cursing him at the top of his voice for a "pander," a "Jew," a "Christian," and a "son of the one-eyed, whose portion is eternal punishment." "O chick pease! O pips!" sings the vender of parched grains, rattling the unsavoury load in his basket. "Out of the way, and say, 'there is one God,'" pants the industrious water-carrier, laden with a skin, fit burden for a buffalo. "Sweetwater, and gladden thy soul, O lemonade!" pipes the seller of that luxury, clanging his brass cups together. Then come the beggars, intensely Oriental. "My supper is in Allah's hands, my supper is in Allah's hands! whatever thou givest, that will go with thee!" chaunts the old vagrant, whose wallet perhaps contains more provision than the basket of many a respectable shopkeeper. "Naal 'abuk —curse thy father—O brother of a naughty sister!" is the response of some petulant Greek to the touch of the old man's staff. "The grave is darkness, and good deeds are its lamp!" sings the blind woman, rapping two sticks together: "upon Allah! upon Allah! O daughter!" cry the by-standers, when the obstinate "bint"* of sixty years seizes their hands, and will not let go without a farthing. "Bring the sweet and take the full,"† cry the long-mustachioed, fierce-browed Arnauts to the coffee-house keeper, who stands

* A daughter, a girl. In Egypt, every woman expects to be addressed as "O lady!" "O female-pilgrim!" "O bride!" or, "O daughter!" even though she be on the wrong side of fifty. In Arabia, you may say "y'al mara!" (O woman); but if you attempt it near the Nile, the answer of the offended fair one will be "may Allah cut out thy heart!" or, "the *woman*, please Allah, in thine eye!" And if you want a violent quarrel, "y'al aguz!" (O old woman!) pronounced drawlingly,—"y'al ago-o-ooz,"—is sure to satisfy you. On the plains of Sorrento, in my day, it was always customary, when speaking to a peasant girl, to call her "bella fé," (beautiful woman), whilst the worst of insults was "vecchiarella." So the Spanish Calesero, under the most trying circumstances, calls his mule "Vieja, reveija," (old woman, very old woman). Age, it appears, is as unpopular in Southern Europe as in Egypt.

† "Fire" is called the "sweet" by euphuism, as to name it directly would be ill-omened. So in the Moslem law, flame and water, being the instruments of Allah's wrath, are forbidden to be used by temporal rulers. The "full" means an empty coffee cup, as we say in India *mez barhao*, ("increaso the table,") when ordering a servant to remove the dishes.

by them charmed by the rhyming *repartie* that flows so readily from their lips.

"*Hanien*," may it be pleasant to thee!* is the signal for encounter.

"Thou drinkest for *ten*," replies the other, instead of returning the usual religious salutation.

"I am the cock and thou art the *hen!*" is the rejoinder,—a tart one.

"Nay, I am the thick one and thou art the *thin!*" resumes the first speaker, and so on till they come to equivoques which will not bear a literal English translation.

And sometimes, high above the hubbub, rises the melodious voice of the blind muezzin, who from his balcony in the beetling tower rings forth, "Hie ye to devotion! Hie ye to salvation! Devotion is better than sleep! Devotion is better than sleep!" Then good Moslems piously stand up, and mutter, previous to prayer, "Here am I at thy call, O Allah! here am I at thy call!"

Sometimes I walked with my friend to the citadel, and sat upon a high wall, one of the out-

* Or, "pleasurably and health:" hanien is a word taken from the Koran. The proper answer to this is "May Allah cause thee to have pleasure!" "Allah yehannik!" which I have heard abominably perverted by Arnaut and other ruffians.

works of Mahommed Ali's mosque, enjoying a view which, seen by night, when the summer moon is near the full, has a charm no power of language can embody. Or escaping from "stifled Cairo's filth*," we passed, through the Gate of Victory, into the wilderness beyond the city of the dead.† Seated upon some mound of ruins, we inhaled the fine air of the desert, inspiriting as a cordial, when

* This in these days must be said comparatively: Ibrahim Pacha's order, that every housekeeper should keep the space before his house properly swept and cleaned, has made Cairo the least filthy city in the East.

† Here lies the Swiss Burckhardt, who enjoyed a wonderful immunity from censure, until a certain pseudo-orientalist of the present day seized the opportunity of using the "unscrupulous traveller's" information, and of abusing his memory.

Some years ago, the sum of 20*l.* (I am informed) was collected, in order to raise a fitting monument over the discoverer of Petra's humble grave. Some objection however, was started, because Moslems are supposed to claim Burckhardt as one of their own saints. Only hear the Egyptian account of his death! After returning from El-Hejar, he taught Tazwid (Koran chaunting) in the Azhar mosque, where the learned, suspecting him to be at heart an infidel, examined his person, and found the formula of the Mahommedan faith written in token of abhorrence upon the soles of his feet. Thereupon, the principal of the mosque, in a transport of holy indignation, did decapitate him with one blow of the sword. It only remains to be observed, that nothing can be more ridiculous than the popular belief, except it be our hesitating to offend the prejudices of such believers.

star-light and dew mists diversified a scene, which, by day, is one broad sea of yellow loam with billows of chalk rock, thinly covered by a film-like spray of sand floating in the fiery wind. There, within a mile of crowded life, all is desolate, the town walls seem crumbling to decay, the hovels are tenantless, and the paths untrodden ; behind you lies the wild, before, the thousand tomb-stones, ghastly in their whiteness, and beyond them the tall dark forms of the Mameluke Sultan's towers rise from the low and hollow ground like the spirits of kings guarding ghostly subjects in the shadowy realm. Nor less weird than the scene are the sounds! — the hyæna's laugh, the howl of the wild dog and the screech of the low-flying owl. Or we spent the evening at some Takiyah*, generally preferring that called the "Gulshani," near the Muayyid Mosque outside the Mutawallis' saintly door. There is nothing attractive in its appearance. You mount a flight of ragged steps, and enter a low verandah enclosing an open stuccoed terrace, where stands the holy man's domed tomb: the two stories contain small dark rooms in which the Dervishes dwell, and the

* A Takiyah is a place where Dervishes have rooms, and perform their devotions.

ground-floor doors open into the verandah. During the fast-month, zikrs* are rarely performed in the Takiyahs: the inmates pray there in congregations, or they sit conversing upon benches in the shade. And a curious medley of men they are, composed of the choicest vagabonds from every nation of Islam. Beyond this I must not describe the Takiyah or the doings there, for the "path" of the Dervish may not be trodden by profane feet.

Curious to see something of my old friends the Persians, I called with Haji Wali upon one Mirza Husayn, who by virtue of his dignity as "Shahbandar†," (he calls himself "consul-general,") ranks with the dozen little diplomatic kings of Cairo He suspends over his lofty gate a sign-board in which the Lion and the Sun, (Iran's proud ensign,) are by some Egyptian "limner's" art metamorphosed into a preternatural tabby-cat grasping a scimitar, with the jolly fat face of a "gay" young lady, curls and all complete, resting fondly upon her pet's concave back. This high dignitary's reception room was a court-yard *sub dio*: fronting the door were benches and cushions composing

* Certain forms of worship peculiar to Dervishes. For a description see Lane, (Modern Egyptians, ch. 24.).

† Shahbandar is here equivalent to our "consul."

the sadr or high place, with the parallel rows of divans spread down the less dignified sides, and a line of naked boards, the lowest seats, ranged along the door wall. In the middle stood three little tables supporting three huge lanterns—as is their size so is the owner's dignity—each of which contained three of the largest spermaceti candles.

The Haji and I entering took our seats upon the side benches with humility, and exchanged salutations with the great man on the Sadr. When the Darbar or levee was full, in stalked the Mirza, and all arose as he calmly divested himself of his shoes and with all due solemnity ascended his proper cushion. He is a short thin man about thirty-five, with regular features and the usual preposterous lamb-skin cap and beard, two peaked black cones at least four feet in length, measured from the tips, resting on a slender basement of pale yellow face. After a quarter of an hour of ceremonies, polite mutterings and low bendings with the right hand on the left breast, the Mirza's pipe was handed to him first, in token of his dignity—at Teheran he was probably an under-clerk in some government office. In due time we were all served with kalioons and coffee by the servants, who made royal *congés* whenever they passed the great man, and more than once the janissary, in dignity of belt and crooked sabre, entered the court to quicken our awe.

The conversation was the usual oriental thing. It is, for instance, understood that you have seen strange things in strange lands.

"Voyaging—is—victory," quotes the Mirza; the quotation is a hackneyed one, but it steps forth majestic as to pause and emphasis.

"Verily," you reply with equal ponderousness of pronunciation and novelty of citation, "in leaving home one learns life, yet a journey is a bit of Jehannum."

Or if you are a physician the "*lieu commun*" will be,

> "Little-learn'd doctors the body destroy:
> Little-learn'd parsons the soul destroy."

To which you will make answer, if you would pass for a man of *belles lettres*, by the well-known lines,

> "Of a truth, the physician hath power with drugs,
> Which, long as the sick man hath life, may relieve him;
> But the tale of our days being duly told,
> The doctor is daft, and his drugs deceive him."

After sitting there with dignity, like the rest of the guests, I took my leave, delighted with the truly Persian "apparatus" of the scene. The Mirza, having no salary, lives by fees, which he extorts from his subjects, who pay him rather than lack some protection, and his dragoman for a counter-fee will sell their interests shamelessly. He is a hidalgo of blue blood in pride, pompousness and poverty. There is not a sheet of writing-paper in the "consulate"—when they want one a farthing is sent to the grocer's—yet the consul drives out in an old carriage with four out-riders, two tall-capped men preceding and two following the crazy vehicle. And the Egyptians laugh heartily at this display, being accustomed by Mohammed Ali to consider all such parade obsolete.

About half an hour before midnight sounds the Abrar * or call to prayer, at which time the latest wanderers return home to prepare for the Sahur, their morning meal. You are careful on the way to address each sentinel with a "peace be upon thee"! especially if you have no lantern, otherwise you may chance to sleep in the guard-house. And, *chemin faisant*, you cannot but stop to gaze at streets as little like what civilised Europe under-

* See Lane (Modern Egyptians, chap. 24.).

stands by that name as an Egyptian temple to the new Houses of Parliament.

There are certain scenes, cannily termed "Kenspeckle," that print themselves upon memory, and endure as long as memory endures, — a thunder-cloud bursting upon the Alps, a night of stormy darkness off the Cape, and, perhaps, most awful of all, a solitary journey over the sandy desert.

Of this class is a stroll through the streets of old Cairo by night. All is squalor in the brilliancy of noon-day. In darkness you see nothing but a mere silhouette. But when the moon is high in the heavens, with the summer stars raining light upon God's world, there is something not of earth in the view. A glimpse at the strip of pale blue sky above scarcely reveals "three ells of breadth:" in many places the interval is less; here the copings meet, and there the outriggings of the houses seem to be interlaced. Now they are parted by a pencil, then by a flood of silvery splendour, while under the projecting cornices and the huge hanging windows of fantastic wood-work, supported by gigantic corbels, and deep verandas, and gateways huge enough for Behemoth to pass through, and blind wynds and long cul-de-sacs, lie patches of thick darkness, made visible by the dimmest of oil lights. The arch is a favourite figure: in one place you see it a mere skeleton of stone opening into some huge deserted hall; in another it is full of fretted stone aud carved wood. Not a line is straight, the huge dead walls of the mosques slope over their massy buttresses, and the thin minarets seem about to fall across your path. The cornices project crookedly from the houses, and the great gables stand merely by force of cohesion. And that the line of beauty may not be wanting, the graceful bending form of the palm, on whose topmost feathers, quivering in the breeze, the moonbeam glistens, springs from a gloomy mound, or from the darkness of a mass of houses almost level with the ground. Briefly the whole view is so drear, so fantastic, so ghostly, that it seems rather preposterous to imagine that in such places human beings like ourselves can be born, and live through life, to carry out the command "increase and multiply," and die.

CHAP. VI.

THE MOSQUE.

WHEN the Byzantine Christians, after overthrowing the temples of Paganism, meditated re-building and remodelling them, poverty of invention and artistic impotence reduced them to group the spoils in a heterogeneous mass.* The sea-ports of Egypt and the plains of Syria abounding in pillars of granite, basalt, and precious marbles, in Pharaonic, Greek, and Roman statuary, and in all manner of structural ornaments, the architects were at no loss for material. Their Syncretism, the result of chance and precipitancy of extravagance, and incuriousness, fell under eyes too ignorant to be hurt by the irregularity of the hybrid: it was perpetuated in the so-called Saracenic style, a plagiarism from the Byzantine †, and reiterated in the Gothic, which is an off-shoot from the Saracenic.‡ This fact accounts in the

* In the capitals of the columns, for instance.

† This direct derivation is readily detected in the mosques at Old Cairo.

‡ The roof supported by arches resting on pillars, was unknown to classic antiquity, and in the earliest ages of El-Islam,

Gothic style for the manifold incongruity in the architecture, for the phenomena, — not solely attributable to the buildings having been erected piece-meal,— of its most classic period being that of its greatest irregularity.

Such "architectural lawlessness," such disregard for symmetry,—the result, I believe, of an imperfect "amalgamation and enrichment,"— may doubtless be defended upon the grounds both of cause and of effect. Architecture is one of the imitative arts, and nature, the myriomorphous, elsewhere delighting in variety, appears to abhor nothing so much as perfect similarity and precise uniformity. To copy her exactly we must therefore seek that general analogy compatible with individual variety; in fact, we should avoid the over-display of order and regularity. And again it may be asserted that, however incongruous these disorderly forms may appear to the conventional eye, we find it easy to surmount our first antipathy to them because we are accustomed to diversity by the physical world. Perhaps we end in admiring it the more, as we love those forms in which irregularity

the cloisters were neither arched nor domed. A modern writer justly observes, "A compound of arcade and colonnade was suggested to the architects of the Middle Ages by the command that ancient buildings gave them of marble columns."

of feature is compensated for by diversity and piquancy of expression.

There is nothing, I believe, new in the Arab mosque; it is an unconscious revival of the forms used from the earliest ages to denote by symbolism the worship of the generative and the creative gods. The reader will excuse me if I only glance at a subject of which the investigation would require a volume, and which, discussed at greater length, would be out of place in such a narrative as this.

The first mosque in El-Islam was erected by Mohammed Kuba at El Medinah: shortly afterwards, when he entered Meccah as a conqueror, he destroyed the idols of the Arab pantheon, and purified that venerable building of its abominations. He had probably observed in Syria the two forms appropriated by the Christians to their places of worship, the cross and the Basilica; he therefore preferred a square to a parallelogram, some authors say with, others, without a cloister, for the prayers of the "saving faith." At length in the reign of El Walid (about A.H. 90) the cupola, the niche, and the minaret made their appearance, and what is called the Saracenic style became the order of the Moslem world.

The Hindoos I believe to have been the first who symbolised by an equilateral triangle their peculiar cult, the Yoni-Lingam: in their temple architecture, it became either a conoid or a perfect pyramid. Egypt denoted it by the obelisk, peculiar to that country; and the form appeared in different parts of the world:—thus in England it was a mere upright stone, and in Ireland a round tower. This we might expect to see. D'Hancarville has successfully traced the worship itself, in its different modifications, to all people: the symbol would therefore be found everywhere. The old Arab minaret is a plain conoid or polygonal tower, without balcony or stages, widely different from the Turkish, modern Egyptian, and Hejazi combinations of cylinder and prism, happily compared by a French traveller to "*une chandelle coiffée d'un eteignoir.*" And finally the ancient minaret, made solid as all Gothic architecture is, and provided with a belfry, became the spire and pinnacle of our ancestors.

From time immemorial, in hot and rainy lands, a hypæthral court surrounded by a covered portico, either circular or square, was used for the double purpose of church and mart,—a place where God and Mammon were worshipped turn by turn. In some places we find rings of stones, like the

Persian Pyrœtheia, in others, round concave buildings representing the vault of heaven, where fire, the divine symbol, was worshipped, and in Arabia, columnal aisles, which, surmounted by the splendid blue vault, resemble the palm-grove. The Greeks adopted this area in the fanes of Creator Bacchus; and at Puzzuoli, near Naples, it may be seen in the building vulgarly called the Temple of Serapis. It was equally well known to the Celts: in some places the Temenos was circular, in others a quadrangle. And such to the present day is the mosque of El-Islam.

Even the Riwak or porches surrounding the area in the mosque are a revival of older forms. "The range of square building which enclose the temple of Serapis are not, properly speaking, parts of the fane, but apartments of the priests, places for victims, and sacred utensils, and chapels dedicated to subordinate deities, introduced by a more complicated and corrupt worship, and probably unknown to the founders of the original edifice." The cloisters in the mosque became cells, used as lecture rooms, and libraries for books, bequeathed to the college. They are unequal, because some are required to be of larger, others to be of smaller dimensions. The same reason causes difference of size when the distribution of the building is into four hyposteles which open upon the area: that in the direction of the Kaabah, where worshippers mostly congregate, demanding greater depth than the other three. The wings were not unfrequently made unequal, either from want of building materials, or because the same extent of accommodation was not required in both. The columns were of different substances; some of handsome marble, others of rough stone meanly plastered over with dissimilar capitals, vulgarly cut shafts of various sizes, here with a pediment, there without, now turned upside down, now joined together by halves in the centre, and almost invariably nescient of intercolumnar rule. This is the result of Byzantine syncretism, carelessly and ignorantly grafted upon Arab ideas of the natural and the sublime. Loving and admiring the great, or rather the huge in plan *, they care little for the execution of mere

* "The Oriental mind," says a clever writer on Indian subjects, "has achieved everything save real greatness of aim and execution." That the Arab mind always aimed, and still aims, at the physically great is sufficiently evident. Nothing affords the Meccans greater pride than the vast size of their temple. Nothing is more humiliating to the people of El Medinah than the comparative smallness of their mosque. Still, with a few exceptions, Arab greatness is the vulgar huge, not the grand.

details, and they have not the acumen to discern the effect which clumsy workmanship, crooked lines, and visible joints,—parts apparently insignificant,—exercise upon the whole of an edifice. Their use of colours was a false taste, commonly displayed by mankind in their religious houses, and statues of the gods. The Hindus paint their pagodas, inside and outside; and rub vermilion, in token of honour, over their deities. The Persian Colossi of Kaiomars and his consort on the Balkh road, and the Sphynx of Egypt, as well as the temples of the Nile, still show traces of artificial complexion. The fanes in classic Greece, where we might expect a purer taste, have been dyed. In the Forum Romanum, one of the finest buildings still bears stains of the Tyrian purple. And to mention no other instances, in the churches and belfries of Modern Italy, we see alternate bands of white and black material so disposed as to give them the appearance of giant zebras. The origin of "Arabesque" must be referred to one of the principles of El-Islam. The Moslem, forbidden by his law to decorate his mosque with statuary and pictures *, supplied their place with quotations

* That is to say, imitations of the human form. All the doctors of El-Islam, however, differ on this head: some absolutely

from the Koran, and inscriptions, "plastic metaphysics," of marvellous perplexity. His alphabet lent itself to the purpose, and hence probably arose that almost inconceivable variety of lace-like fret-work of incrustations, Arabesques, and geometric flowers, in which his eye delights to lose itself.*

The Meccan mosque became a model to the world of El-Islam, and the nations that embraced the new faith copied the consecrated building, as religiously as Christendom produced imitations of the Holy Sepulchre.† The mosque of Omar at Jerusalem, of Amr at Babylon on the Nile, and

forbidding any delineation of what has life, under pain of being cast into hell; others permitting pictures even of the bodies, though not of the faces, of men. The Arabs are the strictest of Misiconists; yet even they allow plans and pictures of the Holy Shrines. Other nations are comparatively lax. The Alhambra abounds in paintings and frescoes. The Persians never object to depict in books and on walls the battles of Rustam, and the Turks preserve in the Seraglio treasury of Constantinople portraits, by Greek and other artists, of their Sultans in regular succession.

* This is at least a purer taste than that of our Gothic architects, who ornamented their cathedrals with statuary so inappropriate as to suggest to the antiquary remains of the worship of the Hellespontine god.

† At Bruges, Bologna, (St. Stefano), and Nuremberg, there are, if I recollect right, imitations of the Holy Sepulchre, although the "palmer" might not detect the resemblance at first sight. The Nuremberg-church was built by a merchant,

Taylun at Cairo were erected with some trifling improvements, such as the arched cloisters and inscribed cornices, upon the plan of the Kaabah. From Egypt and Palestine the ichnography spread far and wide. It was modified, as might be expected, by national taste; what in Arabia was simple and elegant became highly ornate in Spain *, florid in Turkey, and effeminate in India. Still divergence of detail had not, even after the lapse of twelve centuries, materially altered the fundamental form.

Perhaps no Eastern city affords more numerous or more accessible specimens of mosque architecture than Cairo. Between 300 or 400 places of worship †, some stately piles, others ruinous

who travelled three times to Palestine in order to ensure correctness, and totally failed.

"Arab art," says a writer in the "Athenæum," "sprang from the Koran, as the Gothic did from the Bible." He should have remembered, that Arab art, in its present shape, was borrowed by El-Walid from the Greeks, and, perhaps, in part from the Persians and the Hindus, but that the model buildings existed at Meccah, and in Yemen, centuries before the people had "luxurious shawls and weavings of Cashmere" to suggest mural decoration.

* See Théophile Gautier's admirable description of the mosque at Cordova.

† Joseph Pitts, of Exeter, declares that Cairo contained in

hovels, many new, more decaying and earthquake-shaken, with minarets that rival in obliquity the Pisan monster, are open to the traveller's inspection. And Europeans by following the advice of their hotel-keeper have penetrated, and can penetrate, into any one they please.* If architecture be really what I believe it to be, the highest expression of a people's artistic feeling,—highest because it includes all others,—to compare the several styles of the different epochs, to observe how each monarch building his own mosque, and calling it by his own name, identified the manner of the monument with himself, and to trace the gradual decadence of art through 1200 years, down to the present day, must be a work of no ordinary interest to orientalists. The limits of my plan, however, compel me to

his day (A.D. 1678-93) 5 or 6000 mosques, public and private; at the same time he corrects Mr. Collins, who enumerated 6000 public, and 20,000 particular buildings, and M. de Thevenot, who (Part 1. p. 129.), supplied the city with 23,000'

* In Niebuhr's time, a Christian passing one of the very holy buildings on foot was liable to be seized and circumcised. All mosques may now be entered with certain precautions. When at Cairo, I heard occasionally of a Frank being spat at and insulted, but the instances were rare, and an order lately issued, I am told, by His Highness the Pacha will effectually prevent any annoyance to future travellers.

place only the heads of the argument before the reader. May I then be allowed to express a hope that it will induce some more learned traveller to investigate a subject in every way worthy his attention?

The Jama Taylun (9th cent.) is simple and massive, yet elegant, and in some of its details peculiar.* One of the four colonnades † still remains to show the original magnificence of the building; the other porches are walled in, and inhabited by paupers.

In the centre of a quadrangle about 100 paces square is a domed building springing from a square which occupies the proper place of the Kaabah. This "Jama ‡" is interesting as a point

* The "Guide Book" contains the story current among the learned concerning the remarkable shape of the minaret.

† The columns support pointed arches, which, therefore, were known at Cairo 200 years before they were introduced into England. By the discoveries of Mons. Mariette, it is now ascertained, that the Egyptians were perfectly acquainted with the round arch and key-stone at a period antecedent to the architectural existence of Greece.

‡ A "jama" is a place where people assemble to pray—a house of public worship. A "masjid" is any place of prayer, private or public. From "masjid" we derive our "mosque:" its changes on the road to Europe are almost as remarkable as that described in the satiric lines,—

of comparison. If it be an exact copy of the Meccan temple, as it stood in A.D. 879, it shows that the latter has greatly altered in this our modern days.

Next in date to the Taylun Mosque is that of the Sultan El Hakim, third Caliph of the Fatimites, and founder of the Drusian mysteries. The minarets are remarkable in shape, as well as size: they are unprovided with the usual outer gallery, are based upon a cube of masonry, and pierced above with apertures apparently meaningless. A learned Cairene informed me that these spires were devised by the eccentric monarch to disperse, like large censers, fragrant smoke over the city during the hours of prayer. The Azhar and Hasanayn * Mosques are simple and artless piles, celebrated

"Alfana vient d'equus, sans doute,
Mais il faut avouer aussi,
Qu'en venant de la jusqu'ici
Il a bien changé sur la route."

* So called, because supposed to contain relics of Hasan and Hosayn, the martyred grandsons of Mohammed. The tradition is little credited, and the Persians ostentatiously avoid visiting the place. "You are the first Ajemi that ever said the Fathah at this holy spot," quoth the Mujawir, or guardian of the tomb, after compelling me, almost by force, to repeat the formula, which he recited with the prospect of a few piastres.

for sanctity, but remarkable for nothing save ugliness. Few buildings, however, are statelier in appearance, or give a nobler idea of both founder and architect than that which bears Sultan Hasan's name.* The stranger stands almost awe-struck before walls high towering without a single break, a hypæthral court, severe in masculine beauty, a gateway that might suit the palace of the Titans, and the massive grandeur of its lofty minaret. This mosque, with its fortress aspect, owns no more relationship to the efforts of a later age than does Canterbury Cathedral to an Anglo-Indian "Gothic." For dignified elegance and refined taste, the mosque and tomb of Kaid Bey and the other Mameluke kings are admirable Even in their present state beauty presides over decay, and the traveller has seldom seen aught more striking than the rich light of the stained glass pouring through the first shades of evening upon the marble floor.

The modern mosques must be visited, to see Moslem architecture in its decline and fall. That of Sittna Zaynab (our Lady Zaynab), founded by Murad Bey, the Mameluke, and interrupted by the

* It was finished about A.D. 1363.

French invasion, shows, even in its completion, some lingering traces of taste. But nothing can be more offensive than the building which every tourist flogs donkey in his hurry to see—old Mohammed Ali's "Folly" in the citadel. Its Greek architect has toiled to caricature a mosque to emulate the glories of our English "Oriental Pavilion." Outside,

> "The shining minarets, thin and high,"

are so thin, so high above the lumpy domes, that they look like the spindles of crouching crones, and are placed in full sight of Sultan Hasan the Giant, so as to derive all the disadvantages of the contrast. Is the pointed arch forgotten by man, that this hapless building should be disgraced by large and small parallelograms of glass and wood*, so placed and so formed as to give its

* This is becoming the fashion for young Egyptians, who will readily receive a pair of common green "persiannes" in exchange for fine old windows of elaborately carved wood. They are as sensible in a variety of other small matters. Natives of a hot climate generally wear slippers of red and yellow leather, because they are cool and comfortable: on the banks of the Nile, the old chaussure is gradually yielding to black shoes, which blister the feet with heat, but are European, and, therefore, "bon ton." It must, however, be confessed, that the fine old carved wood-work of the windows was removed because it was found to be dangerous in cases of fire.

exterior walls the appearance of a European theatre *coiffé* with oriental cupolas ?

Inside, money has been lavished upon alabaster full of flaws; round the bases of pillars run gilt bands; in places the walls are painted with streaks to mock marble, and the woodwork is overlaid with tinsel gold. After a glance at these abominations, one cannot be surprised to hear the old men of Egypt lament that, in spite of European education, and of prizes encouraging geometry and architecture, modern art offers a melancholy contrast to antiquity. It is said that H. H. Abbas Pacha proposed to erect for himself a mosque that should far surpass the boast of the last generation. I venture to hope that the future architects of Egypt will light the "sacred fire" from Sultan Hasan's, not from Mohammed Ali's Turco-Grecian splendours. The former is like the genuine Osmanli of past ages, fierce, cold, with a stalwart frame, index of a strong mind—there was a sullen grandeur about the man. The latter is the pert and puny modern Turk in pantaloons, frock coat, and fez, ill-dressed, and ill-bred, in body and soul.

We will now enter the El Azhar mosque. At the dwarf wooden railing we take off our slippers, hold them in the left hand, sole to sole, that no dirt may fall from them, and cross the threshold with the right foot, ejaculating Bismillah, &c. Next we repair to the Meyzaah, or large tank, for ablution, without which it is scarcely lawful to appear in the house of Allah. We then seek some proper place for devotion, place our slippers on some other object in front of us to warn the lounger, and perform a prayer of two prostrations in honour of the mosque.* This done, we may wander about, and consider the several objects of curiosity.

The moon shines splendidly upon a vast hypæthral court, paved with stones which are polished like glass by the feet of the Faithful. There is darkness in the body of the building, a large parallelogrammic hall, at least twice too long for its height, supported by a forest of pillars, thin, poor-looking, crooked marble columns, planted avenue-like, and lined with torn and dirty matting. A few oil lamps shed doubtful light upon scanty groups, who

* Irreligious men neglect this act of propriety. There are many in Egypt who will habitually transgress one of the fundamental orders of their faith, namely, never to pray when in a state of religious impurity. In popular *Argot*, prayer without ablution is called Salat Mamlukiyah, or "slaves' prayers," because such men perform their devotions only in order to avoid the master's staff. Others will touch the Koran when impure, a circumstance which highly disgusts Indian Moslems.

are debating some point of grammar, or listening to the words of wisdom that fall from the mouth of a Waiz.* Presently they will leave the hypostyle, and throw themselves upon the flags of the quadrangle, where they may enjoy the open air, and avoid some fleas. It is now "long vacation:" so the holy building has become a kind of caravanserai for travellers; perhaps a score of nations meet in it; there is a confusion of tongues, and the din at times is deafening. Around the court runs a tolerably well-built colonnade, whose entablature is garnished with crimson arabesques, and in the inner wall are pierced apartments, now closed with plank doors. Of the Riwaks, as they are called, the Azhar contains twenty-four, one for each recognised nation in El-Islam, and of these, fifteen are still open to students.† Inside them we find nothing but matting, and a pile of large dingy wooden boxes, which once contained the

* An "adviser," or "lecturer,"—any learned man who, generally in the months of Ramazan and Muharram, after the Friday service and sermon, delivers a discourse upon the principles of El-Islam.

† Amongst them is a foundation for Jawi scholars. Some of our authors, by a curious mistake, have confounded Moslem Jawa (by the Egyptians pronounced Gáwa), with "Goa," the Christian colony of the Portuguese.

college library, but are now, generally speaking, empty.*

There is nothing worth seeing in the cluster of little dark chambers that form the remainder of the Azhar. Even the Zawiyat el Umyán, (or the blind men's oratory,) a place whence so many "gown-rows" have emanated, is rendered interesting only by the fanaticism of its inmates, and the certainty that, if recognised in this sanctum, we shall run the gauntlet under the staves of its proprietors, the angry blind.

The Azhar is the grand collegiate mosque of this city,— the Christ Church, in fact, of Cairo, — once

* Cairo was once celebrated for its magnificent collections of books. Besides private libraries, each large mosque had its bibliotheca, every MS. of which was marked with the word "Wakf" (entailed bequest), or "Wukifa lillahi taala" (bequeathed to God Almighty). But Cairo has now for years supplied other countries with books, and the decay of religious zeal has encouraged the unprincipled to steal and sell MSS. marked with the warning words. The Hejaz, in particular, has been inundated with books from Egypt. Cairo has still some large libraries, but most of them are private property, and the proprietors will not readily lend or give access to their treasures. The principal opportunity of buying books is during the month Ramazan, when they are publicly sold in the Azhar mosque. The Orientalist will, however, meet with many disappointments; besides the difficulty of discovering good works, he will find in the booksellers, scribes, *et hoc genus omne*, a finished race of scoundrels.

celebrated throughout the world of El-Islam. It was built, I was told, originally in poor style by one Jauhar *, the slave of a Moorish merchant, in consequence of a dream that ordered him to "erect a place whence the light of science should shine upon El-Islam."

It gradually increased by "Wakf" of lands, money, and books; and pious rulers made a point of adding to its size and wealth. Of late years it has considerably declined, the result of sequestrations, and of the diminished esteem in which the purely religious sciences are now held in the land of Egypt.† Yet it is calculated that between 2000

* Lane (Mod. Egyptians) has rectified Baron von Hammer's mistake concerning the word "Azhar;" our English Orientalist translates it the "splendid mosque." I would venture to add, that the epithet must be understood in a spiritual and not in a material sense. Wilkinson attributes the erection of the building to Jauhar El Kaid, general under El Moez, about A. D. 970. Wilson ascribes it partly to El Moez the Fatimite, (A. D. 973), partly to his general and successor, El Hakim (?).

† If I may venture to judge, after the short experience of a few months, there is now a slight re-action in favour of the old system. Mohammed Ali managed to make his preparatory, polytechnic, and other schools, thoroughly distasteful to the people, and mothers blinded their children, to prevent their being devoted for life to infidel studies. The printing-press, contrasting in hideousness with the beauty of the written character, and the contemptible Arabic style of the various

and 3000 students of all nations and ages receive instruction here gratis. Each one is provided with bread, in a quantity varying with the amount of endowment in the Riwak set apart for his nation*, with some article of clothing on festival days, and a few piastres once a year. The professors, who are about 150 in number, may not take fees from their pupils; some lecture on account of the religious merit of the action, others to gain the high title of "Teacher in El Azhar." † Six officials receive stipends from the government,—the Shaykh el Jama or dean, the Shaykh el Sakka, who regulates the provision of water for ablution, and others that may be called heads of departments.

works translated by order of government from the European languages, have placed arms in the hands of the orthodox party.

* Finding the Indian Riwak closed, and hearing that an endowment still belonged to it, I called twice upon the Shaykh or Dean, wishing to claim the stipend as a precedent But I failed in finding him at home, and was obliged to start hurriedly for Suez. The Indians now generally study in the Sulaymaniyah, or Afghan College.

† As the attending of lectures is not compulsory, the result is that the lecturer is always worth listening to. May I commend this consideration to our college reformers at home? In my day, men were compelled to waste—notoriously to waste—an hour or two every morning, for the purpose of putting a few pounds sterling into the pocket of some droning Don.

The following is the course of study in the Azhar. The school-boy of four or five years' standing has been taught, by a liberal application of the maxim "the green rod is of the trees of Paradise," to chaunt the Koran without understanding it, the elementary rules of arithmetic, and, if he is destined to be a learned man, the art of writing.* He then registers his name in El

* The would-be calligrapher must go to a Constantinople Khojah (schoolmaster), and after writing about two hours a day regularly through a year or two, he will become, if he has the necessary disposition, a skilful penman. This acquirement is but little valued in the present day, as almost nothing is to be gained by it.

The Turks particularly excel in the ornamental character called "Suls." I have seen some Korans beautifully written; and the late Pacha gave an impetus to this branch of industry, by forbidding, under the plea of religious scruples, the importation of the incorrect Korans cheaply lithographed by the Persians at Bombay.

The Persians surpass the Turks in all but the Suls writing. Of late years, the Pachas of Cairo have employed a gentleman from Khorasan, whose travelling name is "Mirza Sanglakh" to decorate their mosques with inscriptions. I was favoured with a specimen of his art, and do not hesitate to rank him the first of his age, and second to none amongst the ancients but those Raphaels of calligraphy, Mir of Shiraz, and Rahman of Herat

The Egyptians and Arabs, generally speaking, write a coarse and clumsy hand, and, as usual in the East, the higher the rank of the writer is, the worse his scrawl becomes.

Azhar, and applies himself to the branches of study most cultivated in El-Islam, namely Nahw (syntax), Fikh (divinity), Hadis (the traditions of the Prophet), and Tafsir, or exposition of the Koran.

The young Egyptian reads at the same time the Sarf, or the Grammar of the Verb, and El Nahw, or the Grammar and Syntax of the Noun. But as Arabic is his mother-tongue, he is not required to study the former so deeply as are the Turks, the Persians, and the Indians. If he desire, however, to be a proficient, he must carefully peruse five books in El Sarf*, and six in El Nahw.†

* The popular volumes are, 1, El Amsilah, showing the simple conjugation of the triliteral verb; 2. Bisia, the work of some unknown author, explaining the formation of the verb into increased infinities, the quadrilateral verb, &c.; 3. The Maksua, a well-known book written by the great Imam Abu' Hanifah; 4. The "Izzi," an explanatory treatise, the work of a Turk, "Izzah Effendi." And lastly, the Marah of Ahmed el Saudi. These five tracts are bound together in a little volume, printed at the government establishment.

El Amsilah is explained in Turkish, to teach boys the art of "parsing:" Egyptians generally confine themselves in El Sarf to the Izzi, and the Lamiyat el Afal of the grammarian Ibn Malik.

† First, the well-known "Ajrumiyah" (printed by M. Vaucelle), and its commentary, El Kafrawi. Thirdly, the Alfiyyah (Thousand Distichs) of Ibn Malik, written in verse for mnemonic purposes, but thereby rendered so difficult as to

Master of grammar, our student now applies himself to its proper end and purpose, Divinity. Of the four schools those of Abu Hanifah and El Shafei are most common in Cairo ; the followers of Ibn Malik abound only in Southern Egypt and the Berberah country, and the Hanbali is almost unknown. The theologian begins with what is called a Matn or text, a short, dry, and often obscure treatise, a mere string of precepts; in fact, the skeleton of the subject. This he learns by repeated perusal, till he can quote almost every passage literally. He then passes to its "Sharh," or commentary, generally the work of some other savant, who explains the difficulty of the text, amplifies its Laconicisms, enters into exceptional cases, and deals with principles and reasons, as well as with mere precept. A difficult work will sometimes require "Hashiyah," or "marginal notes"; but this aid has a bad name.

"Who readeth with note,
But learneth by rote,"

says a popular doggrel. The reason is, that the student's reasoning powers being little exercised, he

require the lengthy commentary of El Ashmumi. The fifth is the well-known work called the Katr el Nidu (the Dew Drop), celebrated from Cairo to Cabul; and last of all the "Azhari."

learns by notes to depend upon the dixit of a master rather than to think for himself. It also leads to the neglect of another practice, highly advocated by the Eastern pedagogue.

"The lecture is one.
The dispute (upon the subject of the lecture) is one thousand."

In order to become a Fakih, or divine of distinguished fame, the follower of Abu Hanifah must peruse about ten volumes*, some of huge size, written in a diffuse style: the Shafei's reading

* I know little of the Hanafi school; but the names of the following popular works were given to me by men upon whose learning I could depend.

The book first read is the Text, called Marah el Falah, containing about twenty pages, and its commentary, which is about six times more lengthy. Then comes the Matn el Kanz, a brief text of from 35 to 40 pages, followed by three long Sharh. The shortest of these, "El Tai," contains 500 pages; the next, "Mulla Miskin," at least 900; and the "Sharh Ayni" nearly 2000. To these succeeds the Text "El Durar," the work of the celebrated Khusraw, (200 pages), with a large commentary by the same author; and last is the Matn Tanwir El Absar, containing about 500 pages, and its Sharh, a work upwards of four times the size.

Many of these books may be found—especially when the MS. is an old one—with Hashiyah, or marginal notes, but most men write them for themselves, so that there is no generally used collection. The above-mentioned are the works containing a full course of theological study: it is rare, however, to is not quite so extensive.* Theology is much studied, because it leads directly to the gaining of daily bread, as priest or tutor; and other scientific pursuits are neglected for the opposite reason.

The theologian in Egypt, as in other parts of El-Islam, must have a superficial knowledge of the Prophet's traditions. Of these there are eight well known collections †, but the three first only are those generally read.

find a man who reads beyond the "El Kanz," with the shortest of its commentaries, the "El Tai."

* He begins with a little text called, after the name of its author, Abu Shujaa of Isfahan, and proceeds to its commentary, a book of about 250 pages, by Ibn Kasim of Gaza. There is another Sharh, nearly four times larger than this, "El-Khatib;" it is seldom read. Then comes El Tahrir, the work of Zakariya el Ansari,—a celebrated divine buried in the mosque of El Shafei,—and its commentary by the same author, a goodly MS. of 600 pages. Most students here cry; "Enough!" The ambitious pass on to El Minhaj and its commentary, (1600 pages). Nor need they stop at this point. A man may addle his brains over Moslem theology, as upon Aristotle's schoolmen, till his eyesight fails him—both subjects are all but interminable.

† The three best known are the Arbain el Nawawi, and the Sahihain—"the two (universally acknowledged to be) trustworthy,"—by El Muslim and El Bokhari, celebrated divines. The others are El Jami el Saghir, "the smaller collection," so called to distinguish it from a rarer book, El Jami el Kabir, the "greater collection;" both are the work of El Siyuti.

The full course includes, with El Shifa, Shamail, and the labours of Kazi Ayyaz.

School-boys are instructed, almost when in their infancy, to intone the Koran; at the university they are taught a more exact system of chaunting. The style called "Hafs" is most common in Egypt, as it is indeed throughout the Moslem world. And after learning to read the holy volume, some savans are ambitious enough to wish to understand it: under these circumstances they must dive into the Ilm el Tafsir*, or the exposition of the Koran.

Our student is now a perfect Fakih or Mulla.†

* Two Tafsirs are known all over the modern world. The smaller one is called Jelalani, ("the two Jelals," *i.e.* the joint work of Jelal el Siyuti and Jelal el Mahalli), and fills two stout volumes octavo. The larger is the Exposition of El Baizawi, which is supposed to contain the whole subject. Some few divines read El Khazin.

† To conclude the list of Moslem studies, not purely religious. Mautik (or logic) is little valued; it is read when judged advisable, after El Nahw, from which it flows, and before Maani Bayan (rhetoric) to which it leads. In Egypt, students are generally directed to fortify their memories, and give themselves a logical turn of mind, by application to El Jebr (algebra). The only logical works known are the Isaghuyi (the εἰσαγωγη of Porphyry), El-Shamsiyah, the book El-Sullam, with its Sharh El Akhzari, and, lastly, Kazi Mir. Equally neglected are the Tawarikh (history) and the Hikmat (or philosophy), once so ardently cultivated by Moslem savans; indeed, it is now all but impossible to get books upon these subjects. For upwards of six weeks, I ransacked the stalls and the bazar, in order to find

But the poor fellow has no scholarship or fellowship—no easy tutorship—no fat living to look

some one of the multitudinous annals of El Hejaz, without seeing for sale anything but the fourth volume of a large biographical work called El Akd el Samin fi Tarikh el Balad El Amin.

The Ilm el Aruz, or Prosody, is not among the Arabs, as with us, a chapter hung on to the tail of grammar. It is a long and difficult study, prosecuted only by those who wish to distinguish themselves in "Arabiyat,"—the poetry and the eloquence of the ancient and modern Arabs. The poems generally studied, with the aid of commentaries, which impress every verse upon the memory, are the Burdah and the Hamziyah, well-known odes by Mohammed of Abusir. They abound in obsolete words, and are useful at funerals, as on other solemn occasions. The Banat Suadi, by Kaab el Ahbar (or Akhbar), a companion of the Prophet, and the Diwan Umar ibn Fariz, a celebrated mystic, are also learned compositions. Few attempt the bulky volume of El Mutanabbi—though many place it open upon the sofa,—fewer still the tenebrous compositions of El Hariri; nor do the modern Egyptians admire those fragments of ancient Arab poets, which seem so sweetly simple to the European ear. The change of faith has altered the national taste to such an extent, that the decent bard must now sing of woman in the masculine gender. For which reason, a host of modern poetasters can attract the public ear, which is deaf to the voices of the "Golden Song."

In the exact sciences, the Egyptian Moslems, a backward race according to European estimation, are far superior to the Persians and the Moslems of India. Some of them become tolerable arithmeticians, though very inferior to the Coptic Christians; they have good and simple treatises on algebra, and still display some of their ancestors' facility in the acquisition of geometry.

forward to. After wasting seven years, or twice seven years, over his studies, and reading till his

The Ilm el-Mikat, or "Calendar-calculating," was at one time publicly taught in the Azhar: the printing-press has doomed that study to death.

The natural sciences find but scant favour on the banks of the Nile. Astronomy is still astrology, geography a heap of names, and natural history a mass of fables. Alchemy, geo mancy, and summoning of fiends, are pet pursuits; but the former has so bad a name, that even amongst friends it is always alluded to as Ilm el Kaf,—the "science of K," so called from the initial letter of the word "Kimiya." Of the state of therapeutics I have already treated at length.

Aided by the finest of ears, and flexible organs of articulation, the Egyptian appears to possess many of the elements of a good linguist. The stranger wonders to hear a Cairene donkey-boy shouting sentences in three or four European dialects, with a pronunciation as pure as his own. How far this people succeed in higher branches of language, my scanty experience does not enable me to determine. But even for students of Arabic, nothing can be more imperfect than those useful implements, Vocabularies and Dictionaries. The Cairenes have, it is true, the Kamús of Fizurabadi, but it has never been printed; it is therefore rare, and when found, lost pages and clerical errors combined with the intrinsic difficulty of the style, exemplify the saying of Golius, that the most learned Orientalist must act the part of a diviner, before he can perform that of interpreter. They have another Lexicon, the Sihah, and an abbreviation of the same, the Sihah el Saghir (or the lesser), both of them liable to the same objections as the Kamús. For the benefit of the numerous students of Turkish and Persian, short grammars and vocabularies have been printed at a cheap price, but the former are upon the model of Arabic, a language essentially different in formation, and the latter are mere strings of words.

brain is dizzy, his digestion gone, and his eyes half blind, he must either starve upon college alms, or squat, like my old Shaykh Mohammed, in a druggist's shop, or become pedagogue and curate in some country place, on the pay of 8*l.* per annum. With such prospects it is wonderful how the Azhar can present any attractions; but the southern man is essentially an idler, and many become Olema, like Capuchins, in order to do nothing. A favoured few rise to the degree of Mudarris, (professors,) and thence become Kazis and Muftis. This is another inducement to matriculate; every undergraduate having an eye upon the Wazi-ship, with as much chance of obtaining it as the country *paroco* has to become a cardinal. Others again devote themselves to laical pursuits, degenerate into Wakils (lawyers), or seek their fortunes as Katibs — public or private accountants.

As a specimen of the state of periodical literature, I may quote the history of the "Bulak Independent," as Europeans facetiously call it. When Mohammed Ali, determining to have an "organ," directed an officer to be editor of a weekly paper, the officer replied, that no one would read it, and consequently that no one would pay for it. The Pacha remedied this by an order that a subscription should be struck off from the pay of all employés, European and Egyptian, whose salary amounted to a certain sum. Upon which the editor accepted the task, but being paid before his work was published, he of course never supplied his subscribers with their copies.

To conclude this part of the subject, I cannot agree with Dr. Bowring when he harshly says, upon the subject of Moslem education: "The instruction given by the Doctors of the Law in the religious schools, for the formation of the Mohammedan priesthood, is of the most worthless character."* His opinion is equally open to objection with that of those who depreciate the law itself because it deals rather in precepts than in principle, in ceremonies and ordinances, rather than in ethics and æsthetics. Both are what Eastern faiths and Eastern training have ever been,—both are eminently adapted for the child-like state of the Oriental mind. When the people learn to appreciate ethics, and to understand psychics and æsthetics, the demand will create a supply. Meanwhile they leave transcendentalism to their poets, and busy themselves with preparing for heaven by practising the only part of their faith now intelligible to them — the material.

It is not to be supposed that a people in this stage of civilisation could be so fervently devout as the Egyptians are without the bad leaven of

* Would not a well-educated, but hasty, and somewhat prejudiced Turk say exactly the same thing about the systems of Christ Church and Trinity College?

bigotry. The same tongue which is employed in blessing the Almighty, is, it is conceived, doing its work equally well in cursing his enemies. Wherefore the Kafir is denounced by every sex, age, class, and condition, by the man of the world*, as by the boy at the school, out of, as well as in, the mosque. If you ask your friend who is the person with a black turban, he replies,

"A Christian. Allah make his countenance cold!"

If you inquire of your servant, who are the people singing in the next house, it is ten to one that his answer will be,

"A Jew. May his lot be Jehannum!"

It appears unintelligible, still it is not less true, that Egyptians who have lived as servants under European roofs for years, retain the liveliest loathing for the manners and customs of their masters. Few Franks, save those who have mixed with the Egyptians in Oriental disguise, are aware of their repugnance to, and contempt for, Europeans, —so well is the feeling veiled under the garb of in-

* And when the man of the world, as sometimes happens, professes to see no difference in the forms of faith, or whispers that his residence in Europe has made him friendly to the Christian religion, you will be justified in concluding his opinions to be latitudinarian.

nate politeness, and so great is their reserve, when conversing with those of strange religions. I had a good opportunity of ascertaining the truth when the first rumour of a Russian war arose. Almost every able-bodied man spoke of hastening to the Jihad*, and the only thing that looked like apprehension was the too eager depreciation of their foes. All seemed delighted at the idea of French cooperation, for, somehow or other, the Frenchman is everywhere popular. When speaking of England, they were not equally easy: heads were rolled, pious sentences were ejaculated, and finally out came the old Eastern cry, "Of a truth they are Shaitans, those English." † The Austrians are despised, because the East knows nothing of them since the days when Osmanlee hosts threatened the gates of Vienna. The Greeks are hated as clever scoundrels, ever ready to do El-Islam a mischief. The Maltese, the greatest of cowards off their own ground, are regarded with a profound contempt: these are the protégés which bring the British

* A crusade, a holy war.

† I know only one class in Egypt favourable to the English,—the donkey boys,—and they found our claim to the possession of the country upon a base scarcely admissible by those skilled in casuistry, namely, that we hire more asses than any other nation.

nation into disrepute at Cairo. And Italians are known only as "*istruttori*" and "*distruttori** " — doctors, druggists, and pedagogues.

Yet Egyptian human nature is, like human nature everywhere, contradictory. Hating and despising Europeans, they still long for European rule. This people admire an iron-handed and lion-hearted despotism; they hate a timid and a grinding tyranny.† Of all foreigners, they would prefer the French yoke, — a circumstance which I attribute to the diplomatic skill and national dignity of our neighbours across the Channel.‡ But whatever

* The story is, that Mohammed Ali used to offer his flocks of foreigners their choice of two professions, — "destruction," that is to say, physic, or "instruction."

† Of this instances abound. Lately an order was issued to tax the villages of the Bedouins settled upon the edge of the Western desert, who, even in Mohammed Ali's time, were allowed to live free of assessment. The Aulad Ali, inhabitants of a little village near the Pyramids, refused to pay, and turned out with their matchlocks, defying the Pacha. The government then insisted upon their leaving the houses, and living under hair-cloth like Bedouins, since they claimed the privileges of Bedouins. The sturdy fellows at once pitched their tents, and when I returned to Cairo (in December, 1853), they had deserted their village. I could offer a score of such cases, proving the present debased condition of Egypt.

‡ At Constantinople the French were the first to break through the shameful degradation to which the ambassadors of infidel powers were bribed, by 300 or 400 rations a day, to

European nation secures Egypt will win a treasure. Moated on the north and south by seas, with a glacis of impassable deserts to the eastward and westward, capable of supporting an army of 180,000 men, of paying a heavy tribute, and yet able to show a considerable surplus of revenue, this country in western hands will command* India, and by a ship-

submit. M. de Saint Priest refused to give up his sword. General Sebastiani insisted upon wearing his military boots; and the Republican Aubert Dubajet rejected the dinner, and the rich dress, with which "the naked and hungry barbarian who ventured to rub his brow upon the Sublime Porte," was fed and clothed before being admitted to the presence, saying that the ambassadors of France wanted neither this nor that. At Cairo, M. Sabatier, the French Consul-general, has had the merit of doing away with some customs prejudicial to the dignity of his nation. The next English envoy will, if anxious so to distinguish himself, have an excellent opportunity. It is usual, after the first audience, for the Pacha to send, *in token of honour*, a sorry steed to the new comer. This custom is a mere relic of the days when Mohammed the Second threatened to stable his charger in St. Peter's, and when a ride through the streets of Cairo exposed the Inspector-general Tott, and his suite, to lapidation and an "*Avanie.*" To send a good horse is to imply degradation, but to offer a bad one is a positive insult.

* As this canal has become a question of national interest, its advisability is surrounded with all the circumstance of unsupported assertion and bold denial. The English want a railroad, which would confine the use of Egypt to themselves. The French desire a canal that would admit the hardy cruisers of the Mediterranean into the Red Sea. The cosmopolite will hope that both projects may be carried out. Even in the seventh

canal between Pelusium and Suez would open the whole of Eastern Africa.

There is no longer much to fear from the fanaticism of the people, and a little prudence would suffice to command the interests of the mosque.*

The chiefs of corporations †, in the present state

century Omar forbade Amr to cut the Isthmus of Suez for fear of opening Arabia to Christian vessels.

As regards the feasibility of the ship-canal, I heard M. Linant de Bellefonds—the best authority upon all such subjects in Egypt—expressly assert, after levelling and surveying the line, that he should have no dfficulty in making it.

* There are at present about eighteen influential Shaykhs at Cairo, too fanatic to listen to reason. These it would be necessary to banish. Good information about what goes on in each mosque, especially on Fridays, when the priests preach to the people, and a guard of honour placed at the gates of the Kazi, the three Muftis, and the Shaykh of the Azhar, are simple precautions sufficient to keep the Ulema in order.

† These Rakaiz El Usab, as they are called, are the most influential part of the immense mass of dark intrigue which Cairo, like most Oriental cities, conceals beneath the light surface. They generally appear in the ostensible state of barbers and dyers. Secretly, they preside over their different factions, and form a kind of small Vehm. The French used to pay these men, but Napoleon detecting them in stirring up the people, whilst appearing to maintain public tranquillity, shot eighteen or twenty, (about half their number,) and thereby improved the conduct of the rest. They are to be managed, as Sir Charles Napier governed Sindh,—by keeping a watchful eye upon them, a free administration of military law, disarming the population, and forbidding large bodies of men to assemble.

of popular feeling, would offer even less difficulty to an invader or a foreign ruler than the "Ulema." Briefly, Egypt is the most tempting prize which the East holds out to the ambition of Europe, not excepting even the Golden Horn.*

* England, at least, wants neither Egypt nor Constantinople: a free passage to India *for all* is what we claim.—Ed.

CHAP. VII.

PREPARATIONS TO QUIT CAIRO.

At length the slow "month of blessings" passed away. We rejoiced like Romans finishing their Quaresima, when a salvo of artillery from the citadel announced the end of our Lenten woes. On the last day of Ramazan all gave alms to the poor, at the rate of a piastre, and a half for each member of the household — slave, servant, and master. The next day, first of the three composing the festival, we arose before dawn, performed our ablutions, and repaired to the mosque, to recite the peculiar prayer of the Eed*, and to hear the sermon which bade us be "merry and wise." After which we ate and drank heartily, then with pipes and tobacco, pouches in hand, we

* Festival. It lasts the three first days of Shawwal, the month immediately following Ramazan, and therefore, among Moslems, corresponds with our Paschal holidays, which succeed Lent. It is called the "Lesser Festival," the "Greater" being in Zu 'l Hijjah, the pilgrimage-month.

sauntered on, to enjoy the contemplation of smiling faces and street scenery.

The favourite resort on this occasion is the large cemetery outside the Bab el Nasr * — that stern, old, massive gateway which opens upon the Suez road. Here we found a scene of jollity. Tents and ambulant coffee-houses were full of men equipped in their *anglicè* "Sunday best," listening to singers and musicians, smoking, chatting, and looking at jugglers, buffoons, snake-charmers, dervishes, ape-leaders, and dancing boys habited in women's attire. Eating-stalls and lollipop-shops, booths full of playthings, and sheds for lemonade and syrups, lined the roads, and disputed with swings and merry-go-rounds the regards of the little Moslems and Moslemahs. The chief item of the crowd,—fair Cairenes,—carried in their hands huge palm branches, intending to ornament therewith the tombs of parents and friends. Yet, even on this solemn occasion, there is, they say, not a little flirtation and love-making; parties of policemen are posted, with orders to interrupt all such irregularities with a long cane; but their vigilance is notoriously unequal to the task. I could not help

* In Chap. VI. of this Volume, I have mentioned this cemetery as Burckhardt's last resting-place.

observing that frequent pairs — doubtless cousins or other relations — wandered to unusual distances among the sand-hills, and that sometimes the confusion of a distant bastinado struck the ear. These trifles did not, however, by any means interfere with the general joy Every one wore something new; most people were in the fresh suits of finery intended to last through the year, and so strong is personal vanity in the breasts of Orientals, men and women, young and old, that from Cairo to Calcutta it would be difficult to find a sad heart under a handsome coat. The men swaggered, the women minced their steps, rolled their eyes, and were eternally arranging, and coquetting with their head-veils. The little boys strutting about foully abused any one of their number who might have a richer suit than his neighbours. And the little girls ogled every one in the ecstacy of conceit, and glanced contemptuously at other little girls their rivals.

Weary of the country, the Haji and I wandered about the city, paying visits, which at this time are like new-year calls in continental Europe.* I

* You are bound also to meet even your enemies in the most friendly way — for which mortification you afterwards hate them more cordially than before.

can describe the operation in Egypt only as the discussion of pipes and coffee in one place, and of coffee and pipes in another. But on this occasion whenever we meet a friend we throw ourselves upon each other's breast, placing right arms over left shoulders, and *vice versâ*, squeezing like wrestlers, with intermittent hugs, then laying cheek to cheek delicately, at the same time making the loud noise of many kisses in the air. The compliment of the season was, "Kull'am Antum bil Khair" — "Every year may you be well!" — in fact, our "Many happy returns of the day to you!" After this came abundant good wishes, and kindly prophecics, and from a "religious person" a blessing, and a short prayer. To complete the resemblance between a Moslem and a Christian festival, we had dishes of the day, fish, Shurayk, the cross-bun, and a peculiarly indigestible cake, called in Egypt Kabk, the plum-pudding of El-Islam.

This year's Eed was made gloomy, comparatively speaking, by the state of politics. Report of war with Russia, with France, with England, that was going to land 3,000,000 men at Suez, and with Infideldom in general, rang through Egypt, and the city of Mars* became unusually martial. The government armories, arsenals, and manufactories, were crowded with kidnapped workmen. Those who purposed a pilgrimage feared forcible detention. Wherever men gathered together, in the mosques, for instance, or the coffee-houses, the police closed the doors, and made forcible capture of the able-bodied. This proceeding, almost as barbarous as our impressment law, filled the main streets with detachments of squalid-looking wretches, marching with collars round their necks and handcuffed to be made soldiers. The dismal impression of the scene was deepened by crowds of women, who, habited in mourning, and scattering dust and mud upon their rent garments, followed their sons, brothers, and husbands, with cries and shrieks. The death-wail is a peculiar way of cheering on the patriot departing *pro patriâ mori*, and the origin of the custom is characteristic of the people. The principal public amusements

* With due deference to the many of a different opinion, I believe "Kahirah" (corrupted through the Italian into Cairo) to mean, not the "victorious," but the "City of Kahir," or Mars. It was so called because, as Richardson has informed the world, it was founded in A.D. 968 by one Jauhar when the warlike planet was in the ascendant.

allowed to Oriental women are those that come under the general name of "Fantasia," — birth-feasts, marriage festivals, and funerals. And the early campaigns of Mohammed Ali's family in Syria, and El Hejaz having, in many cases, deprived the bereaved of their sex-right to *keen* for the dead, they have now determined not to waste the opportunity, but to revel in the luxury of woe at the live man's wake.*

Another cloud hung over Cairo. Rumours of conspiracy were afloat. The Jews and Christians, — here as ready to take alarm as the English in Italy, — trembled at the fancied preparations for insurrection, massacre, and plunder. And even the Moslems whispered that some hundred desperadoes had resolved to fire the city, beginning with the bankers' quarter, and to spoil the wealthy Egyptians. Of course H. H. Abbas Pasha was absent at the time, and, even had he been at Cairo, his presence would have been of little use: for the

* "There were no weeping women; no neighbours came in to sit down in the ashes, as they might have done had the soldier died at home; there was no Nubian dance for the dead, no Egyptian song of the women lauding the memory of the deceased, and beseeching him to tell why he had left them alone in the world to weep."—(Letter from Widdin, March 25, 1854, describing a Turkish soldier's funeral.)

ruler can do nothing towards restoring confidence to a panic-stricken Oriental nation.

At the end of the Eed or Festival, as a counter-irritant to political excitement, the police magistrates began to bully the people. There is a standing order in the chief cities of Egypt, that all who stir abroad after dark without a lantern shall pass the night in the station-house.* But at Cairo in certain quarters, the Ezbekiyah † for instance, a little laxity is usually allowed. Before I left the capital the licence was withdrawn, and the sudden strictness caused many ludicrous scenes.

If by chance you had sent on your lantern to a friend's house by your servant, and had leisurely followed it five minutes after the hour of eight,—you were sure to be met, stopped, collared, questioned, and captured by the patrol. You probably punched three or four of them, but found the dozen too strong for you. Held tightly by the sleeves, skirts, and collar of your wide outer garment, you

* Captain Haines wisely introduced the custom into Aden. I wonder that it is not made universal in the cities of India, where so much iniquity is perpetrated under the shadow of night.

† The reason being that respectable Europeans, and the passengers by the Overland Mail, live and lodge in this quarter.

were hurried away on a plane of about nine inches above the ground, your feet mostly treading the air. You were dragged along with a rapidity which scarcely permitted you to answer strings of questions concerning your name, nation, dwelling, faith, profession, and self in general,— especially concerning the present state of your finances. If you lent an ear to the voice of the charmer that began by asking a crown to release you, and gradually came down to two-pence half-penny, you fell into a simple trap; the butt-end of a musket applied *à posteriori*, immediately after the transfer of property, convicted you of wilful waste. But if, more sensibly, you pretended to have forgotten your purse, you were reviled, and dragged with increased violence of shaking to the Zabit's office.* You were spun through the large archway leading to the court, every fellow in uniform giving you, as you passed, a kafa, "cuff," on the back of the neck. Despite your rage, you were forced up the stairs to a long gallery full of people in a predicament like your own. Again your name, nation,— I suppose you to be masquerading,— offence, and other particulars were asked, and carefully noted in a folio by a ferocious-looking clerk. If you

* The "Zabit" is the police magistrate.

knew no better, you were summarily thrust into the Hasil or condemned cell, to pass the night with pickpockets and ruffians, pell-mell; but if an adept in such matters, you insisted upon being conducted before the "Pasha of the night," and the clerk feared to refuse, you were hurried to the great man's office, hoping for justice, and dealing out ideal vengeance to your captors,— the patrol. Here you found the dignitary sitting with pen, ink, and paper before him, and pipe and coffee-cup in hand, upon a wide divan of dingy chintz, in a large dimly-lit room, with two guards by his side, and a semicircle of recent seizures vociferating before him. When your turn came, you were carefully collared, and led up to the presence, as if even at that awful moment you were mutinously and murderously disposed. The Pasha, looking at you with a vicious sneer, turned up his nose, ejaculated "Ajemi," and prescribed the bastinado. You observed that the mere fact of being a Persian did not give mankind a right to capture, imprison, and punish you; you declare moreover that you were no Persian, but an Indian under British protection. The Pasha, a man accustomed to obedience, then stared at you, to frighten you, and you, we will suppose, stared at him, till, with an oath, he turned to the patrol, and asked them your offence. They all simultaneously swore by Allah, that you had been found without a lantern, dead-drunk, beating respectable people, breaking into houses, robbing and invading harems. You openly told the Pasha, that they were eating abominations; upon which he directed one of his guards to smell your breath,—the charge of drunkenness being a tangible one. The fellow, a comrade of your capturers, advanced his nose to your lips; as might be expected, cried, "Kikh," contorted his countenance, and answered, by the beard of "Effendina"* that he perceived a pestilent odour of distilled waters. This announcement probably elicited a grim grin from the "Pasha of the night," who loves Curaçoa, and is not indifferent to the charms of cognac. Then by his favour, (for you improved the occasion,) you were allowed to spend the hours of darkness on a wooden bench, in the adjacent long gallery, together with certain little parasites, for which polite language has no name.† In the

* "Our lord," *i. e.* H.H. the Pasha. "Kikh" is an interjection noting disapproval, or disgust,—"Fie," or "Ugh."

† Shortly after the Ramazan of 1853, the consul, I am told, obtained an order that British subjects should be sent directly from the police office, at all hours of the night, to the consulate. This was a most sensible measure.

morning the janissary of your consulate was sent for; he came, and claimed you; you were led off criminally; again you gave your name and address, and if your offence was merely sending on your lantern, you were dismissed with advice to be more careful in future. And assuredly your first step was towards the bath.

But if, on the other hand, you had declared yourself a European, you would either have been dismissed at once, or sent to your consul, who is here judge, jury, and jailor. Egyptian authority has of late years lost half its prestige. When Mr. Lane first settled at Cairo, all Europeans accused of aggression against Moslems were, he tells us, surrendered to the Turkish magistrates. Now, the native powers have no jurisdiction over strangers, nor can the police enter their houses. If the West would raise the character of its Eastern co-religionists, it will be forced to push the system a point further, and to allow all Christians to register their names at the different consulates whose protection they might prefer. This is what Russia has so "unwarrantably and outrageously" attempted. We confine ourselves to a lesser injustice, which deprives Eastern states of their right as indepen dent Powers to arrest, and judge foreigners, who for interest or convenience settle in their dominions. But we still shudder at the right of arrogating any such claim over the born subjects of Oriental Powers. What, however, would be the result were Great Britain to authorise her sons resident at Paris, or Florence, to refuse attendance at a French or an Italian court of justice, and to demand that the police should never force the doors of an English subject? I commend this consideration to all those who "stickle for abstract rights" when the interest and progress of others are concerned, and who become somewhat latitudinarian and concrete in cases where their own welfare and aggrandisement are at stake.

Besides patients I had made some pleasant acquaintances at Cairo. Anton Zananire, a young Syrian of considerable attainments as a linguist, paid me the compliment of permitting me to see the fair face of his "Hareem." Mr. Hatchadoor Noory, an Armenian gentleman, well known in Bombay, amongst other acts of kindness, introduced me to one of his compatriots, Khwayah Yusuf, whose advice, as an old traveller, was most useful to me. He had wandered far and wide, picking up everywhere some scrap of strange knowledge, and his history was a romance. Expelled for a youthful peccadillo from Cairo, he started upon his travels, qualified himself for sanctity at Meccah and El Medinah, became a religious beggar at Bagdad, studied French at Paris, and finally settled down as a professor of languages *, under an amnesty, at Cairo. In his house I saw an Armenian marriage. The occasion was a memorable one: after the gloom and sameness of Moslem society, nothing could be more gladdening than the unveiled face of a pretty woman. Some of the guests were undeniably charming brunettes, with the blackest possible locks, and the brightest conceivable eyes; only one pretty girl wore the national costume †; yet they all smoked chibouques

* Most Eastern nations, owing to their fine ear for sounds, are quick at picking up languages; but the Armenian is here, what the Russian is in the West, the *facile princeps* of conversational linguists. I have frequently heard them speak with the purest accent, and admirable phraseology, besides their mother tongue, Turkish, Arabic, Persian, and Hindoostanee, nor do they evince less aptitude for acquiring the Occidental languages.

† It has been too frequently treated of, to leave room for a fresh description. Though pretty and picturesque, it is open to the reproach of Moslem dressing, namely, that the in-door toilette admits of a display of bust, and is generally so scanty and flimsy that it is unfit to meet the eye of a stranger. This, probably the effect of secluding women, has now become a cause for concealing them.

and sat upon the divans, and as they entered the room, with a sweet simplicity, kissed the hands of the priest, and of the other old gentlemen present.

Among the number of my acquaintances was a Meccan boy, Mohammed El Basyuni, from whom I bought the pilgrim-garb called "El-ihram" and the Kafan or shroud, with which the Moslem usually starts upon such a journey as mine was. He, being in his way homewards after a visit to Constantinople, was most anxious to accompany me in the character of a "companion." But he had travelled too much to suit me; he had visited India, seen Englishmen, and lived with the "Nawwab Baloo" of Surat. Moreover he showed signs of over-wisdom. He had been a regular visitor, till I cured one of his friends of an ophthalmia, after which he gave me his address at Meccah, and was seen no more. Haji Wali described him and his party to be "Nas jarrár," (extractors,) and certainly he had not misjudged them. But the sequel will prove how Providence disposes of what man proposes, and as the boy, Mohammed, eventually did become my companion throughout the pilgrimage, I will place him before the reader as summarily as possible.

He is a beardless youth, of about eighteen, chocolate brown, with high features, and a bold profile; his bony and decided Meccan cast of face is lit up by the peculiar Egyptian eye, which seems to descend from generation to generation.* His figure was short and broad, with a tendency to be obese, the result of a strong stomach and the power of sleeping at discretion. He could read a little, write his name, and was uncommonly clever at a bargain. Meccah had taught him to speak excellent Arabic, to understand the literal dialect, to be eloquent in abuse, and to be profound at prayer and pilgrimage. Constantinople had given him a taste for Anacreontic singing, and female society of the questionable kind, a love of strong waters,—the hypocrite looked positively scandalised when I first suggested the subject,—and an off-hand latitudinarian mode of dealing with serious subjects in general. I found him to be the youngest son of a widow, whose doting fondness had moulded his disposition; he was selfish and affectionate, as spoiled children usually are, volatile, easily offended and

* He was from the banks of the Nile, as his cognomen, El Basyani, proves, but his family, I was told, had been settled for three or four generations at Meccah.

as easily pacified (the Oriental), coveting other men's goods, and profuse of his own (the Arab), with a matchless intrepidity of countenance (the traveller), brazen lunged, not more than half brave, exceedingly astute, with an acute sense of honour, especially where his relations were concerned (the individual). I have seen him in a fit of fury because some one cursed his father; and he and I nearly parted because on one occasion I applied to him an epithet which etymologically considered might be exceedingly insulting to a high-minded brother, but which in popular *parlance* signifies nothing. This "*point d'honneur*" was the boy Mahommed's strong point.

During the Ramazan I laid in my stores for the journey. These consisted of tea, coffee, rice, loaf-sugar, dates, biscuit, oil, vinegar, tobacco, lanterns and cooking utensils, a small bell-shaped tent, costing twelve shillings, and three water skins for the desert.* The provisions were placed in a "Kafas" or hamper artistically made of palm

* Almost all the articles of food were so far useful, that they served every one of the party at least as much as they did their owner. My friends drank my coffee, smoked my tobacco, and ate my rice. I bought better tea at Meccah than at Cairo, and found as good sugar there. It would have been wiser to lay in a small stock merely for the voyage to Yambu, in which case

sticks, and in a huge Sahharah, or wooden box, about three feet each way, covered with leather or skin, and provided with a small lid fitting into the top.* The former, together with my green box containing medicines, and saddle-bags full of clothes, hung on one side of the camel, a counterpoise to the big Sahharah on the other flank, Bedouins always requiring a tolerably equal balance of weight. On the top of the load

there might have been more economy. But I followed the advice of those interested in setting me wrong. Turks and Egyptians always go pilgrimaging with a large outfit, as notably as the East-Indian cadet of the present day, and your outfitter at Cairo, as well as Cornhill, is sure to supply you with a variety of superfluities. The tent was most useful to me; so were the water-skins, which I preferred to barrels, as being more portable, and less liable to leak. Good skins cost about a dollar each; they should be bought new, and always kept half full of water.

* This shape secures the lid, which otherwise, on account of the weight of the box, would infallibly be torn off, or burst open. Like the Kafas, the Sahharah should be well padlocked, and if the owner be a saving man, he does not entrust his keys to a servant. I gave away my Kafas at Yambu, because it had been crushed during the sea voyage, and I was obliged to leave the Sahharah at El Medinah, as my Bedouin camel-shaykh positively refused to carry it to Meccah. So that both these articles were well nigh useless to me. The Kafas cost four shillings, and the Sahharah about twelve. When these large boxes are really strong and good, they are worth about a pound sterling each.

transversely was placed a Shibriyah or cot, in which Shaykh Nur squatted like a large crow. This worthy had strutted out into the streets armed with a pair of horse-pistols and a sword almost as long as himself. No sooner did the mischievous boys of Cairo—they are as bad as the *gamins* of Paris and London—catch sight of him than they began to scream with laughter at the sight of the "Hindi (Indian) in arms," till like a vagrant owl pursued by a flight of larks he ran back into the caravanserai.

Having spent all my ready money at Cairo I was obliged to renew the supply. My native friends advised me to take at least eighty pounds, and considering the expense of outfit for desert travelling, the sum did not appear excessive. I should have found some difficulty in raising the money had it not been for the kindness of a friend at Alexandria and a compatriot at Cairo. My Indians scrutinised the diminutive square of paper*

* At my final interview with the committee of the Royal Geographical Society, one member, Sir Woodbine Parish, advised an order to be made out on the Society's bankers; another, Sir Roderick Murchison, kindly offered to give me one on his own, Coutts & Co.; but I, having more experience in Oriental travelling, begged only to be furnished with a most diminutive piece of paper, permitting me to draw upon the Society, which was at once given by Dr. Shaw, the Secretary, and which proved of so much use eventually.

—my letter of credit—as a raven may sometimes be seen peering, with head askance, into the interior of a suspected marrow-bone. "Can this be a *bonâ fide* draft?" they mentally inquired. And finally they offered, most politely, to write to England for me to draw the money, and to forward it in a sealed bag directed "El Medinah." I need scarcely say that such a style of transmission would, in the case of precious metals, have left no possible chance of its safe arrival. When the difficulty was overcome, I bought fifty pounds worth of German dollars (Maria Theresas), and invested the rest in English and Turkish sovereigns.* The gold I myself carried; part of the silver I sewed up in Shaykh Nur's leather waist-belt, and part was packed in the boxes, for this

It was purposely made as small as possible, in order to fit into a talisman case. But the traveller must bear in mind, that if his letters of credit be addressed to Orientals, the sheet of paper should always be large, and grand-looking. These people have no faith in notes,—commercial, epistolary, or diplomatic.

* Before leaving Cairo, I bought English sovereigns for 112, and sold them in Arabia for 122 piastres. "Abu Takahs," (pataks, or Spanish pillar-dollars,) as they are called in El Hejaz, cost me 24 piastres, and in the Holy City were worth 28. The "Sinkee" (French five franc piece) is bought for 22 piastres in Egypt, and sells at 24 in Arabia. The silver Majídi costs 20 at Cairo, and is worth 22 in the Red Sea, and finally I gained 3 piastres upon the gold "Ghazi" of 19. Such was the

reason,—when Bedouins begin plundering a respectable man, if they find a certain amount of ready money in his baggage, they do not search his person. If they find none they proceed to a personal inspection, and if his waist-belt be empty they are rather disposed to rip open his stomach, in the belief that he must have discovered some peculiarly ingenious way of secreting valuables. Having got through this difficulty I immediately fell into another. My hardly-earned Alexandrian passport required a double visa, one at the Zabit's office, the other at the consul's. After returning to Egypt I found it was the practice of travellers who required any civility from the English official at Cairo to enter the presence furnished with an order from the Foreign Office.

I had neglected the precaution, and had ample reason to regret having done so. Failing at the British consulate, and unwilling to leave Cairo without being "*en regle*,"—the Egyptians warned me that Suez was a place of obstacles to pilgrims * — I was obliged to look elsewhere for protection. My friend Haji Wali was the first consulted: after a long discussion he offered to take me to his

rate of exchange in 1853. It varies, however, perpetually, and in 1863 may be totally different.

* The reason of this will be explained in a future chapter.

consul, the Persian, and to find out for what sum I could become a temporary subject of the Shah. We went to the sign of the "Lion and the Sun," and found the dragoman*, a subtle Syrian Christian, who, after a rigid inquiry into the state of my

* The consular dragoman is one of the greatest abuses I know. The tribe is, for the most part, Levantine and Christian, and its connections are extensive. The father will perhaps be interpreter to the English, the son to the French consulate. By this means, the most privy affairs will become known to every member of the department, except the head, and eventually to that best of spy-trainers, the Turkish government. This explains how a subordinate, whose pay is 200*l.* per annum, and who spends double that sum, can afford, after twelve or thirteen years' service, to purchase a house for 2000*l.* and to furnish it for as much more. Besides which the condition, the ideas, and the very nature of these dragomans are completely Oriental. The most timid and cringing of men, they dare not take the proper tone with a government to which, in case of the expulsion of a consul, they and their families would become subject. And their prepossessions are utterly Oriental. Hanna Massara, dragoman to the consul-general at Cairo, in my presence, and before others, advocated the secret murder of a Moslem girl who had fled with a Greek, on the grounds that an adulteress must always be put to death, either publicly or under the rose. Yet this man is an "old and tried servant" of the state.

Such evils might be in part mitigated by employing English youths, of whom an ample supply, if there were any demand, would soon be forthcoming. This measure has been advocated by the best authorities, but without success. Most probably, the reason of the neglect is the difficulty how to begin, or where to end, the Augean business of consular reform.

purse, (my country was no consideration at all,*) introduced me to the Great Man. I have described this personage once already, and truly he merits not a second notice. The interview was a ludicrous one. He treated us with exceeding *hauteur*, motioned me to sit almost out of hearing, and after rolling his head in profound silence for nearly a quarter of an hour, vouchsafed the information that though my father *might* be a Shirazi, and my mother an Afghan, he had not the honour of my acquaintance. His companion, a large old Persian with Polyphemean eyebrows and a mulberry beard put some gruff and discouraging questions. So I quoted the verses

"He is a man who benefits his fellow men,
Not he who says 'why,' and 'wherefore,' and 'how much?'"

---

* In a previous chapter I have alluded to the species of protection formerly common in the East. Europe, it is to be feared, is not yet immaculate in this respect, and men say that were a list of "protected" furnished by the different consulates at Cairo, it would be a curious document. As no one, Egyptian or foreigner, would, if he could possibly help it, be subject to the Egyptian government, large sums might be raised by the simple process of naturalising strangers. At the Persian consulate 110*l* — the century for the consul, and the decade for his dragoman, — is the tariff for protection. A stern fact this for those who advocate the self-government of the childish East.

upon which an imperious wave of the arm directed me to return to the dragoman, who had the effrontery to ask me four pounds sterling for a Persian passport. I offered one. He derided my offer, and I went away perplexed. On my return to Cairo some months afterwards, he sent to say that had he known me as an Englishman, I should have had the document gratis, — a civility for which he was duly thanked.

At last my Shaykh Mohammed hit upon *the* plan. "Thou art," said he, "an Afghan, I will fetch hither the principal of the Afghan college at the Azhar, and he, if thou make it worth his while" (this in a whisper) "will be thy friend." The case was looking desperate; my preceptor was urged to lose no time.

Presently Shaykh Mohammed returned in company with the principal, a little thin, ragged-bearded, one-eyed, hare-lipped divine, dressed in very dirty clothes, of nondescript cut Born at Muscat of Afghan parents, and brought up at Meccah, he was a kind of cosmopolite, speaking five languages fluently, and full of reminiscenes of toil and travel. He refused pipes and coffee, professing to be ascetically disposed: but he ate more than half my dinner, to reassure me I presume, should

I have been fearful that abstinence might injure his health. We then chatted in sundry tongues. I offered certain presents of books, which were rejected, (such articles being valueless), and the Shaykh Abd el Wahhab having expressed his satisfaction at my account of myself, told me to call for him at the Azhar mosque next morning.

Accordingly at six P. M. Shaykh Mohammed and Abdullah Khan *, — the latter equipped in a gigantic sprigged-muslin turban, so as to pass for a student of theology — repaired to El Azhar. Passing through the open quadrangle we entered the large hall which forms the body of the mosque. In the northern wall was a dwarf door, leading by breakneckstairs to a pigeon-hole, the study of the learned Afghan Shaykh. We found him ensconced behind piles of musty and greasy manuscripts, surrounded by scholars and scribes, with whom he was cheapening books. He had not much business to transact; but long before he was ready, the stifling atmosphere drove us out of the study, and we repaired to the hall. Presently the Shaykh joined us, and we all rode on away to the citadel,

* Khan is a title assumed in India and other countries by all Afghans, and Pathans, their descendants, simple as well as gentle.

and waited in a mosque till the office hour struck. When the doors were opened we went into the "divan," and sat patiently till the Shaykh found an opportunity of putting in a word. The officials were two in number; one an old invalid, very thin and sickly-looking, dressed in the Turco-European style, whose hand was being severely kissed by a troop of religious beggars, to whom he had done some small favours; the other was a stout young clerk, whose duty it was to engross, and not to have his hand kissed.

My name and other essentials were required, and no objections were offered, for who holier than the Shaykh Abd el Wahhab ibn Yunus el Sulaymani? The clerk filled up a printed paper in the Turkish language, apparently borrowed from the European methodfor spoiling the traveller, certified me, upon the Shaykh's security, to be one Abdullah, the son of Yusuf, (Joseph,) originally from Cabool, described my person, and in exchange for five piastres handed me the document. I received it with joy, and still keep it as a trophy.

With bows, and benedictions, and many wishes that Allah might make it the officials' fate to become pilgrims, we left the office, and returned towards El Azhar. When we had nearly reached the mosque, Shaykh Mohammed lagged behind, and made the sign. I drew near the Afghan, and asked for his hand. He took the hint, and muttering "it is no matter!"—"it is not necessary!" —"by Allah it is not required"! extended his fingers, and brought the musculus "*guineorum*" to bear upon three dollars.

Poor man! I believe it was his necessity that consented to be paid for the doing a common act of Moslem charity; he had a wife and children, and the calling of an Alim* is no longer worth much in Egypt.

My departure from Cairo was hastened by an accident. I lost my reputation by a little misfortune that happened in this wise.

At Haji Wali's room in the caravanserai, I met a Yuzbashi, or captain of Albanian Irregulars, who was in Egypt on leave from El Hejaz. He was a tall, bony, and broad-shouldered mountaineer, about forty years old, with the large "bombé" brow, the fierce eyes, thin lips, lean jaws, and peaky chin of his race. His mustachios were enormously long and tapering, and the rest of his face, like his head, was close shaven. His "fustan" † was none of the

* A theologian, a learned man.

† The stiff, white, plaited kilt worn by Albanians.

cleanest, nor was the red cap, which he wore rakishly pulled over his frowning forehead, quite free from stains. Not permitted to carry the favourite pistols, he contented himself with sticking his right hand in the empty belt, and stalking about the house with a most military mien. Yet he was as little of a bully, as carpet knight, that same Ali Agha; his body showed many a grisly scar, and one of his shin bones had been broken by a Turkish bullet, when he was playing tricks on the Albanian hills,— an accident inducing a limp, which he attempted to conceal by a heavy swagger. When he spoke, his voice was affectedly gruff; he had a sad knack of sneering, and I never saw him thoroughly sober.

Our acquaintance began with a kind of storm, which blew over, and left fine weather. I was showing Haji Wali my pistols with Damascene barrels when Ali Agha entered the room. He sat down before me with a grin, which said intelligibly enough, "What business have you with weapons?" —snatched the arm out of my hand, and began to inspect it as a *connoisseur*. Not admiring this procedure, I wrenched it away from him, and, addressing myself to Haji Wali, proceeded quietly with my dissertation. The captain of Irregulars and I then looked at each other. He cocked his cap on one side, in token of excited pugnacity. I twirled my mustachios to display a kindred emotion. Had he been armed, and in El Hajaz, we should have fought it out at once, for the Arnaouts are "*terribili colla pistola,*" as the Italians say, meaning that upon the least provocation, they pull out a horse-pistol, and fire it in the face of friend or foe. Of course, the only way under these circumstances is to anticipate them; but even this desperate prevention seldom saves a stranger, as whenever there is danger, these men go about in pairs. I never met with a more reckless brood. Upon the line of march, indeed, Albanian troops are not allowed ammunition; for otherwise there would be half a dozen duels a day. When they quarrel over their cups, it is the fashion for each man to draw a pistol, and to place it against his opponent's breast. The weapons being kept accurately clean seldom miss fire, and if one combatant draw trigger before the other, he would immediately be shot down by the by-standers.* In Egypt these

* Those curious about the manners of these desperadoes may consult the pages of Giovanni Finati, (Murray, London, 1830), and I will be answerable that he exaggerates nothing.

men, — who are used as irregulars, and often quartered upon the hapless villagers, when unable or unwilling to pay up their taxes, — were the terror of the population. On many occasions they have quarrelled with foreigners, and insulted European women. In El Hejaz their recklessness awes even the Bedouins. The townspeople say of them that, "tripe-sellers, and bath servants at Stamboul, they become Pharaohs * in Arabia." At Jeddah the Arnaouts have amused themselves with firing at the English consul (Mr. Ogilvie) when he walked upon his terrace. And this man-shooting appears a favourite sport with them: at Cairo many stories illustrate the *sang froid* with which they used to knock over the camel-drivers, if any one dared to ride past their barracks. The Albanians vaunt their skill in using weapons, and their pretensions impose upon Arabs as well as Egyptians; yet I have never found them wonderful with any arm, (the pistol alone excepted,) and our officers, who have visited their native hills, speak of them as tolerable, but by no means first-rate rifle shots.

The captain of Irregulars being unhappily debarred the pleasure of shooting me, after looking

* That is to say, tyrants, ruffians.

fierce for a time, rose, and walked majestically out of the room. A day or two afterwards, he called upon me civilly enough, sat down, drank a cup of coffee, smoked a pipe, and began to converse. But as he knew about a hundred Arabic words, and I as many Turkish, our conversation was carried on under difficulties. Presently he asked me in a whisper for "Araki." * I replied that there was none in the house, which induced a sneer, and an ejaculation sounding like "himar," (ass,) the slang synonym amongst fast Moslems for water-drinker. After rising to depart he seized me

* The cognac of Egypt and Turkey. Generically the word means any spirit; specifically, it is applied to that extracted from dates, or dried grapes. The latter is more expensive than the former, and costs from 5 to 7 piastres the bottle. It whitens the water like Eau de Cologne, and being considered a stomachic, is patronised by Europeans as much as by Asiatics. In the Ezbekiyah gardens at Cairo, the traveller is astonished by perpetual calls for "sciroppo di gomma," as if all the Western population was afflicted with sore throat. The reason is that spirituous liquors in a Moslem land must not be sold in places of public resort; so the infidel asks for a "syrup of gum," and obtains a "dram" of Araki. The favourite way of drinking it, is to swallow it neat, and to wash it down with a mouthful of cold water. Taken in this way it acts like the "petit verre d'absinthe." Egyptian women delight in it, and Eastern topers of all classes and sexes prefer it to brandy and cognac, the smell of which, being strange, is offensive to them.

waggishly, with an eye to a trial of strength. Thinking that an Indian doctor and a temperance man would not be very dangerous, he exposed himself to what is professionally termed a "cross-buttock," and had his head come in contact with the stone floor instead of my bed, he might not have drunk for many a day. The fall had a good effect upon his temper. He jumped up, patted my head, called for another pipe, and sat down to show me his wounds, and to boast of his exploits. I could not help remarking a ring of English gold, with a bezel of bloodstone, sitting strangely upon his coarse sun-stained hand. He declared that it had been snatched by him from a Konsol (a consul) at Jeddah, and volubly related, in a mixture of Albanian, Turkish, and Arabic, the history of his acquisition. Unfortunately I could not follow the thread of his discourse. He begged me to supply him with a little poison that "would not lie," for the purpose of quieting a troublesome enemy, and he carefully stowed away in his pouch five grains of calomel, which I gave him for that laudable purpose. Before taking leave he pressed me strongly to go and drink with him: I refused to do so during the day, but, wishing to see how these men sacrifice to Bacchus, promised compliance that night. About 9 o'clock, when the caravanserai was quite quiet, I took a pipe, and a tobacco-pouch*, stuck my dagger in my belt, and slipped into Ali Agha's room. He was sitting on a bed spread upon the ground: in front of him stood four wax candles, (all Orientals hate drinking in any but a bright light,) and a tray containing a basin of stuff like soup maigre, a dish of cold stewed meat, and two bowls of Salatah † and curds. The "materials" peeped out of an iron pot filled with water; one was a long, thin, white-glass flask of Araki, the other a bottle of some strong perfume. Both were wrapped up in wet rag, the usual refrigerator.

Ali Agha welcomed me politely, and seeing me admire the preparations, bade me beware how I suspected an Albanian of not knowing how to drink; he made me sit by him on the bed, threw his dagger to a handy distance, signalled me to do

* When Egyptians of the middle classes call upon one another, the visitor always carries with him his tobacco-pouch, which he hands to the servant, who fills his pipe.

† The "Salatah" is made as follows. Take a cucumber, pare, slice and place it in a plate, sprinkling it over with salt. After a few minutes, season it abundantly with pepper, and put it in a bowl containing some peppercorns, and about a pint of curds. When the dish is properly mixed, a live coal is placed upon the top of the compound to make it bind, as the Arabs say. It is considered a cooling dish, and is esteemed by the abstemious, as well as by the toper.

the same, and prepared to begin the bout. Taking up a little tumbler, in shape like those from which French postilions used to drink "la goutte," he inspected it narrowly, wiped out the interior with his fore-finger, filled it to the brim, and offered it to his guest * with a bow. I received it with a low salaam, swallowed its contents at once, turned it upside down in proof of fair play, replaced it upon the floor, with a jaunty movement of the arm, somewhat like a "British pugilist" delivering a "rounder," bowed again, and requested him to help himself. The same ceremony followed on his part. Immediately after each glass,—and rapidly the cup went about,—we swallowed a draught of water, and ate a spoonful of the curds or the Salatah in order to cool our palates. Then we re-applied ourselves to our pipes, emitting huge puffs, —a sign of being "fast" men,—and looked facetiously at each other,—drinking being considered by Moslems a funny and pleasant manner of sin.

* These Albanians are at most half Asiatic as regards manner. In the East generally, the host drinks of the cup, and dips his hand into the dish before his guest, for the same reason that the master of the house precedes his visitor over the threshold. Both actions denote that no treachery is intended, and to reverse them, as amongst us, would be a gross breach of custom, likely to excite the liveliest suspicions.

The Albanian captain was at least half seas over when we began the bout, yet he continued to fill and to drain without showing the least progress in ebriety. I in vain for a time expected the "bad-masti," (as the Persians call it,) the horse play, and gross facetiæ, which generally accompany southern and eastern tipsiness. Ali Agha, indeed, occasionally took up the bottle of perfume, filled the palm of his right hand, and dashed it in my face: I followed his example, but our pleasantries went no further.

Presently my companion started a grand project, namely, that I should entice the respectable Haji Wali into the room, where we might force him to drink. The idea was facetious; it was making a Bow-street magistrate polk at a casino. I started up to fetch the Haji: and when I returned with him Ali Agha was found in a new stage of "freshness." He had stuck a green-leaved twig upright in the floor, and had so turned over a goblet of water, that its contents trickled slowly, in a tiny stream under the verdure, and he was sitting before it mentally gazing, with an outward show of grim Quixotic tenderness, upon the shady trees and the cool rills of his fatherland. Possibly he had peopled the place with "young barbarians at play;" for verily I thought that a tear "which had no business there" was glistening in his stony eye.

The appearance of Haji Wali suddenly changed the scene. Ali Agha jumped up, seized the visitor by the shoulder, compelled him to sit down, and, ecstasied by the old man's horror at the scene, filled a tumbler, and with the usual grotesque grimaces insisted upon his drinking it. Haji Wali stoutly refused; then Ali Agha put it to his own lips, and drained it, with a hurt feeling and reproachful aspect. We made our unconvivial friend smoke a few puffs, and then we returned to the charge. In vain the Haji protested that throughout life he had avoided the deadly sin; in vain he promised to drink with us to-morrow,—in vain he quoted Koran, and alternately coaxed, and threatened us with the police. We were inexorable. At last the Haji started upon his feet, and rushed away, regardless of any thing but escape, leaving his tarboosh, his slippers, and his pipe, in the hands of the enemy. The host did not dare to pursue his recreant guest beyond the door, but returning he carefully sprinkled the polluting liquid on the cap, pipe, and shoes, and called the Haji an ass in every tongue he knew.

Then we applied ourselves to supper, and dispatched the soup, the stew, and the Salatah. A few tumblers and pipes were exhausted to obviate indigestion, when Ali Agha arose majestically, and said that he required a troop of dancing girls to gladden his eyes with a ballet.

I represented that such persons are no longer admitted into caravanserais.* He inquired, with calm ferocity, "who hath forbidden it?" I replied "the Pasha;" upon which Ali Agha quietly removed his cap, brushed it with his fore-arm, fitted it on his forehead, raking forwards, twisted his mustachios to the sharp point of a single hair, shouldered his pipe, and moved towards the door, vowing, that he would make the Pasha himself come, and dance before us.

I foresaw a brawl, and felt thankful that my boon companion had forgotten his dagger. Prudence whispered me to return to my room, to bolt the

* Formerly these places, like the coffee-houses, were crowded with bad characters. Of late years the latter have been refused admittance, but it would be as easy to bar the door to gnats and flies. They appear as "foot-pages," as washerwomen, as beggars; in fact, they evade the law with ingenuity and impunity.

door, and to go to bed, but conscience suggested that it would be unfair to abandon the Albanian in his present helpless state. I followed him into the outer gallery, pulling him, and begging him, as a despairing wife might urge a drunken husband, to return home. And he, like the British husband, being greatly irritated by the unjovial advice, instantly belaboured with his pipe-stick * the first person he met in the gallery, and sent him flying down the stairs with fearful shouts of "O Egyptians! O ye accursed! O genus of Pharaoh! O race of dogs! O Egyptians!"

He then burst open a door with his shoulder, and reeled into a room where two aged dames were placidly reposing by the side of their spouses, who were basket-makers. They immediately awoke, seeing a stranger, and, hearing his foul words, they retorted with a hot volley of vituperation.

Put to flight by the old women's tongues, Ali Agha, in spite of all my endeavours, reeled down

* Ismail Pasha was murdered by Malik Nimr, chief of Shendy, for striking him with a chibouque across the face. Travellers would do well to remember, that in these lands the pipe-stick and the slipper disgrace a man, whereas a whip or a rod would not do so. The probable reason of this is, that the two articles of domestic use are applied slightingly, not seriously, to the purposes of punishment.

the stairs, and fell upon the sleeping form of the night porter, whose blood he vowed to drink—the Oriental form of threatening "spiflication." Happily for the assaulted, the Agha's servant, a sturdy Albanian lad, was lying on a mat in the doorway close by. Roused by the tumult he jumped up, and found the captain in a state of fury. Apparently the man was used to the master's mood. Without delay he told us all to assist, and we lending a helping hand, half dragged and half carried the Albanian to his room. Yet even in this ignoble plight, he shouted with all the force of his lungs the old war-cry, "O Egyptians! O race of dogs! I have dishonoured all Sikandarijah—all Kahirah—all Suways."* And in this vaunting frame of mind he was put to bed. No Welsh undergraduate at Oxford, under similar circumstances, ever gave more trouble.

"You had better start on your pilgrimage at once," said Haji Wali, meeting me the next morning with a "goguenard" smile.

He was right. Throughout the caravanserai nothing was talked of for nearly a week but the wickedness of the captain of Albanian Irregulars,

* *Anglicè,* Alexandria, Cairo, and Suez,— an extensive field of operations.

and the hypocrisy of the staid Indian doctor. Thus it was, gentle reader, that I lost my reputation of being a "serious person" at Cairo. And all I have to show for it is the personal experience of an Albanian drinking bout.

I wasted but little time in taking leave of my friends, telling them, by way of precaution, that my destination was Meccah *viâ* Jeddah, and firmly determining, if possible, to make El Medinah *viâ* Yambu. "Conceal," says the Arabic proverb, "thy tenets, thy treasure, and thy travelling."

CHAP. VIII.

FROM CAIRO TO SUEZ.

SHAYKH Nassar, a Bedouin of Tur, (Mount Sinai,) being on his way homewards, agreed to let me have two dromedaries for the sum of 50 piastres, or about ten shillings each.* Being desirous to start with a certain display of respectability, I accepted these terms: a man of humble pretensions would have travelled with a single animal, and a camel-man running behind him. But, besides ostentation, I wanted my attendant to be mounted, that we might make a forced march in order to ascertain how much a four years' life of European effeminacy had impaired my powers of endurance. The reader may believe the assertion that there are few better tests than an eighty-four mile ride in mid-summer, on a bad wooden saddle, borne by a worse dromedary, across a desert. Even the squire famed

* The proper hire of a return dromedary from Cairo to Suez is forty piastres. But every man is charged in proportion to his rank, and Europeans generally pay about double.

for being copper-sheeted might not have disdained a trial of the kind.

I started my Indian boy and heavy luggage for Suez two days before the end of the Eed,— laden camels generally taking fifty-five or sixty hours to do the journey, and I spent the intermediate time with Haji Wali. He advised me to mount about 3 P.M., so that I might arrive at Suez on the evening of the next day, and assisted me in making due preparations of water provisions, tobacco, and a bed for the road. Early on the morning of departure the Afghan Shaykh came to the caravanserai, and breakfasted with us, "because Allah willed it." After a copious meal he bestowed upon me a stately benediction, and would have embraced me, but I humbly kissed his hand: sad to relate, immediately that his back was turned, Haji Wali raised his forefinger to a right angle with the palm, and burst into a shout of irreverent laughter. At 3 o'clock Nassar, the Bedouin, came to announce that the dromedaries were saddled. I dressed myself, sticking a pistol in my belt, and passing the crimson silk cord of the hamail or pocket Koran over my shoulder, in token of being a pilgrim—distributing a few trifling presents to friends and servants, and accompanied by the Shaykh Mohammed, and Haji Wali, descended the stairs with an important gait. In the court-yard sat the camels, (dromedaries they could not be called,) and I found that a second driver was going to accompany us. I objected to this, as the extra Bedouin would, of course, expect to be fed by me; but Nassar swore the man was his brother, and, as you rarely gain by small disputes with these people, he was allowed to have his own way.

Then came the preparatory leave-takings. Haji Wali embraced me heartily, and so did my poor old Shayk, who, despite his decrepitude and my objections, insisted upon accompanying me to the city gate. I mounted the camel, crossed my legs before the pommel—stirrups are not used in Egypt* — and, preceding my friend, descended the street leading towards the desert. As we emerged from the huge gateway of the caravanserai all the

* The tender traveller had better provide himself with a pair of stirrups, but he will often find, when on camel back, that his legs are more numbed by hanging down, than by the Arab way of crossing them before and beneath the pommel. He must, however, be careful to inspect his saddle, and should bars of wood not suit him, to have them covered with stuffed leather. And again, for my part, I would prefer riding a camel with a nose ring,—Mongol and Sindhian fashion,—to holding him, as the Egyptians do, with a halter, or to guiding him,—Wahhabi-wise,—with a stick.

bystanders, except only the porter, who believed me to be a Persian, and had seen me with the drunken captain, exclaimed, "Allah bless thee, Y'al Hajj*, and restore thee to thy country and thy friends!" And passing through the Bab el Nasr, where I addressed the salutation of peace to the sentry, and to the officer commanding the guard, both gave me God-speed with great cordiality † — the pilgrim's blessing in Asia, like the old woman's in Europe, being supposed to possess peculiar efficacy. Outside the gate my friends took a final leave of me, and I will not deny having felt a tightening of heart as their honest faces and forms faded in the distance.

But Shaykh Nassar switches his camel's shoulder, and appears inclined to take the lead. This is a trial of manliness. There is no time for emotion. Not a moment can be spared, even for a retrospect.

* "O pilgrim!" The Egyptians write the word Hajj, and pronounce Hagg. In Persia, India, and Turkey, it becomes Hâji. These are mere varieties of form, derived from one and the same Arabic root.

† The Egyptians and Arabs will not address "Salam" to an infidel; the Moslems of India have no such objection. This, on the banks of the Nile, is the revival of an old prejudice. Alexander of Alexandria, in his circular letter, describes the Arian heretics as "men whom it is not lawful to salute, or to bid God-speed."

I kick my dromedary, who steps out into a jog-trot. The Bedouins with a loud ringing laugh attempt to give me the go-by. I resist, and we continue like children till the camels are at their speed, though we have eighty-four miles before us, and above an atmosphere like a furnace blast. The road is deserted at this hour, otherwise grave Moslem travellers would have believed the police to be nearer than convenient to us.

Presently we drew rein, and exchanged our pace for one more seasonable, whilst the sun began to tell on man and beast. High raised as we were above the ground, the reflected heat struck us sensibly, and the glare of a macadamized road added a few extra degrees of caloric.* The Bedouins, to refresh themselves, prepare to smoke. They fill my chibouque, light it with a flint and steel, and cotton dipped in a solution of gunpowder,

* It is Prince Puckler Muskau, if I recollect rightly, who mentions that in his case a pair of dark spectacles produced a marked difference of apparent temperature, whilst travelling over the sultry sand of the desert. I have often remarked the same phenomenon. The Arabs, doubtless for some reason of the kind, always draw their head-kerchiefs, like hoods, far over their brows, and cover up their mouths, even when the sun and wind are behind them. Inhabitants of the desert are to be recognised by the net-work of wrinkles traced in the skin round the orbits, the result of half-closing their eyelids; but this is done to temper the intensity of the light.

and pass it over to me.* After a few puffs I return it to them, and they smoke it turn by turn. Then they begin to while away the tedium of the road by asking questions, which *passe-temps* is not easily exhausted; for they are never satisfied till they know as much of you as you do of yourself. They next resort to talking about victuals, for with this hungry race of Bedouins, food, as a topic of conversation, takes the place of money in more civilised lands. And lastly, even this engrossing subject being exhausted for the moment, they take refuge in singing; and, monotonous and droning as it is, their song has yet an artless plaintiveness, which admirably suits the singer and the scenery. If you listen to the words, you will surely hear allusions to bright verdure, cool shades, bubbling rills, or something which hereabouts man hath not, and yet which his soul desires.

* Their own pipe-tubes were of coarse wood, in shape somewhat resembling the German pipe. The bowl was of soft stone, apparently steatite, which, when fresh, is easily fashioned with a knife. In Arabia the Bedouins, and even the townspeople, use on journeys an earthen tube from five to six inches shorter than the English "clay," thicker in the tube, with a large bowl, and coloured yellowish-red. It contains a handful of tobacco, and the smoker emits puffs like a chimney. In some of these articles the bowl forms a rectangle with the tube; in others, the whole is an unbroken curve, like the old Turkish Meerschaum.

And now while Nassar and his brother are chaunting a duet—the refrain being,

> "W'al arzu mablul bi matar,"
> "And the earth was wet with rain,"—

I must crave leave to say a few words, despite the triteness of the subject, about the modern Sinaitic race of Arabs.

Besides the tribes occupying the northern parts of the peninsula five chief clans are enumerated by Burckhardt.* Nassar, and other authorities at Suez, divided them into six, namely:—

1. Karashi (in the plural Kararishah), who, like the Gara in Eastern Arabia, claim an apocryphal origin from the great Koraysh tribe.

2. Salihi (*pl.* Sawalihah), the principal family of the Sinaitic Bedouins.

3. Arimi (*pl.* Awarimah): according to Burckhardt this clan is merely a sub-family of the Sawalihahs.

4. Saidi. Burckhardt calls them Welad Said and derives them also from the Sawalihahs.

5. Aliki (*pl.* Alaykah, erroneously written Elegat, and Aleykah), and lastly, the

* See Wallin's papers, published in the Journals of the Royal Geographical Society.

6. Muzaynah, generally pronounced M'zaynah. This class is an off-shoot from the great Jehaymah tribe inhabiting the deserts about Yambu. According to oral tradition five persons, the ancestors of the present Muzaynah race, were forced by a blood-feud to fly their native country. They landed at the Shurum *, and have now spread themselves over the Eastern parts of the peninsula. In El Hejaz the Muzaynah is an old and noble tribe. It produced Kaab el Akbar, the celebrated poet, to whom Mohammed gave the cloak which the Ottomans believe to have been taken by Sultan Selim from Egypt, and, under the name of Khirkah Sherif, to have been converted into the national oriflamme.

There are some interesting ethnographical points about these Sinaitic clans—interesting at least to those who would trace the genealogy of the great Arabian family. Any one who knows the Bedouins can see that the Muzaynah are pure blood. Their brows are broad, their faces narrow, their features regular, and their eyes of a moderate size: whereas the other Tawarah † clans are as pal-

* Shurum, (plural of Sharm, a creek), a word prefixed to the proper names of three small forts in the Sinaitic peninsula.

† Tawarah, plural of Turi, an inhabitant of Tur or Sinai.

pably Egyptian. They have preserved that round ness of face which may still be seen in the Sphynx as in the modern Copt, and their eyes have that peculiar size, shape, and look, which the old Egyptian painters attempted to express by giving to the profile eye the form of the full eye. Upon this feature, so characteristic of the Nilotic race, I would lay great stress. No traveller familiar with the true Egyptian eye, long, almond-shaped, deeply fringed, slightly raised at the outer corner and dipping in front like the Chinese *, can ever mistake it. It is to be seen in half-castes, and, as I have before remarked, families originally from the banks of the Nile, but settled in El Hejaz for generations, retain the peculiarity in all its integrity.

I therefore believe the Turi Bedouin to be an impure race, Egypto-Arab †, whereas his neighbour the Hejazi is the pure Syrian or Mesopotamian.

* This feature did not escape the practised eye of Denon. "Eyes long, almond-shaped, half shut, and languishing, and turned up at the outer corner, as if habitually fatigued by the light and heat of the sun; cheeks round, &c.," (*Voyage en Egypt*). The learned Frenchman's description of the ancient Egyptians applies in most points to the Tur Bedouins.

† "And he (Ishmael) dwelt in the wilderness of Paran, (Wady Firan?) and his mother took him a wife, out of the

A wonderful change has taken place in the Tawarah tribes, whilome pourtrayed by Sir John Mandeville as "folke fulle of alle evylle condiciouns." Niebuhr notes the trouble they gave him, and their perpetual hankering for both murder and pillage. Even in the late Mohammed Ali's early reign, no governor of Suez dared to flog, or to lay hands upon a Turi, whatever offence he might have committed within the walls of the town. Now the wild man's sword is taken from him, before he is allowed to enter the gates, and my old ac-

land of Egypt," (Gen. xxi. 21.) I wonder that some geographers have attempted to identify Massa the son of Ishmael, (Gen. xxv. 14.), with Meccah, when in verse 18. of the same chapter we read, "And they (the twelve princes, sons of Ishmael) *dwelt from Havilah unto Shur.*" This asserts, as clearly as language can, that the posterity of, or the race typified by Ishmael,—the Egypto-Arab,—occupied only the northern parts of the peninsula. Their *habitat* is not even included in Arabia by those writers who bound the country on the north by an imaginary line drawn from Ras Mohammed to the mouths of the Euphrates.

Dr. Wilson (Lands of the Bible), repeated by Eliot Warburton, (Crescent and Cross,) lays stress upon the Tawarah tradition, that they are Beni Israel converted to El Islam, considering it a fulfilment of the prophecy, "that a remnant of Israel shall dwell in Edom." With due deference to so illustrious an orientalist and Biblical scholar as Dr. Wilson, I believe that most modern Moslems, being ignorant that Jacob was the first called "prince with God," apply the term Beni-Israel to all the posterity of Abraham.

quaintance, Giaffar Bey, would think no more of belabouring a Bedouin than of flogging a Fellah.* Such is the result of Mohammed Ali's rigorous policy, and such the effects of even semi-civilisation, when its influence is brought to bear direct upon barbarism.

To conclude this subject, the Tawarah still retain many characteristics of the Bedouin race. The most good-humoured and sociable of men, they delight in a jest, and may readily be managed by kindness and courtesy. Yet they are passionate, nice upon points of honour, revenge-

* In the mouth of a Turk, no epithet is more contemptuous than that of "Fellah ibn Fellah,"—"boor, son of a boor!" The Osmanlis have, as usual, a semi-religious tradition to account for the superiority of their nation over the Egyptians. When the learned doctor, Abu Abdullah Mahommed ben Idris el Shafei, returned from Meccah to the banks of the Nile, he mounted, it is said, a donkey belonging to one of the *Asinarii* of Bulak. Arriving at the caravanserai, he gave the man ample fare, whereupon the Egyptian putting forth his hand, and saying "haat," called for more. The doctor doubled the fee; still the double was demanded. At last the divine's purse was exhausted, and the proprietor of the donkey waxed insolent. A wandering Turk seeing this, took all the money from the Egyptian, paid him his due, solemnly kicked him, and returned the rest to El Shafei, who asked him his name—"Osman"—and his nation—the "Osmanli,"—blessed him, and prophesied to his countrymen supremacy over the Fellahs and donkey boys of Egypt.

ful and easily offended, where their peculiar prejudices are misunderstood. I have always found them pleasant companions, and deserving of respect, for their hearts are good, and their courage is beyond a doubt. Those travellers who complain of their insolence and extortion may have been either ignorant of their language or offensive to them by assumption of superiority, —in the Desert man meets man,—or physically unfitted to acquire their esteem.

We journeyed on till near sunset through the wilderness without ennui. It is strange how the mind can be amused amid scenery that presents so few objects to occupy it. But in such a country every slight modification of form or colour rivets observation: the senses are sharpened, and perceptive faculties, prone to sleep over a confused shifting of scenery, act vigorously when excited by the capability of embracing each detail. Moreover desert views are eminently suggestive; they appeal to the future, not to the past; they arouse because they are by no means memorial. To the solitary wayfarer there is an interest in the wilderness unknown to Cape seas and Alpine glaciers, and even to the rolling prairie, — the effect of continued excitement on the mind stimulating its powers to their pitch. Above, through a sky terrible in its stainless beauty, and the splendours of a pitiless blinding glare, the Simoom caresses you like a lion with flaming breath. Around lie drifted sand heaps, upon which each puff of wind leaves its own trace in solid waves, flayed rocks, the very skeletons of mountains, and hard unbroken plains, over which he who rides is spurred by the idea that the bursting of a water skin, or the pricking of a camel's hoof would be a certain death of torture,—a haggard land infested with wild beasts, and wilder men,—a region whose very fountains murmur the warning words "Drink and away!" What can be more exciting? what more sublime? Man's heart bounds in his breast at the thought of measuring his puny force with nature's might, and of emerging triumphant from the trial. This explains the Arab's proverb, "Voyaging is a victory." In the desert even more than upon the ocean, there is present death: hardship is there, and piracies, and shipwreck—solitary, not in crowds, where, as the Persians say, "death is a festival,"—and this sense of danger, never absent, invests the scene of travel with an interest not its own.

Let the traveller who suspects exaggeration leave the Suez road for an hour or two, and gallop northwards over the sands: in the drear silence, the solitude, and the fantastic desolation of the place, he will feel what the Desert may be.

And then the Oases *, and little lines of fertility —how soft and how beautiful!—even though

* Hugh Murray derives this word from the Egyptian, and quoting Strabo and Abulfeda makes it synonymous with Auasis and Hyasis. I believe it to be a mere corruption of the Arabic Wady, وادى.

Nothing can be more incorrect than the vulgar idea of an Arabian Oasis, except it be the popular conception of an Arabian desert. One reads of "isles of the sandy sea," but one never sees them. The real "wady" is, generally speaking, a rocky valley bisected by the bed of a mountain torrent, dry during the hot season. In such places the Bedouins love to encamp, because they find food and drink,—water being always procurable by digging.

When the supply is perennial, the wady becomes the site of a village. The Desert is as unaptly compared to a "sandy sea." Most of the wilds of Arabia resemble the tract between Suez and Cairo; only the former are of primitive formation, whereas the others are of a later date. Sand heaps are found in every desert, but sand plains are merely a local feature, not the general face of the country. The wilderness, east of the Nile, is generally a hard dry earth, which requires only a monsoon to become highly productive: even where silicious sand covers the plain, the waters of a torrent, depositing *humus* or vegetable mould, bind the particles together, and fit it for the reception of seed.

the Wady El Ward (the Vale of Flowers) be the name of some stern flat upon which a handful of wild shrubs blossom while struggling through a cold season's ephemeral existence. In such circumstances the mind is influenced through the body. Though your mouth glows, and your skin is parched, yet you feel no languor, the effect of humid heat; your lungs are lightened, your sight brightens, your memory recovers its tone, and your spirits become exuberant; your fancy and imagination are powerfully aroused, and the wildness and sublimity of the scenes around you stir up all the energies of your soul—whether for exertion, danger, or strife. Your *morale* improves: you become frank and cordial, hospitable, and single-minded: the hypocritical politeness and the slavery of civilisation are left behind you in the city. Your senses are quickened: they require no stimulants but air and exercise,—in the Desert spirituous liquors excite only disgust. There is a keen enjoyment in a mere animal existence. The sharp appetite disposes of the most indigestible food, the sand is softer than a bed of down, and the purity of the air suddenly puts to flight a dire cohort of diseases. Hence it is that both sexes, and every age, the most material as well as the most imaginative of minds, the tamest citizen, the most peaceful student, the spoiled child of civilisation, all feel their hearts dilate, and their pulses beat strong as they look down from their dromedaries upon the "glorious Desert." Where do we hear of a "traveller" being disappointed by it? It is another illustration of the ancient truth that nature returns to man, however unworthily he has treated her. And believe me, gentle reader, that when once your tastes have conformed to the tranquillity of such travel, you will suffer real pain in returning to the turmoil of civilisation. You will anticipate the bustle and the confusion of artificial life, its luxury and its false pleasures, with repugnance. Depressed in spirits, you will for a time after your return feel incapable of mental or bodily exertion. The air of cities will suffocate you, and the care-worn and cadaverous countenances of citizens will haunt you like a vision of judgment.*

As the black shadow· mounted in the East†,

* The intelligent reader will easily understand that I am speaking of the Desert in the temperate season, not during the summer heats, when the whole is one vast furnace, or in winter, when the Sarsar wind cuts like an Italian Tramontana.

† This, as a general rule in El Islam, is a sign that the

I turned off the road, and was suddenly saluted by a figure rising from a little hollow with an "As' Salamo Alaykum" of truly Arab sound.* I looked at the speaker for a moment without recognising him. He then advanced with voluble expressions of joy, invited me to sup, seized my camel's halter without waiting for an answer, "nakh'd †," him, led me hurriedly to a carpet spread in a sandy hollow, pulled off my slippers, gave me cold water for ablution, told me that he had mistaken me at a distance for a "Sherif" of the Arabs, but was delighted to find himself in error, and urged me to hurry over ablution, otherwise that night would come on before we could say our prayers. It was Mohammed El Basyuni, the Meccan boy of whom I had bought my pilgrim-garb at Cairo. There I had refused

Maghrib or evening prayer must not be delayed. The Shafei school performs its devotions immediately after the sun has disappeared.

* This salutation of peace is so differently pronounced by every eastern nation that the observing traveller will easily make of it a shibboleth.

† To "nakh" in vulgar, as in classical, Arabic is to gurgle "Ikh! ikh!" in the bottom of one's throat till the camel kneels down. We have no English word for this proceeding; but Anglo-oriental travellers are rapidly naturalising the "nakh."

his companionship, but here for reasons of his own —one of them was an utter want of money,—he would take no excuse. When he prayed he stood behind me *, thereby proving pliancy of conscience, for he suspected me from the first of being at least a heretic.

After prayer he lighted a pipe, and immediately placed the snake-like tube in my hand; this is an argument which the tired traveller can rarely resist. He then began to rummage my saddle-bags; drew forth stores of provisions, rolls, water-melons, boiled eggs, and dates, and whilst lighting the fire and boiling coffee, managed to distribute his own stock, which was neither plentiful nor first-rate, to the camel-men. Shaykh Nassar and his brother looked aghast at this movement, but the boy was inexorable. They tried a few rough hints, which he noticed by singing a Hindostani couplet that asserts the impropriety of anointing rats' heads with jasmine oil. They suspected abuse, and waxed cross; he acknowledged this by deriding them. "I have heard of Nasrs and Nasirs, and Mansúrs, but may Allah spare me the mortification of a Nassár!" said the boy, relying upon my support. And I

* There are many qualifications necessary for an Imaun, — a leader of prayer; the first condition, of course, is orthodoxy.

urged him on, wanting to see how the city Arab treats the countryman. He then took my tobacco-pouch from the angry Bedouins, and in a stage whisper reproved me for entrusting it to such thieves; insisting, at the same time, upon drinking all the coffee, so that the poor guides had to prepare some for themselves. He improved every opportunity of making mischief. "We have eaten water-melon!" cried Nassar, patting its receptacle in token of repletion. "Dost thou hear, my lord, how they grumble?—the impudent ruffians!" remarked Mohammed—"*We have eaten water-melon!* that is to say, we ought to have eaten meat!" The Bedouins, completely out of temper, told him not to trust himself among their hills. He seized a sword, and began capering about after the fashion of the Indian school of arms, and boasted that he would attack single-handed the whole clan, which elicited an ironical "Allah! Allah!" from the hearers.

After an hour most amusingly spent in this way I arose, much to the dissatisfaction of my guides, who wished to sleep there, and insisted upon mounting. Shaykh Nassar and his brother had reckoned upon living gratis, for at least three days, judging it improbable that a soft Effendi would hurry himself. When they saw the fair vision dissolve, they began to finesse: they induced the camel-man, who ran by the side of Mohammed's dromedary, to precede the animal—a favourite manœuvre to prevent over-speed. Ordered to fall back, the man pleaded fatigue, and inability to walk. The boy Mohammed immediately asked if I had any objection to dismount one of my guides, and to let his weary attendant ride for an hour or so. I at once assented, and the Bedouins obeyed me with ominous grumblings. When we resumed our march the melancholy Arabs had no song left in them, whereas Mohammed chanted vociferously, and quoted bad Hindostani and worse Persian till silence was forcibly imposed upon him. The camel-men lagged behind, in order to prevent my dromedary advancing too fast, and the boy's guide, after dismounting, would stride along in front of us, under pretext of showing the way. And so we jogged on, now walking, then trotting, till the dromedaries began to grunt with fatigue, and the Arabs clamoured for a halt.

At midnight we reached the centre station, and lay down under its walls to take a little rest. The dews fell heavily, wetting the sheets that covered us; but who cares for such trifles in the

Desert? The moon shone bright *; the breeze blew coolly, and the jackal sang a lullaby which lost no time in inducing the soundest sleep. As the wolf's tail † appeared in the heavens we arose. Grey mists floating over the hills northwards gave the Dar el Baida ‡ the look of some old feudal castle. There was a haze in the atmosphere, which beautified even the face of desolation. The swift flying Káta § rose in noisy coveys from the road, and

* "The sun shall not smite thee by day, nor the moon by night," (Psalm cxxi. 6.). Easterns still believe firmly in the evil effects of moonlight upon the human frame,—from Sindh to Abyssinia, the traveller will hear tales of wonder concerning it.

† The Dum i Gurg, or wolf's tail, is the Persian name for the first brushes of grey light which appear as forerunners of dawn.

‡ The Egyptians pronounce this word "Bay*da*," although Baidtha or Baydtha is the proper way of writing it,—the letter being in fact the English th, as we pronounce it, "soft" (dth) in "this." Indeed, the Bedouin Arabs universally so pronounce it. Dar el Baida is a palace belonging to H.H. Abbas Pacha. This "white house" was formerly called the "red house,"—I believe from the colour of its windows,—but the name was changed, as being not particularly good-omened.

§ The Tetrao Kata or sand-grouse, (Pterocles melanogaster) (in Sindh it is called the rock pigeon,) is a fast-flying bird, not unlike a grey partridge whilst upon the wing. When, therefore, Shanfara boasts "The ash-coloured Kátas can only drink my leavings, after hastening all night to slake their thirst in the morning," it is a hyperbole to express exceeding swiftness. Káta, in Arabic pronounced Gatta or Gutta. Unfortunately in English we have no way of writing the ق k, which is our g, a stray gazelle paced daintily over the stony plain. As we passed by the Pilgrims' tree, I added another rag to its coat of tatters.* We then invoked the aid of the holy saint El Dakruri † from his cream-coloured abode, mounted our camels, and resumed

though not followed by any a. It is the same letter that the ancient Greeks had, and which occurs in the names of "*Corinth*," "*Hector*," and which was written Ϙ — ϘΟΡΙΝΘΟΣ, ΕϘΤΩΡ.

* I have already, when writing upon the subject of Sindh, alluded to this system as prevalent throughout El Islam, and professed, like Mr. Lane, ignorance of its origin and object.

In Huc's travels, we are told that the Tartars worship mountain spirits by raising an "obo,"—dry branches hung with bones and strips of cloth, and planted in enormous heaps of stones. Park, also, in Western Africa, conformed to the example of his companions, in adding a charm or shred of cloth on a tree (at the entrance of the Wilderness), which was completely covered with these guardian symbols. And, finally, the Tarikh Tabari mentions it as a practice of the Pagan Arabs, and talks of evil spirits residing in the date-tree.

May not, then, the practice in El Islam be one of the many debris of fetish-worship which entered into the heterogeneous formation of the saving faith? Some believe that the Prophet permitted the practice, and explain the peculiar name of the expedition called Zat el Rikaa, (place of shreds of cloth,) by supposing it to be a term for a tree to which the Moslems hung their *ex-voto* rags.

† The saint lies under a little white-washed dome, springing from a square of low walls — a form of sepulchre now common to El Hejaz, Egypt, and the shores and islands of the Red Sea. As regards his name my informants told me it was that of a Hejazi Shaykh. The subject is by no means an interesting

the march in real earnest. The dawn passed away in its delicious coolness, and sultry morning came on. Then day arose in its fierceness, and the noontide sun made the plain glow with terrible heat. Still we pressed onwards.

At 3 P.M. we turned off the road into a dry water-course, which is not far from No. 13 station. The sand was dotted with the dried-up leaves of the Datura, and strongly perfumed by a kind of Absinthe *, the sweetest herb of the Desert. A Mimosa was there, and although its shade at this season is little better than a cocoa tree's †, the Bedouins would not neglect it. We lay down upon the sand, to rest among a party of Maghrabi pilgrims travelling to Suez. These wretches, who were about a dozen in number, appeared to be of the lowest class; their garments consisted of a Burnoos and a pair of sandals, their sole weapon a long knife,

one; but the exact traveller will find the word written Takroore, and otherwise explained by Sir Gardner Wilkinson.

* Called by the Arabs Shih or Shíëh, شيح which the dictionaries translate "wormwood of Pontus." It is an *artemisia*. We find Wallin in his works, speaking of *Ferashat al shih*, or wormwood carpets.

† We are told in verse of "a cocoa's feathery shade," and "sous l'ombre d'un cocotier." But to realise the prose picture, let the home reader, choosing some sultry August day, fasten a large fan to a long pole, and enjoy himself under it.

and their only stock a bag of dry provisions. Each had his large wooden bowl, but none carried water with him. It was impossible to help pitying their state, nor could I eat, seeing them hungry, thirsty, and way-worn. So Nassar served out about a pint of water and a little bread to each man. Then they asked for more. None was to be had, so they cried out that money would do as well. I had determined upon being generous to the extent of a few pence. Custom, as well as inclination, was in favour of the act; but when the alms became a demand, and the demand was backed by fierce looks and a derisive sneer and a kind of reference to their knives, gentle charity took the alarm and fled. My pistols kept them at bay, for they were only making an attempt to intimidate, and, though I took the precaution of sitting apart from them, there was no real danger. The Suez road, by the wise regulations of Mohammed Ali, has become as safe to European travellers as that between Hampstead and Highgate, and even Easterns have little to fear but what their cowardice creates. My Indian servant was full of the dangers he had run, but I did not believe in them. I afterwards heard that the place where the Maghrabis attempted to frighten what they thought a timid Effendi was once notorious for plunder and murder. Here the spurs of two opposite hills almost meet upon the plain, a favourable ground for Bedouin ambuscade. Of the Maghrabis I shall have more to say when relating my voyage in the Pilgrim Ship: they were the only travellers from whom we experienced the least annoyance. Numerous parties of Turks, Arabs, and Afghans, and a few Indians * were on the same errand as ourselves. All, as we passed them, welcomed us with the friendly salutation that so becomes men engaged in a labour of religion.

About half an hour before sunset, I turned off the road leftwards, and, under pretext of watering the dromedaries, rode up to inspect the El Ajrúdi †

* On a subsequent occasion, I met a party of Panjabis, who had walked from Meccah to Cairo in search of "Abu Tabilah," (General Avitabile,) whom report had led to the banks of the Nile. Some were young, others had white beards—all were weary and wayworn; but the saddest sight was an old woman, so decrepid that she could scarcely walk. The poor fellows were travelling on foot, carrying their wallets, with a few pence in their pockets, utterly ignorant of route and road, and actually determined in this plight to make Lahore by Baghdad, Bushire, and Kurrachee. Such—so incredible—is Indian improvidence!

† Upon this word cacography has done her worst—"Haji Rood" may serve for a specimen. My informants told me that El Ajrudi is the name of a Hejazi Shaykh whose mortal remains repose under a little dome near the fort. This, if it be

fort. It is a quadrangle with round towers at the gateway, and at the corners, newly built of stone and mortar; the material is already full of crevices, and would not stand before a twelve-pounder. Without guns or gunners, it is occupied by about a dozen Fellahs, who act as hereditary "ghafirs," (guardians); they were expecting at that time to be reinforced by a party of Bash Buluks—irregulars from Cairo. The people of the country were determined that an English fleet would soon appear in the Red Sea, and this fort is by them ridiculously considered the key of Suez. As usual in these Vauban-lacking lands, the well, supplying the stronghold, is in a detached and distant building, which can be approached by an enemy with the greatest security. Over the gateway of the well was an ancient inscription reversed; the water was brackish, and of bad quality.*

true, completely nullifies the efforts of etymology to discern in it a distinct allusion to "the overthrow of Pharaoh's chariots, whose Hebrew appellation, 'Ageloot,' bears some resemblance to this modern name."

* The only sweet water in Suez is brought on camel back from the Nile, across the Desert. The "Bir Suez" is fit for beasts only; the Uyun Musa (Moses' Wells) on the Eastern side, and that below Abu Deraj, on the Western shore of the Suez Gulf, are but little better. The want of sweet water is the reason why no Hammam (or Bath) is found at Suez.

We resumed our way: Suez was now near. In the blue distance rose the castellated peaks and the wide sand-tracts over which lies the land route to El Hejaz. Before us the sight ever dear to English eyes, —a strip of sea gloriously azure, with a gallant steamer walking the waters. On the right-hand side lay the broad slopes of Jebel Mukuttum, a range of hills which flanks the road all the way from Cairo. It was at this hour a spectacle not easily to be forgotten. The near range of chalk and sandstone wore a russet suit, gilt where the last rays of the sun seamed it with light, and the deep folds were shaded with the richest purple; whilst the background of the higher hill, Abu Déraj, (the Father of Steps) was sky blue streaked with the lightest plum colour. We drew up at a small building called Bir Suways (well of Suez), and under pretext of watering the cattle, I sat for half an hour admiring the charms of the Desert. The eye never tires of loveliness of hue, and the memory of the hideousness of this range, when a sun in front exposed each barren and deformed feature, supplied the evening view with another element of attraction.

It was already night when we passed through the tumbling gateway of Suez; and there still remained the task of finding my servant and effects. After wandering in and out of every Wakálat in the village, during which peregrination the boy Mohammed proved himself so useful that I determined to make him my companion at all risks, we accidentally heard that an Indian had taken lodgings at a hostelry bearing the name of Jirjis.* On arriving there our satisfaction was diminished by the intelligence that the same Indian, after locking the door, had gone out with his friends to a ship in the harbour; in fact, that he had made all preparations for running away. I dismounted, and tried to persuade the porter to break open the wooden bolt, but he absolutely refused, and threatened the police. Meanwhile Mohammed had found a party of friends, men of El Medinah, returning to the pilgrimage after a begging tour through Egypt and Turkey. The meeting was characterised by vociferous inquiries, loud guffaws, and warm embraces. I was invited to share their supper, and their dormitory,—an uncovered platform pro-

* The "George:" so called after its owner, a Copt. There are 36 caravanserais at Suez, 33 small ones for merchandise, and 3 for travellers; of these the best is that of Sayyid Hashim. The pilgrim, however, must not expect much comfort or convenience, even at Sayyid Hashim's.

jecting from the gallery over the square court below,—but I had neither appetite nor spirits to be sociable. The porter, after persuasion, showed me an empty room, in which I spread my carpet. That night was a sad one. My eighty-four mile ride had made every bone ache; I had lost much epidermis, and the sun had seared every portion of skin exposed to it. So, lamenting my degeneracy and the ill effects of four years' domicile in Europe, and equally disquieted in mind about the fate of my goods and chattels, I fell into an uncomfortable sleep.

CHAP. IX.

SUEZ.

Early on the morning after my arrival, I arose, and consulted my new acquaintances about what steps should be taken towards recovering the missing property. They unanimously advised a visit to the governor, whom, however, they described to be a "Kelb ibn Kelb," (dog, son of a dog,) who never returned Moslems' salutations, and thought all men dirt to be trodden under foot by the Turks. The boy Mohammed showed his *savoir faire* by extracting from his huge box a fine embroidered cap, and a grand peach-coloured coat, with which I was instantly invested; he dressed himself with similar magnificence, and we then set out to the "palace."

Giaffar Bey,—he has since been deposed,—then occupied the position of judge, officer commanding, collector of customs, and magistrate of Suez. He was a Mirliwa, or brigadier-general, and had some reputation as a soldier, together with a slight tincture of European science and language.

The large old Turk received me most superciliously, disdained all return of salaam, and fixing upon me two little eyes like gimlets demanded my business. I stated that one Shaykh Nur, my Indian servant, had played me false; therefore I required permission to break into the room supposed to contain my effects. He asked my profession. I replied the medical. This led him to inquire if I had any medicine for the eyes, and being answered in the affirmative, he sent a messenger with me to enforce obedience on the part of the porter. The obnoxious measure was, however, unnecessary. As we entered the caravanserai there appeared at the door the black face of Shaykh Nur, looking, though accompanied by sundry fellow countrymen, uncommonly as if he merited and expected the bamboo. He had, by his own account, been seduced into the festivities of a coal hulk manned by Indian Lascars, and the vehemence of his self-accusation saved him from the chastisement which I had determined to administer.

I must now briefly describe the party into which fate threw me: the names of these men will so frequently appear in the following pages, that a few words about their natures will not be misplaced.

First of all comes Omar Effendi,—so called in honour,—a Daghistani or Circassian, the grandson of a Hanafi Mufti at El Medinah, and the son of a Shayk Rakl, an officer whose duty it is to lead dromedary-caravans. He sits upon his cot, a small, short, plump body, of yellow complexion and bilious temperament, grey-eyed, soft-featured, and utterly beardless,—which affects his feelings, —he looks fifteen, and owns to twenty-eight. His manners are those of a student; he dresses respectably, prays regularly, hates the fair sex, like an Arab, whose affections and aversions are always in extremes, is serious, has a mild demeanour, an humble gait, and a soft slow voice. When roused he becomes furious as a Bengal tiger. His parents have urged him to marry, and he, like Camaralzaman, has informed his father that he is a person of great age, but little sense. Urged moreover by a melancholy turn of mind, and the want of leisure for study at El Medinah, he fled the paternal domicile, and entered himself a pauper Talib ilm (student) in the Azhar mosque. His disconsolate friends and afflicted relations sent a confidential man to fetch him home by force, should it be necessary; he has yielded, and is now awaiting the first opportunity of travelling, if possible, gratis to El Medinah.

That confidential man is a negro-servant, called Saad, notorious in his native city as El Jinni, the devil. Born and bred a slave in Omar Effendi's family, he obtained manumission, became a soldier in El-Hejaz, was dissatisfied with pay perpetually in arrears, turned merchant, and wandered far and wide, to Russia, to Gibraltar, and to Baghdad. He is the pure African, noisily merry at one moment, at another silently sulky, affectionate and abusive, brave and boastful, reckless and crafty, exceedingly quarrelsome, and unscrupulous to the last degree. The bright side of his character is his love for, and respect to, the young master Omar Effendi; yet even him he will scold in a paroxysm of fury, and steal from him whatever he can lay his hands on. He is generous with his goods, but is ever borrowing and never paying money; he dresses like a beggar, with the dirtiest tarboosh upon his tufty poll, and only a cotton shirt over his sooty skin, whilst his two boxes are full of handsome apparel for himself and the three ladies his wives at El Medinah. He knows no fear but for those boxes. Frequently during our search for a vessel he forced himself into Giaffar Bey's presence, and demeaned himself so impudently, that we expected to see him lamed by the bastinado; his forwardness, however, only amused the dignitary. He wanders all day about the bazaar, talking about freight and passage, for he has resolved, cost what it will, to travel gratis, and, with doggedness like his, he must succeed.

Shaykh Hamid el Lamman derives his cognomen, the "clarified butter-seller," from a celebrated saint and Sufi of the Kadiriyah order, who left a long line of holy descendants at El Medinah. This Shaykh squats upon a box full of presents for the daughter of his paternal uncle*, a perfect specimen of the town Arab. His head is crowned with a rough Shushah or tuft of hair on the poll†;

* His wife.

† When travelling, the Shushah is allowed to spread over the greatest portion of the scalp, to act as a protection against the sun; and the hair being shaved off about two inches all round the head, leaves a large circular patch. Nothing can be uglier than such tonsure, and it is contrary to the strict law of the Prophet, who ordered a clean shave, or a general growth of the hair. The Arab, however, knows by experience, that though habitual exposure of the scalp to a burning sun may harden the skull, it seldom fails to damage its precious contents. He, therefore, wears a Shushah during his wanderings, and removes it on his return home.

his face is of a dirty brown, his little goat's beard untrimmed; his feet are bare, and his only garment is an exceedingly unclean ochre-coloured blouse, tucked at the waist into a leathern girdle beneath it. He will not pray, because he is unwilling to take pure clothes out of his box; but he smokes when he can get other people's tobacco, and groans between the whiffs, conjugating the verb all day, for he is of active mind. He can pick out his letters, and he keeps in his bosom a little dog's-eared MS. full of serious romances and silly prayers, old and exceedingly ill written: this he will draw forth at times, peep into for a moment, devoutly kiss, and restore to its proper place with all the veneration of the vulgar for a book. He can sing all manner of songs, slaughter a sheep with dexterity, deliver a grand call to

Abu Hanifah, if I am rightly informed, wrote a treatise advocating the growth of a long lock of hair on the Nasiyah, or crown of the head, lest the decapitated Moslem's mouth or beard be exposed to defilement by an impure hand. This would justify the comparing it to the "chivalry-lock," by which the American brave facilitates the removal of his own scalp. But I am at a loss to discover the origin of our old idea, that the "angel of death will, on the last day, bear all true believers, by this important tuft of hair on the crown, to Paradise." Probably this office has been attributed to the Shushah by the ignorance of the West.

prayer, shave, cook, fight, and he excels in the science of vituperation: like Saad, he never performs his devotions, except when necessary to "keep up appearances," and though he has sworn to perish before he forgets his vow to the "daughter of his uncle," I shrewdly suspect he is no better than he should be. His brow crumples at the word wine, but there is quite another expression about the region of the mouth; and Stamboul, where he has lived some months, without learning ten words of Turkish, is a notable place for displaying prejudice. And finally, he has not more than a piastre or two in his pocket, for he has squandered the large presents given to him at Cairo and Constantinople by noble ladies, to whom he acted as master of the ceremonies, at the tomb of the Prophet.

Stretched on a carpet, smoking a Persian Kalioon all day, lies Salih Shakkar, a Turk on the father's, and Arab on the mother's side, born at El Medinah. This lanky youth may be 16 years old, but he has the ideas of 40; he is thoroughly greedy, selfish, and ungenerous, coldly supercilious as a Turk, and energetically avaricious as an Arab. He prays more often, and dresses more respectably, than the descendant of the clarified-butter-seller;

he affects the Constantinople style of toilette, and his light yellow complexion makes people consider him a "superior person." We were intimate enough on the road, when he borrowed from me a little money. But at El Medinah he cut me pitilessly, as a "town man" does a continental acquaintance accidentally met in Hyde Park, and of course he tried, though in vain, to evade repaying his debt. He had a tincture of letters, and appeared to have studied critically the subject of "largesse." "The generous is Allah's friend, aye, though he be a sinner, and the miser is Allah's foe, aye, though he be a saint," was a venerable saying always in his mouth. He also informed me that Pharaoh, although the quintessence of impiety, is mentioned by name in the Koran, by reason of his liberality, whereas Nimrod, another monster of iniquity, is only alluded to, because he was a stingy tyrant. It is almost needless to declare that Salih Shakkar was, as the Indians say, a very "fly-sucker."* There were two other men of El Medinah in the Wakalat Girgis; but I omit description, as we left them, they being penniless, at Suez. One of them, Mahommed Shiklibha, I afterwards met at Meccah, and seldom have I seen a more honest and warm-

* "Makhi-chus," equivalent to our "skin-flint."

hearted fellow. When we were embarking at Suez, he fell upon Hamid's bosom, and both of them wept bitterly, at the prospect of parting even for a few days.

All the individuals above mentioned lost no time in opening the question of a loan. It was a lesson in oriental metaphysics to see their condition. They had a twelve days' voyage, and a four days' journey, before them; boxes to carry, custom-houses to face, and stomachs to fill; yet the whole party could scarcely, I believe, muster two dollars of ready money. Their boxes were full of valuables, arms, clothes, pipes, slippers, sweet-meats, and other "notions," but nothing short of starvation would have induced them to pledge the smallest article.

I foresaw that their company would be an advantage, and therefore I hearkened favourably to the honeyed request for a few crowns. The boy Mohammed obtained six dollars; Hamid about five pounds,—I intended to make his house at El Medinah my home; Umar Effendi three dollars; Saad the Devil, two — I gave the money to him at Yambu,—and Salih Shakkar fifty piastres. But since in these lands, as a rule, no one ever lends coins, or borrowing ever returns them, I took care to exact service from the first, to take two rich coats from the second, a handsome pipe from the third, a "bala" or yataghan from the fourth, and from the fifth an imitation Cashmere shawl. After which, we sat down and drew out the agreement. It was favourable to me: I lent them Egyptian money, and bargained for repayment in the currency of El Hejaz, thereby gaining the exchange, which is sometimes 16 per cent. This was done, not so much for the sake of profit, as with the view of becoming a Hatim*, by a "never mind" on settling day. My companions having received these small sums, became affectionate, and eloquent in my praise: they asked me to make one of their number for the future at meals, overwhelmed me with questions, insisted upon a present of sweetmeats, detected in me a great man under a cloud, — perhaps my claims to being a Dervish assisted them to this discovery, — and declared that I should perforce be their guest at Meccah and El Medinah. On all occasions precedence was forced upon me; my opinion was the first consulted, and no project was settled without my concurrence: briefly, Abdullah the Dervish suddenly

* A well-known Arab chieftain, whose name has come to stand for generosity itself.

found himself a person of consequence. This sudden elevation led me into an imprudence which might have cost me dear, and aroused the only suspicion about me ever expressed during the summer's trip. My friends had looked at my clothes, overhauled my medicine chest, and criticised my pistols; they sneered at my copper-cased watch *, and remembered having seen a compass at Constantinople. Therefore I imagined they would think little about a sextant. This was a mistake. The boy Mohammed I afterwards learned † waited only my leaving the room to declare that

* This being an indispensable instrument for measuring distances, I had it divested of gold case, and provided with a facing carefully stained and figured with Arabic numerals. In countries where few can judge of a watch by its works, it is as well to secure its safety by making the exterior look as mean as possible. The watches worn by respectable people in El Hejaz are almost always old silver pieces, of the turnip shape, with hunting cases and an outer *etui* of thick leather. Mostly they are of Swiss or German manufacture, and they find their way into Arabia *viâ* Constantinople and Cairo.

† On my return to Cairo, Umar Effendi, whom I met accidentally in the streets, related the story to me. I never owned having played a part, to avoid shocking his prejudices; and though he must have suspected me,—for the general report was, that an Englishman, disguised as a Persian, had performed the pilgrimage, measured the country, and sketched the buildings,—he had the gentlemanly feeling never to allude to the past. We parted, when I went to India, on the best of terms.

the would-be Haji was one of the infidels from India, and a council sat to discuss the case. Fortunately for me Umar Effendi had looked over a letter which I had written to Haji Wali that morning, and he had at various times received categorical replies to certain questions in high theology. He felt himself justified in declaring, *ex cathedrâ*, the boy Mohammed's position perfectly untenable. And Shaykh Hamid, who looked forward to being my host, guide, and debtor in general, and probably cared scantily for catechism or creed, swore that the light of El-Islam was upon my countenance, and consequently that the boy Mohammed was a pauper, a "fakir," an owl, a cut-off one *, a stranger, and a Wahhabi, for daring to impugn the faith of a brother believer.† The scene ended with a general abuse of the acute

* Munkatia—one cut off (from the pleasures and comforts of life). In El Hejaz, as in England, any allusion to poverty becomes highly offensive.

† The Koran expressly forbids a Moslem to discredit the word of any man who professes his belief in the Saving Faith. The greatest offence of the Wahhabis is their habit of designating all Moslems that belong to any but their own sect by the opprobrious name of Kafirs or infidels. This, however, is only the Koranic precept; in practice a much less trustful spirit prevails.

youth, who was told on all sides that he had no shame and was directed to fear Allah. I was struck with the expression of my friends' countenances when they saw the sextant, and, determining with a sigh to leave it behind, I prayed five times a day for nearly a week.

We all agreed not to lose an hour in securing places on board some vessel bound to Yambu, and my companions, hearing that my passport as a British Indian was scarcely "en régle," earnestly advised me to have it signed by the governor without delay, whilst they occupied themselves about the harbour. They warned me that if I displayed the Turkish Tezkireh given to me at the citadel of Cairo, I should infallibly be ordered to await the caravan, and lose their society and friendship. Pilgrims arriving at Alexandria, be it known to the reader, are divided into bodies, and distributed by means of Tezkirehs to the three great roads, namely, Suez, Cosseir, and the Haj route by land round the Gulf of Akabah. After the division has once been made, government turns a deaf ear to the representations of individuals. The Bey of Suez has an order to obstruct pilgrims as much as possible till the end of the season, when they are hurried down that way, lest they should arrive at

Meccah too late.* As most of the Egyptian high officials have boats, which sail up the Nile laden with pilgrims and return freighted with corn, the government naturally does its utmost to force the delays and discomforts of this line upon strangers.† And as those who travel by the Haj route must spend money in the Egyptian territories, at least fifteen days longer than they would if allowed to embark at once from Suez, the Pacha very properly assists them in the former and obstructs them in the latter case. Knowing these facts, I felt that a difficulty was at hand. The first thing was to take Shaykh Nur's passport, which was "en régle," and my own which was not, to the Bey for signature. He turned the papers over and over, as if unable to read them, and raised false hopes high by referring me to his clerk. The under

* Towards the end of the season, poor pilgrims are forwarded gratis, by order of government. But, to make such liberality as inexpensive as possible, the Pacha compels shipowners to carry one pilgrim per 9 ardebbs in small, and 1 per 11 in large vessels. The ardebb is about 5 bushels.

† I was informed by a Prussian gentleman, holding an official appointment under His Highness the Pacha, at Cairo, that 300,000 ardebbs of grain were annually exported from Cosseir to Jeddah. The rest is brought down the Nile fon consumption in Lower Egypt, and export to Europe.

official at once saw the irregularity of the document, asked me why it had not been visé at Cairo, swore that under such circumstances nothing would induce the Bey to let me proceed, and when I tried persuasion, waxed insolent. I feared that it would be necessary to travel *viâ* Cosseir, for which there was scarcely time, or to transfer myself on camel back to the harbour of Tur, and there to await the chance of finding a place in some half-filled vessel to El Hejaz,— which would have been relying upon an accident. My last hope at Suez was to obtain assistance from Mr. George West, H. B. M. sub-vice-consul. I therefore took the boy Mohammed with me, choosing him on purpose, and excusing the step to my companions by concocting an artful fable about my having been, in some part of Afghanistan, a benefactor to the British nation. We proceeded to the consulate. Mr. West, who had been told by an imprudent friend to expect me, saw through the disguise, despite jargon assumed to satisfy official scruples, and nothing could be kinder than the part he took. His clerk was directed to place himself in communication with the Bey's factotum, and when objections to signing the Alexandrian Tezkireh were offered, the vice consul said that he would, at his own risk, give me a fresh passport as a

British subject from Suez to Arabia. His firmness prevailed, and on the second day, the documents were returned to me in a satisfactory state. I take a pleasure in owning this obligation to Mr. West: in the course of my wanderings, I have often received from him hospitality and the most friendly attentions.

Whilst these passport difficulties were being solved, the rest of the party was as busy in settling about passage and passage money. The peculiar rules of the port of Suez require a few words of explanation.* "About thirty-five years ago, the ship-owners proposed to the then government, with the view of keeping up freight, a Fazzeh, or system of rotation. It might be supposed that the Pacha, whose object notoriously was to retain all monopolies in his own hands, would have refused his sanction to such a measure. But it so happened in those days that all the court had ships at Suez. Ibrahim Pacha alone owned four or five. Consequently, they expected to

* The information here offered to the reader was kindly supplied to me by Henry Levick, Esq., (late vice-consul, and now postmaster at Suez), and may be depended upon, as coming from a resident of 16 years' standing. All the passages marked with inverted commas are extracts from a letter with which that gentleman favoured me.

share profits with the merchants, and thus to be compensated for the want of port dues. From that time forward all the vessels in the harbour were registered, and ordered to sail in rotation. This arrangement benefits the owner of the craft 'en départ,' giving him in his turn a temporary monopoly, with the advantage of a full market; and freight is so high that a single trip often clears off the expense of building and the risk of losing the ship — a sensible *succedaneum* for insurance companies. On the contrary, the public must always be a loser by the 'Fazzeh.' Two of a trade do not agree elsewhere; but at Suez even the Christian and the Moslem ship-owner are bound by a fraternal tie, in the shape of this rotation system. It injures the general merchant, and the Red Sea trader, not only by perpetuating high freight*, but also by causing at one period of the

* The rate of freight is at present about forty shillings per ton — very near the same paid by the P. and O. Company for coals carried from Newcastle *viâ* the Cape to Suez. Were the "Fazzeh" abolished, freight to Jeddah would speedily fall to 15 or 16 shillings per ton. Passengers from Suez to Jeddah are sometimes charged as much as 6 or even 8 dollars for standing-room — personal baggage forming another pretext for extortion — and the higher orders of pilgrims, occupying a small portion of the cabin, pay about 12 dollars.

year a break in the routine of sales and in the supplies of goods for the Jeddah market.* At this moment (Nov. 1853), the vessel to which the turn belongs happens to be a large one; there is a deficiency of export to El Hejaz,—her owner will of course wait any length of time for a full cargo; consequently no vessel with merchandise has left Suez for the last seventy two days. Those who have bought goods for the Jeddah market at three months' credit will therefore have to meet their acceptances for merchandise still warehoused at the Egyptian port. This strange contrast to free-trade principle is another proof that protection benefits only one party, the protected, while it is detrimental to the interests of the other party, the public." To these remarks of Mr. Levick's, I have only to add that the government supports the Fazzeh with all the energy of protectionists. A letter from Mr. Drummond Hay was insufficient to induce the Bey of Suez to break through the rule of rotation in favour of certain princes from Morocco.

These first and second class fares would speedily be reduced, by abolishing protection, to 3 and 6 dollars.

* The principal trade from Suez is to Jeddah, Cosseir supplying Yambu. The latter place, however, imports from Suez wheat, beans, cheese, biscuit, and other provisions for return pilgrims.

The recommendations of Lord Stratford de Redcliffe met with no better fate; and all Mr. West's good will could not procure me a vessel out of her turn.* We were forced to rely upon our own exertions, and the activity of Saad the Devil. This worthy, after sundry delays and differences, mostly caused by his own determination to travel gratis, and to make us pay too much, finally closed with the owner of the Golden Thread. He took places for us upon the poop,—the most eligible part of the vessel at this season of the year; he premised that we should not be very comfortable, as we were to be crowded with Maghrabi pilgrims, but that "Allah makes all things easy!" Though not penetrated with the conviction that this would happen in our case, I paid for two deck passages eighteen Riyals †, my companions seven each, whilst

* My friends were strenuous in their exertions for me to make interest with Mr. West. In the first place, we should have paid less for the whole of a privileged vessel, than we did for our wretched quarters on the deck of the pilgrim-ship; and, secondly, we might have touched at any port we pleased, so as to do a little business in the way of commerce.

† For the "Sath," or poop, the sum paid by each was seven Riyals. I was, therefore, notably cheated by Saad the Devil. The unhappy women in the "Kamrah," or cabin, bought suffocation at the rate of 6 dollars each, as I was afterwards informed, and the third class, in the "Taht," or amidships and forward,

Saad secretly entered himself as an able seaman. Mohammed Shiklibha we were obliged to leave behind, as he could, or would, not afford the expense, and none of us would afford it for him. Had I known him to be the honest, true-hearted fellow he was — his kindness at Meccah quite won my heart — I should not have grudged the small charity.

Nothing more comfortless than our days and nights in the "George" Inn. The ragged walls of our rooms were clammy with dirt, the smoky rafters foul with cobwebs, and the floor, bestrewed with kit, in terrible confusion, was black with hosts of ants and flies. Pigeons nestled on the shelf, cooing amatory ditties the live-long day, and cats like tigers crawled through a hole in the door, making night hideous with their cat-a-waulings. Now a curious goat, then an inquisitive jackass, would walk stealthily into the room, remark that it was tenanted, and retreat with

contributed from 3 to 5 Riyals. But, as usual on these occasions, there was no *prix fixe;* every man was either overcharged or undercharged, according to his means or his necessities. We had to purchase our own water, but the ship was to supply us with fuel for cooking. We paid nothing extra for luggage, and we carried an old Maghrabi woman gratis for good luck.

dignified demeanour, and the mosquitoes sang Io Pæans over our prostrate forms throughout the twenty-four hours. I spare the reader the enumeration of the other Egyptian plagues that infested the place. After the first day's trial, we determined to spend the hours of light in the passages, lying upon our boxes or rugs, smoking, wrangling, and inspecting one another's chests: the latter occupation was a fertile source of disputes, for nothing was more common than for a friend to seize an article belonging to another, and to swear by the Prophet's beard that he admired it, and, therefore, would not return it. The boy Mohammed and Shaykh Nur, who had been intimates the first day, differed in opinion on the second, and on the third, came to pushing each other against the wall. Sometimes we went into the Bazar, a shady street flanked with poor little shops, or we sat in the coffee-house *, drinking hot salt

* We were still at Suez, where we could do as we pleased. But respectable Arabs in their own country, unlike Egyptians, are seldom to be seen in the places of public resort. "Go to the coffee-house and sing there!" is a reproach sometimes addressed to those who have a habit of humming in decent society.

water tinged with burnt bean, or we prayed in one of the three tumble-down old mosques, or we squatted upon the pier, lamenting the want of Hammams, and bathing in the tepid sea.* I presently came to the conclusion that Suez as a "watering-place" is duller even than Dover. The only society we found,—excepting an occasional visitor,—was that of a party of Egyptian women, who with their husbands and families occupied some rooms adjoining ours. At first they were fierce, and used bad language, when the boy Mohammed and I, whilst Omar Effendi was engaged in prayer, and the rest were wandering about the town, ventured to linger in the cool passage, where they congregated, or to address a facetious phrase to them. But hearing that I was a Hakim-bashi—for fame had pro-

* It was only my prestige as physician that persuaded my friend to join me in these bathings. As a general rule, the western Arabs avoid cold water, from a belief that it causes fever. When Mr. C. Cole, H. B. M.'s vice-consul, arrived at Jeddah, the people of the place, seeing that he kept up his Indian habits, advised him strongly to drop them. He refused; but unhappily he soon caught a fever, which confirmed them all in their belief. When Arabs wish to cool the skin after a journey, they wash with a kind of clay called "Tafl," or with a thin paste of henna, and then anoint the body with oil or butter.

moted me to the rank of a "Physician General" at Suez—all had some ailments; they began prudently with requesting me to display the effects of my drugs by dosing myself, but they ended submissively by swallowing nauseous compounds in a body. To this succeeded a primitive form of flirtation, which mainly consisted of the demand direct: the most charming of the party was one Fattúmah*, a plump-personed dame fast verging upon her thirtieth year, fond of a little flattery, and possessed, like all her people, of a most voluble tongue. The refrain of every conversation was "Marry me, O Fattumah! O daughter! O female pilgrim!" In vain the lady would reply, with a coquettish movement of the sides, and toss of the head, and a flirting manipulation of her head-veil, "I am mated, O young man!"—it was agreed that she being a person of polyandrous propensities could support the weight of at least three matrimonial engagements. Some-

* An incrementative form of the name "Fatimah," very common in Egypt. Fatimah would mean a "weaner"—Fattúmah, a "great weaner." By the same barbarism Khadijah becomes "Khaddújah," and Nafisah, "Naffúsah" on the banks of the Nile.

times the entrance of the male Fellahs * interrupted these little discussions, but people of our respectability and nation were not to be imposed upon by such husbands. In their presence we only varied the style of conversation—inquiring the amount of "Mahr," or marriage settlement, deriding the cheapness of womanhood in Egypt, and requiring to be furnished on the spot with brides at the rate of ten shillings a head.† More often the amiable Fattumah—the fair sex in this country, though passing frail, have the best tempers in the world—would laugh at our impertinences. Sometimes vexed by our imitating her Egyptian accent, mimicking her gestures, and depreciating her country-women ‡, she would wax wroth, and

* The palmy days of the Egyptian husband, when he might use the stick, the sword, or the sack with impunity, are, in civilised places at least, now gone by. The wife has only to complain to the Cadi, or to the governor, and she is certain of redress. This is right in the abstract, but in practice it acts badly. The fair sex is so unruly in this country, that strong measures are necessary to coerce it, and in the arts of deceit men have little or no chance against women.

† The amount of settlement being, among Moslems as among Christians, the test of a bride's value,—moral and physical,—it will readily be understood that our demand was more facetious than complimentary.

‡ The term Misriyah (an Egyptian woman) means in El

order us to be gone, and stretch out her forefinger —a sign that she wished to put out our eyes, or adjure Allah to cut the hearts out of our bosoms. Then the "Marry me, O Fattúmah, O daughter, O female pilgrim!" would give way to Y'al-ago-o-oz! (O old woman and decrepit!) "O daughter of sixty sires, and only fit to carry wood to market!"—whereupon would burst a storm of wrath, at the tail of which all of us, like children, starting upon our feet, rushed out of one another's way. But—"*qui se dispute, s'adore*"—when we again met all would be forgotten, and the old tale be told over *de novo*. This was the amusement of the day. At night we, men, assembling upon the little terrace, drank tea, recited stories, read books, talked of our travels, and indulged in various pleasantries. The great joke was the boy Mohammed's abusing all his companions to their faces in Hindostani, which none but Shaykh Nur and I could understand; the others,

Hejaz and the countries about it, a depraved character. Even the men own unwillingly to being Egyptians, for the free-born never forget that the banks of the Nile have for centuries been ruled by the slaves of slaves. "He shall be called an Egyptian," is a denunciation strikingly fulfilled, though the country be no longer the "basest of kingdoms."

however, guessed his intention, and revenged themselves by retorts of the style uncourteous in the purest Hejazi.

I proceed to offer a few more extracts from Mr. Levick's letter about Suez and the Suezians. "It appears that the number of pilgrims who pass through Suez to Meccah has of late been steadily on the decrease. When I first came here (in 1838) the pilgrims who annually embarked at this port amounted to between 10,000 and 12,000, the shipping was more numerous, and the merchants were more affluent.* I have ascertained from a special register kept in the government archives that in the Moslem year 1268 (from 1851 to 1852) the exact number that passed through was 4893."

"In 1269 A. H. it had shrunk to 3136. The natives assign various causes to the falling off, which I attribute chiefly to the indirect effect of European civilisation upon the Moslem powers immediately in contact with it. The heteroge-

* In those days, merchants depended solely upon the native trade, and the passage of pilgrims. The pecuniary advantage attending what is called the Overland transit benefits chiefly the lowest orders, camel-men, sailors, porters, and others of the same class. Sixteen years ago the hire of a boat from the harbour to the roadstead was a piastre and a half: now it is at least five.

neous mass of pilgrims is composed of people of all classes, colours, and costumes. One sees among them, not only the natives of countries contiguous to Egypt, but also a large proportion of central Asians from Bokhara, Persia, Circassia, Turkey and the Crimea, who prefer this route by way of Constantinople to the difficult, expensive, and dangerous caravan line through the desert from Damascus and Baghdad. The West sends us Moors, Algerines, and Tunisians, and Inner Africa a mass of sable Takrouri *, and others from Bornu, the Sudan †, Ghedamah near the Niger, and Jabarti from the Habash." ‡

* This word, says Mansfield Parkyns (Life in Abyssinia), is applied to the wandering *pilgrim* from Darfur, Dar Borgou, Bayarima, Fellatah, and western Africa. He mentions, however, a tribe called "Tokrouri," settled in Abyssinia near Nimr's country, but he does not appear to know that the ancient Arab settlement in Western Africa, "El Takrúr," (Sakatu?) has handed down its name to a large posterity of small kingdoms. A description of El Takrúr is to be found in El Idrisi (1. climate, 1. section,); but I do not agree with the learned translator in writing the word "Tokrour." Burckhardt often alludes in his benevolent way to the "respectable and industrious Tekrourys." I shall have occasion to mention them at a future time.

† The Sudan (Blacksland) in Arabia is applied to Upper Nubia, Senaar, Kordofan, and the parts adjacent.

‡ Not only in Ghiz, but also in Arabic, the mother of Ghiz,

"The Suez ship-builders are an influential body of men, originally Candiots and Alexandrians. When Mohammed Ali fitted out his fleet for the Hejaz war, he transported a number of Greeks to Suez, and the children now exercise their fathers' craft. There are at present three great builders at this place. Their principal difficulty is the want of material. Teak comes from India* *viâ* Jeddah, and Venetian boards, owing to the expense of camel-transport, are a hundred per cent. dearer here than at Alexandria. Trieste and Turkey supply spars, and Jeddah canvass: the sail-makers are Suez men, and the crews a mongrel mixture of Arabs and Egyptians; the Rais, or captain, being almost invariably, if the vessel be a large one, a Yambu man. There are two kinds of craft, distinguished from each other by tonnage, not by build. The Baghlah † is a vessel above 50 tons

the word "Habash," whence our "Abyssinians," means a rabble, a mixture of people. Abyssinian Moslems are called by the Arabs "Jabarte."

* There is no such thing as a tree, except the date, the tamarisk, and the Mimosa on the western shores of the Red Sea.

† This word, which in Arabic is the feminine form of "Baghl," a mule, is in Egypt, as in India, pronounced and written by foreigners "buggalow." Some worthy Indians have further corrupted it to "bungalow."

burden, the Sambuk from 15 to 50. The shipowner bribes the Amir el Bahr, or port-captain, and the Nazir el Safain, or the captain commanding the government vessels, to rate his ship as high as possible—if he pay the price, he will be allowed 9 ardébs to the ton.* The number of ships belonging to the port of Suez amounts to 92; they vary from 25 to 250 tons. The departures in A.H. 1269 (1852 and 1853) were 38, so that each vessel, after returning from a trip, is laid up for about two years. Throughout the passage of the pilgrims, that is to say, during four months, the departures average twice a week; during the remainder of the year from 6 to 10 vessels may leave the port. The homeward trade is carried on principally in Jeddah bottoms, which are allowed to convey goods to Suez, but not to take in return cargo there: they must not interfere with, nor may they partake in any way of the benefits of the rotation system." †

* "The ardéb, like most measures in this country of commercial confusion, varies greatly according to the grain for which it is used. As a general rule, it may be assumed at 300 lbs."

† Return Arab boats, at any but the pilgrim season, with little difficulty obtain permission to carry passengers, but not

"During the present year the imports were contained in 41,395 packages, the exports in 15,988. Specie makes up in some manner for this preponderance of imports: a sum of from 30,000*l.* to 40,000*l.*, in crown, or Maria Theresa, dollars annually leaves Egypt for Arabia, Abyssinia and other parts of Africa. I value the imports at about 350,000*l.*; the export trade to Jeddah at 300,000*l.* per annum. The former consists principally of coffee and gum Arabic; of these there were respectively 17,460 and 15,132 bales, the aggregate value of each article being from 75,000*l.* to 80,000*l.*, and the total amount 160,000*l.* In the previous year the imports were contained in 36,840 packages, the exports in 13,498: of the staple articles — coffee and gum Arabic —they were respectively 15,499 and 14,129 bales, each bale being valued at about 5*l.* Next in importance comes wax from Yemen and the Hejaz, mother-of-pearl * from the Red Sea, sent to England in rough, pepper from Malabar, cloves

cargo. Two gentlemen, in whose pleasant society I once travelled from Cairo to Suez,—Mons. Charles Didier and the Abbé Hamilton,—paid the small sum of 1000 piastres, (say 10*l.*) for the whole of a moderate sized "Sambuk" returning to Jeddah.

* Mother-of pearl is taken to Jerusalem, and there made

brought by Moslem pilgrims from Java, Borneo, and Singapore*, cherry pipe-sticks from Persia and Bussora, and Persian or Surat 'timbak,' (tobacco) These I value at 20,000*l.* per annum. There were also (A. D. 1853) of cloves 708 packages and of Malabar pepper 948: the cost of these two might be 7,000*l.* Minor articles of exportation are, general spiceries (ginger, cardamoms, &c.), Eastern perfumes, such as aloes wood, ottar of rose, ottar of pink and others, tamarinds from India and Yemen, Banca tin, hides supplied by the nomade Bedouins, senna leaves from Yemen and the Hejaz, and blue chequered cotton Melayahs (women's mantillas,) manufactured in southern Arabia. The total value of these smaller imports may be 20,000*l.* per annum."

"The exports chiefly consist of English and native 'grey domestics,' bleached Madipilams, Paisley lappets, and muslins for turbans; the

into chaplets, saints' figures, and crucifixes for Christian pilgrims. At Meccah it is worked into rosaries for the Hajis.

In Europe, cabinet and ornamental work cause a considerable demand for it. Some good pearls are procurable in the Red Sea. I have seen a drop of fair size and colour sold for seven dollars.

* I was told at Meccah, that the pilgrimage is attended by about 2000 natives of Java and the adjoining islands.

remainder being Manchester prints, antimony, Syrian soap, iron in bars, and common ironmongery, Venetian or Trieste beads, used as ornaments in Arabia and Abyssinia, writing paper, Tarbooshes, Papooshes (slippers), and other minor articles of dress and ornament."

"The average annual temperature of the year at Suez is 67° Fahrenheit. The extremes of heat and cold are found in January and August; during the former month the thermometer ranges from a minimum of 38° to a maximum of 68°; during the latter the variation extends from 68° to 102°, or even to 104°, when the heat becomes oppressive. Departures from these extremes are rare. I never remember to have seen the thermometer rise above 108° during the severest Khamsin, or to have sunk below 34° in the rawest wintry wind. Violent storms come up from the south in March. Rain is very variable*: sometimes three years have passed

* The following popular puerilities will serve to show how fond barbarians are of explaining the natural by the supernatural. The Moslems of Egypt thus account for the absence of St. Swithin from their drought-stricken lands. When Jacob lost his Benjamin, he cursed the land of Misraim, declaring that it should know no rain; Joseph on the other hand blessed it, asserting that it should never want water. So the Sindh Hindus believe that Hiranyakasipu, the demon-tyrant of

without a shower, whereas in 1841 torrents poured for nine successive days, deluging the town, and causing many buildings to fall."

"The population of Suez now numbers about 4,800. As usual in Mohammedan countries no census is taken here. Some therefore estimate the population at 6,000. Sixteen years ago it was supposed to be under 3,000. After that time it rapidly increased till 1850, when a fatal attack of cholera reduced it to about half its previous number. The average mortality is about twelve a month.* The endemic diseases are fevers of typhoid and intermittent types in spring, when strong northerly

Multan, finding Meyha-Raja (the cloud.king) troublesome in his dominions, bound him with chains, and only released him upon his oath not to trouble the Unhappy Valley with his presence.

I would suggest to those Egyptian travellers who believe that the fall of rain has been materially increased at Cairo of late, by plantations of trees, to turn over the volumes of their predecessors; they will find almost every one complaining of the discomforts of rain. In Sindh it appears certain that during the last few years there has been at times almost a monsoon: this novel phenomenon the natives attribute to the presence of their conquerors, concerning whom it cannot be said that they have wooded the country to any extent.

* This may appear a large mortality; but at Alexandria it is said the population is renewed every fourteen years.

winds cause the waters of the bay to recede, and leave a miasma-breeding swamp exposed to the rays of the sun. In the month of October and November febrile attacks are violent; ophthalmia more so. The eye disease is not so general here as at Cairo, but the symptoms are more acute; in some years it becomes a virulent epidemic, which ends either in total blindness or in a partial opacity of the cornea, inducing dimness of vision, and a permanent weakness of the eyes. In one month three of my acquaintances lost their sight. Dysenteries are also common, and so are bad boils, or rather ulcers. The cold season is not unwholesome, and at this period the pure air of the Desert restores and invigorates the heat-wasted frame.

"The walls, gates, and defences of Suez are in a ruinous state, being no longer wanted to keep out the Sinaitic Bedouins. The houses are about 500 in number, but many of the natives prefer occupying the upper stories of the Wakálahs, the rooms on the ground floor serving for stores to certain merchandise, wood, dates, cotton, &c. The Suezians live well, and their bazar is abundantly stocked with meat and clarified butter brought from Sinai, and fowls, corn, and vegetables from the Sharkiyah province; fruit is supplied by Cairo as well as by the Sharkiyah, and wheat conveyed down the Nile in flood to the capital is carried on camel-back across the Desert. At sunrise they eat the Fatur, or breakfast, which in summer consists of a 'fatireh,' a kind of muffin, or of bread and treacle. In winter it is more substantial, being generally a mixture of lentils and rice*, with clarified butter poured over it, and a 'kitchen' of pickled lime or stewed onions. At this season they greatly enjoy the 'ful mudammas,' (boiled horse beans †,) eaten with an abundance of linseed oil, into which they steep bits of bread. The beans form a highly nutritive diet, which, if the stomach can digest it,—the pulse is never shelled,—gives great strength. About the middle of the day comes 'El Ghada,' a light dinner of wheaten bread, with dates, onions or cheese: in the hot season melons and cooling fruits are preferred, especially by those who have to face the

* This mixture, called in India Kichhri, has become common in El Hejaz as well as at Suez. "El Kajari" is the corruption, which denotes its foreign origin, and renders its name pronounceable to Arabs.

† Beans, an abomination to the ancient Egyptians, who were forbidden even to sow them, may now be called the common "kitchen" of the country. The Bedouins, who believe in nothing but flesh, milk, and dates, deride the bean-eaters, but they do not consider the food so disgusting as onions.

sun. 'El Asha,' or supper, is served about half an hour after sunset; at this meal all but the poorest classes eat meat. Their favourite flesh, as usual in this part of the world, is mutton; beef and goat are little prized." *

The people of Suez are a finer and a fairer race than the Cairenes. The former have more the appearance of Arabs: their dress is more picturesque, their eyes are carefully darkened with Kohl, and they wear sandals, not slippers. They are, according to all accounts, a turbulent and somewhat fanatic set, fond of quarrels, and slightly addicted to "pronunciamentos." The general programme of one of these latter diversions is said to be as follows. The boys will first be sent by their fathers about the town in a disorderly mob, and ordered to cry out "Long live the Sultan!" with its usual sequel, "Death to the infidels!" The infidels, Christians or others, must hear and may happen to resent this; or possibly the governor, foreseeing a disturbance, orders an ingenuous youth or two to be imprisoned, or to be caned by the police. Whereupon some person, rendered influential by wealth or religious reputation, publicly complains that the Christians

* Here concludes Mr. Levick's letter. For the following observations, I alone am answerable.

are all in all, and that in these evil days El Islam is going to destruction. On this occasion the speaker conducts himself with such insolence, that the governor must perforce consign him to confinement, which exasperates the populace still more. Secret meetings are now convened, and in them the chiefs of corporations assume a prominent position. If the disturbance be intended by its main spring to subside quietly, the conspirators are allowed to take their own way; they will drink copiously, become lions about midnight, and recover their hare-hearts before noon next day. But if mischief be intended, a case of bloodshed is brought about, and then nothing can arrest the torrent of popular rage.* The Egyptian, with all his good humour, merriment, and nonchalance, is notorious for

* The government takes care to prevent bloodshed in the towns by disarming the country people, and by positively forbidding the carrying of weapons. Moreover, with a wise severity, it punishes all parties concerned in a quarrel, where blood is drawn, with a heavy fine and the bastinado *de rigueur*. Hence it is never safe, except as a European, to strike a man, and the Egyptians generally confine themselves to collaring and pushing each other against the walls. Even in the case of receiving gross abuse, you cannot notice it as you would elsewhere. You must take two witnesses,—respectable men,—and prove the offence before the Zabit, who alone can punish the offender.

doggedness, when, as the popular phrase is, his "blood is up." And this, indeed, is his chief merit as a soldier. He has a certain mechanical dexterity in the use of arms, and an Egyptian regiment will fire a volley as correctly as a battalion at Chobham. But when the head, and not the hands, is required, he notably fails, as all Orientals do. The reason of their superiority in the field is their peculiar stubbornness, and this, together with their powers of digestion and of enduring hardship on the line of march, is the quality that made them terrible to their old conquerors, the Turks.

CHAP. X.

THE PILGRIM SHIP.

THE larger craft anchor some three or four miles from the Suez pier, so that it is necessary to drop down in a skiff or shore-boat.

Immense was the confusion on the eventful day of our departure. Suppose us standing upon the beach, on the morning of a fiery July day, carefully watching our hurriedly-packed goods and chattels, surrounded by a mob of idlers, who are not too proud to pick up waifs and strays, whilst pilgrims rush about apparently mad, and friends are weeping, acquaintances vociferating adieux, boatmen demanding fees, shopmen claiming debts, women shrieking and talking with inconceivable power, children crying,— in short, for an hour or so we were in the thick of a human storm. To confound confusion, the boatmen have moored their skiff half a dozen yards away from the shore, lest the porters should be unable to make more than double their fare from the Hajis. Again the Turkish women raise a hideous howl, as they are carried off struggling vainly in brawny arms; the children howl because their mothers howl; and the men scold and swear, because in such scenes none may be silent. The moment we had embarked, each individual found that he or she had missed something of vital importance,—a pipe, a child, a box, or a water-melon; and naturally all the servants were in the bazaars, when they should have been in the boat. Briefly, despite the rage of the sailors, who feared being too late for a second trip, we stood for some time on the beach before putting off.

From the beach we poled to the little pier, where sat the Bey in person to perform a final examination of our passports. Several were detected without the necessary document. Some were bastinadoed, others peremptorily ordered back to Cairo, and the rest were allowed to proceed. At about 10 A.M. we hoisted sail, and ran down the channel leading to the roadstead. On our way we had a specimen of what we might expect from our fellow passengers, the Maghrabi.* A boat crowded

* Men of the Maghrab, or Western Africa; the vulgar plural is Maghrabin, generally written "Mogrebyn." May not the singular form of this word have given rise to the Latin "maurus," by elision of the Ghain, to Italians an unpronounceable consonant? From maurus comes the Portuguese

with these ruffians caught us up, ran alongside of us, and, before we could organise a defence, about a

"moro," and our "moor." When Vasco de Gama reached Calicut, he found there a tribe of Arab colonists, who in religion and in language were the same as the people of Northern Africa,—for this reason he called them "Moors." This was explained long ago by Vincent (Periplus, lib. 3.), and lately by Prichard (Natural History of Man). I repeat it because it has been my fate to hear, at a meeting of a learned society in London, a gentleman declare, that in Eastern Africa he found a people calling *themselves* Moors.

Maghrabin—Westerns,—then would be opposed to Sharkiyin, Easterns, the origin of our "Saracen." From Gibbon downwards, many have discussed the history of this word; but few expected in the nineteenth century to see a writer on Eastern subjects assert, with Sir John Mandeville, that these people "properly, ben clept Sarrazins of Sarra." The learned M. Jomard, who never takes such original views of things, asks a curious question:—"Mais comment un son aussi distinct que le Chine ش aurait-il pu se confondre avec le Syn س et, pour un mot aussi connu que charq; comment aurait-on pu se tromper à l'omission des points?" Simply because the word Saracens came to us through the Greeks (Ptolemy uses it), who have no such sound as sh in their language, and the Italian which, hostile to the harsh sibilants of Oriental dialects, generally melts sh down into s. So the historical word Hashshashiyun—hemp-drinker,—civilised by the Italians into "assassino," became, as all know, an expression of European use.

But if any one adverse to "etymological fancies" objects to my deriving maurus from "Maghrab," let him remember Johnson's successfully tracing the course of the metamorphosis of "dies" into "jour." An even more peculiar change we may discover in the word "elephant." "Pilu" in Sanscrit became score of them poured into our vessel. They carried things too with a high hand, laughed at us, and seemed quite ready to fight. My Indian boy, who happened to let slip the word "Marras," narrowly escaped a blow with a palm stick, which would have felled a camel. They outnumbered us, and were armed; so that, on this occasion, we were obliged to put up with their insolence, and not murmur.

Our Pilgrim Ship, the Silk el Zahab, or the "Golden Wire," was a Sambuk, of about 400 ardébs (fifty tons), with narrow wedge-like bows, a clean water line, a sharp keel, undecked, except upon the poop, which was high enough to act as a sail in a gale of wind. She carried two masts, imminently raking forward, the main considerably larger than the mizen; the former was provided with a huge triangular latine, very deep in the tack, but the second sail was unaccountably wanting She

"pil;" in old Persian, which ignores short final vowels, "fil," and with the article "El-fil;" in Arabic, which supplies the place of p (an unknown letter to it), by f; and elephas in Greek, which is fond of adding "as" to Arabic words, as in the cases of Aretas (Haris) and Obodas (Ubayd). "A name," says Humboldt, "often becoming a historical monument, and the etymological analysis of language, however it may be divided, is attended by valuable results."

had no means of reefing, no compass, no log, no sounding lines, nor even the suspicion of a chart; and in her box-like cabin and ribbed hold there was a something which savoured of close connection between her model and that of the Indian Toni.* Such, probably, were the craft which carried old Sesostris across the Red Sea to Dire; such the cruisers which once every three years left Ezion-Geber for Tarshish; such the transports of which 130 were required to convey Ælius Gallus, with his 10,000 men; and—the East moves slowly—such most probably in A. D. 1900 will be the "Golden Wire," which shall convey future pilgrims from Suez to El-Hejaz. "Bakhshish" was the last as well as the first odious sound I heard in Egypt. The owner of the shore-boat would not allow us to climb the sides of our vessel before paying him his fare, and when we did so, he asked for Bakhshish. If Easterns would only imitate the example of Europeans,—I never yet saw an Englishman give Bakhshish to a soul,—the nuisance would soon be done away with. But on this

* The Toni or Indian canoe is the hollowed-out trunk of a tree,—near Bombay generally a mango. It must have been the first step in advance from that simplest form of naval architecture, the "Catamaran" of Madras and Aden.

occasion all my companions complied with the request, and at times it is unpleasant to be singular. The first look at the interior of our vessel showed a hopeless sight; for Ali Murad, the greedy owner, had promised to take sixty passengers in the hold, but had stretched the number to ninety-seven. Piles of boxes and luggage in every shape and form filled the ship from stem to stern, and a torrent of Hajis were pouring over the sides like ants into the Indian sugar-basin. The poop, too, where we had taken our places, was covered with goods, and a number of pilgrims had established themselves there by might, not by right.

Presently, to our satisfaction, appeared Saad the Devil, equipped as an able seaman, and looking most unlike the proprietor of two large boxes full of valuable merchandise. This energetic individual instan ly prepared for action. With our little party to back him, he speedily cleared the poop of intruders and their stuff by the simple process of pushing or rather throwing them off it into the hold below. We then settled down as comfortably as we could; three Syrians, a married Turk with his wife and family, the rais or captain of the vessel, with a portion of his crew, and our seven selves, composing a total of eighteen human beings, upon a space certainly not exceeding 10 feet by 8. The cabin —a miserable box about the size of the poop, and three feet high — was stuffed, like the hold of a slave ship, with fifteen wretches, children and women, and the other ninety-seven were disposed upon the luggage or squatted on the bulwarks. Having some experience in such matters, and being favoured by fortune, I found a spare bed-frame slung to the ship's side; and giving a dollar to its owner, a sailor — who flattered himself that, because it was his, he would sleep upon it,— I instantly appropriated it, preferring any hardship outside to the condition of a packed herring inside the place of torment.

Our Maghrabis were fine-looking animals from the deserts about Tripoli and Tunis; so savage that, but a few weeks ago, they had gazed at the cock-boat, and wondered how long it would be growing to the size of the ship that was to take them to Alexandria. Most of them were sturdy young fellows, round-headed, broad-shouldered, tall and large-limbed, with frowning eyes, and voices in a habit of perpetual roar. Their manners were rude, and their faces full of fierce contempt or insolent familiarity. A few old men were there, with countenances expressive of intense ferocity; women as savage and full of fight as men; and handsome boys with shrill voices, and hands always upon their daggers. The women were mere bundles of dirty white rags. The males were clad in Burnooses—brown or striped woollen cloaks with hoods; they had neither turban nor tarboosh, trusting to their thick curly hair or to the prodigious hardness of their scalps as a defence against the sun; and there was not a slipper nor a shoe amongst the party. Of course all were armed; but, fortunately for us, none had anything more formidable than a cut-and-thrust dagger about ten inches long. These Maghrabis travel in hordes under a leader who obtains the temporary title of "Maula,"—the master. He has generally performed a pilgrimage or two, and has collected a stock of superficial information which secures for him the respect of his followers, and the profound contempt of the heaven-made Ciceroni of Meccah and El Medinah. No people endure greater hardships when upon the pilgrimage than these Africans, who trust almost entirely to alms and to other such dispensations of Providence. It is not therefore to be wondered at that they rob whenever an opportunity presents itself. Several cases of theft occurred on board the "Golden Wire;" and as a plunderer seldom allows himself to be baulked by insufficient defence, they are perhaps deservedly accused of having committed some revolting murders.

The first thing to be done after gaining standing-room was to fight for greater comfort; and never a Holyhead packet in the olden time showed a finer scene of pugnacity than did our pilgrim ship. A few Turks, ragged old men from Anatolia and Caramania, were mixed up with the Maghrabis, and the former began the war by contemptuously elbowing and scolding their wild neighbours. The Maghrabis under their leader, "Maula Ali," a burly savage, in whom I detected a ridiculous resemblance to an old and well-remembered schoolmaster, retorted so willingly that in a few minutes nothing was to be seen but a confused mass of humanity, each item indiscriminately punching and pulling, scratching and biting, butting and trampling whatever was obnoxious to such operations, with cries of rage, and all the accompaniments of a proper fray. One of our party on the poop, a Syrian, somewhat incautiously leapt down to aid his countrymen by restoring order. He sank immediately below the surface of the living mass; and when we fished him out, his forehead was cut open, half his beard had disappeared, and a fine sharp set of teeth belonging to some Maghrabi had left their mark in the calf of his leg. The enemy showed no love of fair play, and never appeared contented unless five or six of them were setting upon a single man. This made matters worse. The weaker of course drew their daggers, and a few bad wounds were soon given and received. In a few minutes five men were completely disabled, and the victors began to dread the consequences of their victory.

Then the fighting stopped, and as many could not find places, it was agreed that a deputation should wait upon Ali Murad, the owner, to inform him of the crowded state of the vessel. After keeping us in expectation at least three hours he appeared in a row-boat, and, preserving a respectful distance, informed us that any one who pleased might leave the ship and take back his fare. This left the case exactly as it was before; none would abandon his party to go on shore: so Ali Murad was rowed off towards Suez, giving us a parting injunction to be good, and not fight; to trust in Allah, and that Allah would make all things easy to us. His departure was the signal for a second fray, which in its accidents differed a little from the first. During the previous disturbance we kept our places with weapons in our hands. This time we were summoned by the Maghrabis to relieve their difficulties, by taking about half a dozen of them on the poop. Saad the Devil at once rose with an oath, and threw amongst us a bundle of "Nebut"—goodly ashen staves six feet long, thick as a man's wrist, well greased, and tried in many a rough bout. He shouted to us "Defend yourselves if you don't wish to be the meat of the Maghrabis!" and to the enemy "Dogs and sons of dogs! now shall you see what the children of the Arab are,"—"I am Omar of Daghistan!" "I am Abdullah the son of Joseph!" "I am Saad the Devil!" we exclaimed, "renowning it" by this display of name and patronymic. To do the enemy justice, they showed no sign of flinching; they swarmed towards the poop like angry hornets, and encouraged each other with loud cries of "Allah akbar!" But we had a vantage ground about four feet above them, and their palm-sticks and short daggers could do nothing against our terrible quarter-staves. In vain the "Jacquerie" tried to scale the poop and to overpower us by numbers; their courage only secured them more broken heads.

At first I began to lay on load with *main morte*, really fearing to kill some one with such a weapon; but it soon became evident that the Maghrabis' heads and shoulders could bear and did require the utmost exertion of strength. Presently a thought struck me. A large earthen jar full of drinking water*, —in its heavy frame of wood the weight might have been 100 lbs, —stood upon the edge of the poop, and the thick of the fray took place beneath. Seeing an opportunity I crept up to the jar, and, without attracting attention, by a smart push with the shoulder rolled it down upon the swarm of assailants. The fall caused a shriller shriek to rise above the ordinary din, for heads, limbs, and bodies were sorely bruised by the weight, scratched by the broken potsherds, and

* In these vessels each traveller, unless a previous bargain be made, is expected to provide his own water and fire-wood. The best way, however, is, when the old wooden box called a tank is sound, to pay the captain for providing water, and to keep the key.

wetted by the sudden discharge. A fear that something worse might be forthcoming made the Maghrabis shrink off towards the end of the vessel. After a few minutes, we, sitting in grave silence, received a deputation of individuals in whity-brown Burnooses, spotted and striped with what Mephistopheles calls a "curious juice." They solicited peace, which we granted upon the condition that they would bind themselves to keep it. Our heads, shoulders, and hands were penitentially kissed, and presently the fellows returned to bind up their hurts in dirty rags. We owed this victory entirely to our own exertions, and the meek Omar was by far the fiercest of the party. Our rais, as we afterwards learned, was an old fool who could do nothing but call for the Fát-hăh *, claim Bakhshish at every place where we moored for the night, and spend his leisure hours in the "Caccia del Mediterraneo." Our crew consisted of half a dozen Egyptian lads, who, not being able to defend themselves, were periodically chastised by the Maghrabi, especially when any attempt

* The "opener"—the first chapter of the Koran, which Moslems recite as Christians do the Lord's Prayer; it is also used on occasions of danger, the beginnings of journeys, to bind contracts, &c.

was made to cook, to fetch water, or to prepare a pipe.*

At length, about 3 P.M. on the 6th July, 1854, we shook out the sail, and, as it bellied in the favourable wind, we recited the Fát-hah with upraised hands which we afterwards drew down our faces.† As the "Golden Wire" started from her place, I could not help casting one wistful look upon the British flag proudly floating over the Consulate. But the momentary regret was stifled by the heart-bounding which prospects of an adventure excite, and by the real pleasure of leaving Egypt. I had lived there a stranger in the land, and a hapless life it had been: in the streets every man's face was the face of a foe as he looked upon the Persian. Whenever I came in contact with the native officials ‡, insolence marked the event; and the circumstance of living

* These Maghrabis, like the Somalis, the Wahhabis of the desert, and certain other barbarous races, unaccustomed to tobacco, appeared to hate the smell of a pipe.

† The hands are raised in order to catch the blessing that is supposed to descend from heaven upon the devotee; and the meaning of drawing the palms down the face, is symbolically to transfer the benediction to every part of the body.

‡ As is the case under all despotic governments, nothing can be more intentionally offensive than the official manners

within hail of my fellow countrymen, and yet in an impossibility of enjoying their society, still throws a gloom over the memory of my first sojourn in Egypt.

The ships of the Red Sea—infamous region of rocks, reefs, and shoals—cruise along the coast by day, and for the night lay to in the first cove they can find; they do not sail when it blows hard, and as in winter time the weather is often stormy and the light of day does not last long, the voyage is intolerably slow.* At sunset we stayed our adventurous course, and, still within sight of Suez, comfortably anchored under the lee of Jebel Atakah, the "Mountain of Deliverance."† We were now on classic waters. The

of a superior to his inferior in Egypt. The Indians charge their European fellow-subjects with insolence of demeanour and coarseness of language. As far as my experience goes, our roughness and brusquerie are mere politeness compared with what passes between Easterns. At the same time it must be owned that I have seen the worst of it.

* It was far safer and more expeditious in El Edrisi's day (A. D. 1154), when the captain used to sit on the poop "furnished with numerous and useful instruments;" when he "sounded the shallows, and by his knowledge of the depths could direct the helmsman where to steer."

† In the East it is usual, when commencing a voyage or a journey, to make a short day's work, in order to be at a conve-

Eastern shore was dotted with the little grove of palm trees which clusters around the Uyun Musa, or Moses' Wells; and on the west, between two towering ridges, lay the mouth of the valley down which, according to Father Sicard *, the Israelites fled to the Sea of Sedge.† The view was by no means deficient in a sort of barbarous splendour. Verdure there was literally none, but under the violet and orange tints of the sky the chalky rocks became heaps of topazes, and the black ridges masses of amethyst. The rising mists, here silvery white, there deeply

nient distance for returning, in case of any essential article having been forgotten.

* A Jesuit missionary who visited the place in A.D. 1720, and described it in a well-known volume. As every eminent author, however, monopolises a "crossing," and since the head of the Suez creek, as is shown by its old watermark, has materially changed within no very distant period, it is no wonder that the question is still *sub judice*, and that there it will remain most probably till the end of time. The Christians have two equally favourite lines: the Moslems patronise one so impossible, that it has had attractions enough to fix their choice. It extends from Zafaran Point to Hummum Bluffs, ten miles of deep water.

† The Hebrew name of this part of the Red Sea. In a communication lately made to the Royal Geographical Society, I gave my reasons for believing that the Greeks borrowed their Erythræan Sea from the Arabic "Sea of Himyar."

rosy, and the bright blue of the waves*, lining long strips of golden sand, compensated for the want of softness by a semblance of savage gorgeousness.

Next morning, before the cerulean hue had vanished from the hills, we set sail. It was not long before we came to a proper sense of our position. The box containing my store of provisions, and, worse still, my opium, was at the bottom of the hold, perfectly unapproachable; we had, therefore, the pleasure of breaking our fast on "mare's skin†," and a species of biscuit, hard as a stone and quite as tasteless. During the day, whilst unsufferable splendour reigned above, a dashing of the waters below kept my nest in a state of perpetual drench. At night rose a cold bright moon, with dews falling so thick and

* Most travellers remark that they have never seen a brighter blue than that of the Red Sea. It was the observation of an early age that "the Rede Sea is not more rede than any other sea, but in some place thereof is the gravelle rede, and therefore men clepen it the Rede Sea."

† Jild el Faras (or Kamar el din), a composition of apricot paste, dried, spread out, and folded into sheets, exactly resembling the article after which it is named. Turks and Arabs use it when travelling; they dissolve it in water, and eat it as a relish with bread or biscuit.

clammy that the skin felt as though it would never be dry again. It is, also, by no means pleasant to sleep upon a cot about four feet long by two broad, with the certainty that a false movement would throw you overboard, and a conviction that if you do fall from a Sambuk under sail, no mortal power can save you. And as under all circumstances in the East, dozing is one's chief occupation, the reader will understand that the want of it left me in utter idleness.

The gale was light that day, and the sunbeams were fire; our crew preferred crouching in the shade of the sail to taking advantage of what wind there was. In spite of our impatience we made but little way: near evening time we anchored on a tongue of sand, about two miles distant from the well-known heights called by the Arabs Hammam Faraún *, which

—"like giants stand
To sentinel enchanted land."

The strip of coarse quartz and sandstone gravel

* "Pharaoh's hot baths," which in our maps are called "Hummam Bluffs." They are truly "enchanted land" in Moslem fable: a volume would scarcely contain the legends that have been told and written about them.

is obviously the offspring of some mountain torrent; it stretches southwards, being probably dispersed in that direction by the currents of the sea, as they receive the deposit. The distance of the Bluffs prevented my visiting them, which circumstance I regretted the less as they have been described by pens equal to the task.

That evening we enjoyed ourselves upon clean sand, whose surface, drifted by the wind into small yellow waves, by a little digging and heaping up, was easily converted into the coolest and most comfortable of couches. Indeed, after the canescent heat of the day, and the tossing of our ill conditioned vessel, we should have been contented with lodgings far less luxurious. Fuel was readily collected, and while some bathed, the others erected a hearth—three large stones and a hole open to leeward—lit the fire, and put the pot on to boil. Shaykh Nur had fortunately brought a line with him; we had been successful in fishing; a little rice also had been bought; with this boiled and rock cod broiled upon the charcoal, we made a dinner that caused every one to forget the breakfast of mare's skin and hard biscuit. A few Maghrabis had ventured on shore,—the rais having terrified the others by threatening them with those "bogles," the Bedouins—they offered us Kus Kusu * in exchange for a little fish. As evening came we determined before sleeping, to work upon their "morale" as effectually as we had attacked their physique. Shaykh Hamid stood up and indulged them with the Azan, or call to prayers, pronounced after the fashion of El Medinah.† They performed their devotions in lines ranged behind us as a token of respect, and when worship was over we were questioned about the Holy City till we grew tired of answering. Again our heads and shoulders, our hands and knees ‡, were kissed, but this time in devotion, not in penitence. My companions could scarcely understand half the rugged words

* One of the numerous species of what the Italians generally call "Pasta." The material is wheaten or barley flour rolled into small round grains. In Barbary it is cooked by steaming, and served up with hard boiled eggs and mutton, sprinkled with red pepper. These Bedouin Maghrabis merely boiled it.

† The Azan is differently pronounced, though similarly worded by every orthodox nation in El Islam.

‡ The usual way of kissing the knee is to place the finger tips upon it, and then to raise them to the mouth. It is an action denoting great humility, and the condescending superior who is not an immediate master returns the compliment in the same way.

which the Maghrabis used *, as this dialect was fresh from the distant desert, still we succeeded in making ourselves intelligible to them, vaunting our dignity as the sons of the Prophet, and the sanctity of our land which should protect its children from every description of fraud and violence. We benignantly promised to be their guides at El Medinah, and the boy Mohammed would conduct their devotions at Meccah always provided that they repented their past misdeeds, avoided any repetition of the same, and promised to perform the duties of good and faithful pilgrims. Presently the rais joined our party, and the usual story-telling began. The old man knew the name of each hill, and had a legend for every nook and corner in sight. He dwelt at length upon the life of Abu Zulaymah, the patron saint of these seas, whose little tomb stands at no great distance from our bivouac place, and told us how he sits watching over the

* The Maghrabi dialect is known to be the harshest and most guttural form of Arabic. It owes this unenviable superiority to its frequency of "Sukun," or the quiescence of one or more consonants;—"K'lab," for instance, for "Kilab," and "'Msik" for "Amsik." Thus it is that vowels, the soft and liquid part of language, disappear, leaving in their place a barbarous sounding mass of consonants.

safety of pious mariners in a cave among the neighbouring rocks, and sipping his coffee, which is brought in a raw state from Meccah by green birds, and prepared in the usual way by the hands of ministering angels. He showed us the spot where the terrible king of Egypt, when close upon the heels of the children of Israel, was whelmed in the "hill of waters*," and he warned us that next day our way would be through breakers, and reefs, and dangerous currents, over whose troubled depths, since that awful day the Ifrit of the storm has never ceased to flap his sable wing. The wincing of the hearers proved that the shaft of the old man's words was sharp ; but as night was advancing, we unrolled our rugs, and fell asleep upon the sand, all of us happy, for we had eaten and drunk, and—since man is a hopeful animal—expecting on the morrow that the Ifrit would be merciful, and allow us to eat fresh dates at the harbour of Tur.

Fair visions of dates doomed to the Limbo

* Burckhardt mentions the Arab legend that the spirits of the drowned Egyptians may be seen moving at the bottom of the sea, and Finati adds that they are ever busy recruiting their numbers with shipwrecked mariners.

of things which should have been! The grey dawn looked down upon us in difficulties. The water is deep near this coast; we had anchored at high tide close to the shore, and the ebb had left us high and dry. When this fact became apparent, a storm was upon the point of breaking. The Maghrabis, but for our interference, would have bastinadoed the rais, who, they said with some reason, ought to have known better. When this phase of feeling passed away, they applied themselves to physical efforts. All except the women and children, who stood on the shore encouraging their relatives with shrill quaverings, threw themselves into the water; some pushed, others applied their shoulders to the vessel's side, and all used their lungs with might and main. But the "Golden Wire" was firmly fixed, and their exertions were too irregular. Physical force failed, upon which they changed their tactics. At the suggestion of their "Maula," they prepared to burn incense in honour of the Shaykh Abu Zulaymah. The material not being forthcoming, they used coffee, which perhaps accounts for the short-comings of that holy man. After this the rais remembered that their previous exertions had not begun under the auspices of the Fát-hah. Therefore they prayed, and then re-applied themselves to work. Still they failed. Finally, each man called aloud upon his own particular saint or spiritual guide, and rushed forward as if he alone sufficed for the exploit. Shaykh Hamid unwisely quoted the name, and begged the assistance of his great ancestor, the "clarified-butter-seller;" the obdurate "Golden Wire" was not moved, and Hamid retired in momentary confusion.

It was now about nine A.M., and the water had risen considerably. My morning had been passed in watching the influx of the tide, and the grotesque efforts of the Maghrabis. When the vessel showed some symptoms of unsteadiness, I arose, walked gravely up to her, ranged the pilgrims around her with their shoulders to the sides, and told them to heave with might when they should hear me invoke the revered name of the Indian saint. I raised my hands and voice; "Ya Pirau Pir!" Ya Abd el Kader Jilani* was the signal. Each Maghrabi worked like an Atlas, the "Golden Wire" canted half over, and, sliding heavily

* A celebrated Sufi or mystic, whom many Indians reverence as the Arabs do their Prophet. In Appendix I. the curious reader will find Abd el Kader again mentioned.

through the sand, once more floated off into deep water. This was generally voted a minor miracle, and the Effendi was greatly respected — for a day or two.

The wind was fair, but we had all to re-embark, an operation which went on till noon. After starting, I remarked the natural cause which gives this Birkat Faraún — "Pharaoh's Bay," — a bad name. Here the gulf narrows, and the winds, which rush down the clefts and valleys of the lofty mountains on the Eastern and Western shores, meeting tides and counter-currents, cause a perpetual commotion. That day the foam-tipped waves repeatedly washed over my cot, by no means diminishing its discomforts. In the evening, or rather late in the afternoon, we anchored, to our infinite disgust, under a ridge of rocks, behind which lies the plain of Tur. The rais deterred all from going on shore by terrible stories about the Bedouins that haunt the place, besides which there was no sand to sleep upon. We remained, therefore, on board that night, and, making sail early the next morning, threaded through reefs and sand-banks into the intricate and dangerous entrance of Tur about noon.

Nothing can be meaner than the present appearance of the old Phœnician colony, although its position as a harbour, and its plentiful supply of fruit and fresh water, make it one of the most frequented places on the coast. The only remains of any antiquity — except the wells — are the fortifications which the Portuguese erected to keep out the Bedouins. The little town lies upon a plain that stretches with a gradual rise from the sea to the lofty mountains, which form the axis of the Sinaitic group. The country around reminded me strongly of maritime Sindh — a flat of clay and sand, clothed with sparse tufts of Salsolæ, and bearing strong signs of a (geologically speaking) recent origin. The town is inhabited principally by Greek and other Christians*, who live by selling

* Those people are descendants of Syrians and Greeks that fled from Candia, Scios, the Ionian Islands, and Palestine to escape the persecutions of the Turks. They now wear the Arab dress, and speak the language of the country, but they are easily to be distinguished from the Moslems, by the expression of their countenances and sometimes by their blue eyes and light hair.

There are also a few families calling themselves Jebeliyah, or mountaineers. Originally they were 100 households, sent by Justinian to serve the convent of St. Catherine, and to defend it against the Berbers. Sultan Kansooh el Ghori, called by European writers Campson Gaury, the Mameluke king of Egypt, in A.D. 1501, admitted these people into the Moslem community on condition of their continuing the menial service they had afforded to the monks.

water and provisions to ships. A fleecy cloud hung lightly over the majestic head of Jebel Tur, about eventide, and the outlines of the giant hills stood "picked out" from the clear blue sky. Our rais, weather-wise man, warned us that these were indications of a gale, and that, in case of rough weather, he did not intend to leave Tur. I was not sorry to hear this. We had passed a pleasant day, drinking sweet water, and eating the dates, grapes, and pomegranates, which the people of the place carry down to the beach for the benefit of hungry pilgrims. Besides which, there were various sights to see, and with these we might profitably spend the morrow. We therefore pitched the tent upon the sand, and busied ourselves with extricating a box of provisions — a labour rendered lighter by the absence of the Maghrabis, some of whom were wandering about the beach, whilst others had gone off to fill their bags with fresh water. We found their surliness insufferable; even when we were passing from poop to forecastle, landing or boarding, they grumbled forth their dissatisfaction.

Our rais was not mistaken in his prediction. When morning broke, we found the wind strong, and the sea white with foam. Most of us thought lightly of these terrors, but our valorous captain swore that he dared not for his life cross the mouth of ill-omened Akabah in such a storm. We breakfasted, therefore, and afterwards set out to visit Moses' hot baths, mounted on wretched donkeys with pack-saddles, ignorant of stirrups, and without tails, whilst we ourselves suffered generally from boils, which, as usual upon a journey, make their appearance in localities the most inconvenient. Our road lay northward across the plain towards a long narrow strip of date ground, surrounded by a ruinous mud well. After a ride of two or three miles, we entered the gardens, and came suddenly upon the Hammam. It is a prim little bungalow, built by the present Pasha of Egypt for his own accommodation, glaringly whitewashed, and garnished with divans and calico curtains of a gorgeous hue. The guardian had been warned of our visit, and was present to supply us with bathing-cloths and other necessaries. One by one, we entered the cistern, which is now in an inner room. The water is about four feet deep, warm in winter, cool in summer, of a saltish and bitter taste, but celebrated for its invigorating qualities, when applied externally. On one side of the calcareous rock, near the ground, is the hole opened for the spring by Moses' rod, which must have been like the "mast of some tall Ammiral *," and near it are the marks of Moses' nails — deep indentations in the stone, which were probably left there by some extinct Saurian. Our cicerone informed us that formerly the finger-marks existed, and that they were long enough for a man to lie in. The same functionary attributed the sanitary properties of the spring to the blessings of the Prophet, and when asked why Moses had not made sweet water to flow, informed us that the great law-giver had intended the spring for bathing in, not for drinking. We sat with him, eating the small yellow dates of Tur, which are delicious, melting like honey in the mouth, and leaving a surpassing *arrière goût.* After finishing sundry pipes and cups of coffee, we gave the man a few piastres, and, mounting our donkeys, started eastward for the Bir Musa †,

* Adam's forehead (says the Turikh Tabari) brushed the skies, but this height being inconvenient, the Lord abridged it to 100 cubits. The Moslems firmly believe in Anakim. Josephus informs us that Moses was of "divine form and great tallness;" the Arabs specify his stature, — 300 cubits. They have, moreover, found his grave in some part of the country S. E. of the Dead Sea, and make cups of a kind of bitumen called "Moses' Stones." This people *nescit ignorare* — it *will* know everything.

† "Moses' Well." I have no argument except the untrust-

which we reached in half an hour. It is a fine old well, built round and domed over with roughly squared stones, very like what may be seen in some rustic parts of Southern England. The sides of the pit were so rugged that a man could climb down them, and at the bottom was a pool of water, sweet and abundant. We had intended to stay there, and to dine *al fresco*, but the hated faces of our companions, the Maghrabis, meeting us at the entrance, nipped that project in the bud. Accordingly we retired from the burning sun to a neighbouring coffee-house — a shed of palm leaves kept by a Tur man, and there, seated on mats, we demolished the contents of our basket. Whilst we were eating, some Bedouins came in and joined us, when invited so to do. They were poorly dressed, and all armed with knives and cheap sabres, hanging to leathern bandoleens: in language and demeanour they showed few remains of their old ferocity. As late as Mohammed Ali's time these people were noted wreckers, and formerly they

worthy traditions of the Bedouins, either for or against this having been the identical well near which Moses sat when he fled from the face of Pharaoh to the land of Midian. One thing is certain, namely, that in this part of Arabia, as also at Aden, the wells are of a very ancient date.

were dreaded pirates—now they are lions with their fangs and claws drawn.

In the even, when we returned to our tent, a Syrian, one of our party on the poop, came out to meet us with the information that several large vessels had arrived from Suez, comparatively speaking, empty, and that the captain of one of them would land us at Yambu for three dollars a head. The proposal was a tempting one. But, presently it became apparent that my companions were unwilling to shift their precious boxes, and moreover, that I should have to pay for those who could not or would not pay for themselves,—that is to say, for the whole party. As such a display of wealth would have been unadvisable, I dismissed the idea with a sigh. Amongst the large vessels was one freighted with Persian pilgrims, a most disagreeable race of men on a journey or a voyage. They would not land at first, because they feared the Bedouins. They would not take water from the town people, because some of these were Christians. Moreover, they insisted upon making their own call to prayer, which heretical proceeding—it admits five extra words—our party, orthodox Moslems, would rather have died than permitted. When their crier, a small wizen-faced man, began the Azan with a voice

> —"in quel tenore
> Che fa il cappon quando talvolta canta,"

we received it with a shout of derision, and some, hastily snatching up their weapons, offered him an opportunity of martyrdom. The Maghrabis, too, hearing that the Persians were Rafaz (heretics) crowded fiercely round to do a little Jihad, or fighting, for the faith. The long-bearded men took the alarm. They were twice the number of our small party, and therefore had been in the habit of strutting about with nonchalance, and looking at us fixedly, and otherwise demeaning themselves in an indecorous way. But when it came to the point, they showed the white feather. These Persians accompanied us to the end of our voyage. As they approached the Holy Land, visions of the "nebut" caused a change for the better in their manners. At Mahar they meekly endured a variety of insults, and at Yambu they cringed to us like dogs.

R. BURTON DEL^t HANHART LITH

THE TAKHTRAWAN OR GRANDEE'S LITTER.

CHAP. XI

TO YAMBU.

On the 11th July, about dawn, we left Tur, with the unpleasant certainty of not touching ground for thirty-six hours. I passed the time in steadfast contemplation of the webs of my umbrella, and in making the following meteorological remarks.

Morning. The air is mild and balmy as that of an Italian spring; thick mists roll down the valleys along the sea, and a haze like mother-o'-pearl crowns the headlands. The distant rocks show Titanic walls, lofty donjons, huge projecting bastions, and moats full of deep shade. At their base runs a sea of amethyst, and as earth receives the first touches of light, their summits, almost transparent, mingle with the jasper tints of the sky. Nothing can be more delicious than this hour. But, as

> "—Les plus belles choses
> Ont le pire destin,—"

so morning soon fades. The sun bursts up from

behind the main, a fierce enemy, a foe that will compel every one to crouch before him. He dyes the sky orange, and the sea "incarnadine," where its violet surface is stained by his rays, and mercilessly puts to flight the mists and haze and the little agate-coloured masses of cloud that were before floating in the firmament: the atmosphere is so clear that now and then a planet is visible. For the two hours following sunrise the rays are endurable; after that they become a fiery ordeal. The morning beams oppress you with a feeling of sickness; their steady glow, reflected by the glaring waters, blinds your eyes, blisters your skin, and parches your mouth: you now become a monomaniac; you do nothing but count the slow hours that must "minute by" before you can be relieved.*

Noon. The wind, reverberated by the glowing hills, is like the blast of a lime-kiln. All colour melts away with the canescence from above. The sky is a dead milk-white, and the mirror-like sea

* The reader who has travelled in the East will feel that I am not exaggerating. And to convince those who know it only by description, I will refer them to any account of our early campaigns in Sindh, where many a European soldier has been taken up stone dead after sleeping an hour or two in the morning sun.

so reflects the tint that you can scarcely distinguish the line of the horizon. After noon the wind sleeps upon the reeking shore; there is a deep stillness; the only sound heard is the melancholy flapping of the sail. Men are not so much sleeping as half senseless; they feel as if a few more degrees of heat would be death.

Sunset. The enemy sinks behind the deep cerulean sea, under a canopy of gigantic rainbow which covers half the face of heaven. Nearest to the horizon is an arch of tawny orange; above it another of the brightest gold, and based upon these a semicircle of tender sea green blends with a score of delicate gradations into the sapphire sky. Across the rainbow the sun throws its rays in the form of spokes tinged with a beautiful pink. The Eastern sky is mantled with a purple flush that picks out the forms of the hazy desert and the sharp-cut hills. Language is a thing too cold, too poor, to express the harmony and the majesty of this hour, which is evanescent, however, as it is lovely. Night falls rapidly, when suddenly the appearance of the zodiacal light * restores the

* The zodiacal light on the Red Sea, and in Bombay, is far brighter than in England. I suppose this is the "after-glow" described by Miss Martineau and other travellers: "flashes of

scene to what it was. Again the grey hills and the grim rocks become rosy or golden, the palms green, the sands saffron, and the sea wears a lilac surface of dimpling waves. But after a quarter of an hour all fades once more; the cliffs are naked and ghastly under the moon, whose light falling upon this wilderness of white crags and pinnacles is most strange—most mysterious.

Night. The horizon is all of darkness, and the sea reflects the white visage of the moon as in a mirror of steel. In the air we see giant columns of pallid light, distinct, based upon the indigo-coloured waves, and standing with their heads lost in endless space. The stars glitter with exceeding brilliance. At this hour

> "—River and hill and wood,
> With all the numberless goings on of life,
> Inaudible as dreams—"

the planets look down upon you with the faces of smiling friends. You feel the "sweet influence of

light like coruscations of the Aurora Borealis in pyramidal form" would exactly describe the phenomenon. It varies, however, greatly, and often for some days together is scarcely visible.

* Niebuhr considers that the stars are brighter in Norway than in the Arabian deserts: I never saw them so bright as on the Neilgherry hills.

the Pleiades." You are bound by the "bond of Orion." Hesperus bears with him a thousand things. In communion with them your hours pass swiftly by, till the heavy dews warn you to cover up your face and sleep. And with one look at a certain little star in the north, under which lies all that makes life worth living through—surely it is a venial superstition to sleep with your face towards that Kiblah!—you fall into oblivion.

Those thirty-six hours were a trial even to the hard-headed Bedouins. The Syrian and his two friends were ill. Omar Effendi, it is true, had the courage to say his sunset prayers, but the exertion so altered him that he looked another man. Salih Shakkar in despair ate dates till threatened with a dysentery. Saad the Devil had rigged out for himself a cot three feet long, which, arched with bent bamboo and covered with cloaks, he had slung on the larboard side; but the loud grumbling which proceeded from his nest proved that his precaution had not been a remedy. Even the boy Mohammed forgot to chatter, to scold, to smoke, and to make himself generally disagreeable. The Turkish lady appeared dying, and was not strong enough to wail. How the poor mother stood her trials so well, made every one wonder. The most pleasant trait in my companions' characters was the consideration they showed to her, and their attention to her children. Whenever one of the party drew forth a little delicacy—a few dates or a pomegranate—they gave away a share of it to the children, and most of them took their turns to nurse the baby. This was genuine politeness — kindness of heart. It would be well for those who sweepingly accuse Easterns of want of gallantry to contrast this trait of character with the savage scenes of civilisation that take place among the "Overlands" at Cairo and Suez. No foreigner could be present for the first time without bearing away the lasting impression that the sons of Great Britain are model barbarians.* On board the "Golden Wire" Salih Shakkar was the sole base exception to the general gallantry of my companions.

As the sun starts towards the west, falling harmlessly upon our heads, we arise, still faint and dizzy, calling for water, which before we had not the strength to drink, and pipes, and coffee, and similar luxuries. Our primitive kitchen is a square wooden box, lined with clay, and filled with sand,

* On one occasion I was obliged personally to exert myself to prevent a party of ladies being thrust into an old and bad transit-van; the ruder sex having stationed itself at some distance from the starting-place in order to seize upon the best.

upon which three or four large stones are placed to form a hearth. Preparations are now made for the evening meal, which is of the simplest description. A little rice, a few dates, or an onion, will keep a man alive in our position; a single "good dinner" would justify long odds against his seeing the next evening. Moreover, it is impossible in such cases to have an appetite, fortunately, as our store of provisions is a scanty one. Arabs consider it desirable on a journey to eat hot food once in the twenty-four hours; so we determine to cook, despite all difficulties. The operation, however, is by no means satisfactory; twenty expectants surround the single fire, and there is sure to be a quarrel amongst them every five minutes.

As the breeze, cooled by the dew, begins to fan our parched faces, we recover our spirits amazingly. Songs are sung, and stories are told, and rough jests are bandied about, till not unfrequently Oriental sensitiveness is sorely touched. Or, if we see the prospect of storm or calm, we draw forth, and piously peruse, a "Hizlr el Bahr." As this prayer is supposed to make all safe upon the ocean wave, I will not selfishly withhold it from the British reader. To draw forth all its virtues, the reciter should receive it from the hands of his

Murshid or spiritual guide, and study it during the Chillah, or forty days of fast, of which, I venture to observe, few Britons are capable. "O Allah, O Exalted, O Almighty, O All-pitiful, O All-powerful, thou art my God, and sufficeth to me the knowledge of it! Glorified be the Lord my Lord, and glorified be the faith my faith! Thou givest victory to whom thou pleasest, and thou art the glorious, the merciful! We pray thee for safety in our goings forth and our standings still, in our words and our designs, in our dangers of temptation and doubts, and the secret designs of our hearts. Subject unto us this sea, even as thou didst subject the deep to Musa (Moses), and as thou didst subject the fire to Ibrahim* (Abraham), and as thou didst subject the iron to Dáúd†, (David), and as thou didst subject the wind and the devils and genii and mankind to Sulayman‡, (Solomon), and as thou didst subject the moon and El Burak to Mohammed, upon whom be Allah's mercy and his

* Abraham, for breaking his father's idols, was cast by Nimrod into a fiery furnace, which forthwith became a garden of roses. (See Chapter xxi. of the Koran, called "the Prophets.")

† David worked as an armourer, but the steel was as wax in his hands.

‡ Solomon reigned over the three orders of created beings; the fable of his flying carpet is well known. (See Chapter xxvii. of the Koran, called "the Ant.")

blessing! And subject unto us all the seas in earth and heaven, in the visible and in thine invisible worlds, the sea of this life, and the sea of futurity. O thou who reignest over everything, and unto whom all things return, Khyas! Khyas! Khyas!" * And lastly, we lie down upon our cribs, wrapped up in thickly padded cotton coverlets, and forget the troubles of the past day, and the discomforts of that to come.

Late on the evening of the 11th July we passed in sight of the narrow mouth of Akabah, whose *famosi rupes* are a terror to the voyagers of these latitudes. Like the Gulf of Cambay, here a tempest is said to be always brewing, and men raise their hands to pray as they cross it. We had no storm from without that day, but a fierce one was about to burst within our ship. The essence of Oriental discipline is personal respect based upon fear. Therefore it often happens, that the commanding officer, if a mild old gentleman, is the last person whose command is obeyed,—his only privilege being that of sitting apart from his inferiors. And such was the case with our Rais. On the present occasion, irritated by the refusal

* These are mystic words, and entirely beyond the reach of dictionaries and vocabularies.

of the Maghrabis to stand out of the steerman's way, and excited by the prospect of losing sight of shore for a whole day, he threatened one of the fellows with his slipper. It required all our exertions, even to a display of the dreaded quarter-staves, to calm the consequent excitement. After passing Akabah, we saw nothing but sea and sky, and we spent a weary night and day tossing upon the waters, — our only exercise: every face brightened as, about sunset on the 12th, we suddenly glided into the mooring place.

Marsa Damghah*—"Damghah Anchorage"—is scarcely visible from the sea. An islet of limestone rock defends the entrance, leaving a narrow passage on each side. It is not before he enters that the mariner discovers the extent and the depth of this creek, which indents far into the land, and offers 20 feet of fine clear anchorage which no swell can reach. Inside it looks more like a lake, and at night its colour is gloriously blue as Geneva itself. I could not help calling to mind, after dinner, the old school lines,

> "Est in secessu longo locus. Insula portum
> Efficit objecta laterum, quibus omnis ab alto
> Frangitur inque sinus scindit sese unda reductos."

---

* In Moresby's Survey, "Sherm Demerah," the creek of Demerah. Ali Bey calls it Demeg.

Nothing was wanted but the "atrum nemus." Where, however, shall we find such luxuries in arid Arabia?

The Rais, as usual, attempted to deter us from landing, by romancing about the "Bedoynes and Ascopards," representing them to be "folke ryghte felonouse and foule and of cursed kynde." To which we replied by shouldering our Nebuts and scrambling into the cock-boat. On shore we found a few wretched looking beings, "Jehaynahs*" seated upon heaps of dried wood, which they sold to travellers, and three boat loads of Syrian pilgrims who had preceded us. We often envied them their small swift craft, with their double latine sails disposed in "hare-ears," —which, about evening time in the far distance, looked like white gulls alighting upon the purple wave; and they justified our envy by arriving at

* These men of the Beni Jahaynah, or "Juhaynah" tribe— the "Beni Kalb," as they are also called,—must not be trusted. They extend from the plains north of Yambu into the Sinaitic Peninsula. They boast no connection with the great tribe El Harb; but they are of noble race, are celebrated for fighting, and, it is said, have good horses. The specimens we saw at Marsa Damghah were poor ones, they had few clothes, and no arms except the usual Jambiyah (crooked dagger). By their civility and their cringing style of address it was easy to see they had been corrupted by intercourse with strangers.

Yambu two days before us. The pilgrims had bivouacked upon the beach, and were engaged in drinking their after dinner coffee. They received us with all the rights of hospitality, as natives of the Medinah should every where be received; we sat an hour with them, ate a little fruit, satisfied our thirst, smoked their pipes, and when taking leave blessed them. Then returning to the vessel we fed, and lost no time in falling asleep.

The dawn of the next day saw our sail flapping in the idle air. And it was not without difficulty that in the course of the forenoon we entered Wijh Harbour, distant from Damghah but very few miles. Wijh is also a natural anchorage, in no way differing from that where we passed the night, except in being smaller and shallower. The town is a collection of huts meanly built of round stones, and clustering upon a piece of elevated rock on the northern side of the creek. It is distant about five miles from the inland fort of the same name, which receives the Egyptian caravan, and thrives, like its port, by selling water and provisions to pilgrims. The little bazaar, which the sea almost washes every high tide, provided us with mutton, rice, baked bread, and the other necessaries of life at a moderate rate. Luxuries also were to be found: a druggist sold me an ounce of opium at a Chinese price.

With reeling limbs we landed at Wijh*, and finding a large coffee-house above and over the beach, we installed ourselves there. But the Persians who preceded us had occupied all the shady places outside; we were forced to content ourselves with the interior. It was a building of artless construction, consisting of little but a roof supported by wooden posts, roughly hewn from date trees, and round the tamped earthen floor ran a raised bench of unbaked brick forming a divan for mats and sleeping rugs. In the centre a huge square Mastabah, or platform, answered a similar purpose. Here and there appeared attempts at long and side walls, but these superfluities had been allowed to admit daylight through large gaps. In one corner stood the apparatus of the "Kahvahji," an altar-like elevation, also of earthen work, containing a hole for a charcoal fire, upon which were three huge coffee pots dirtily tinned. Near it were ranged the Shishas, or Egyptian hookahs, old, exceedingly unclean, and worn

* It is written Wish, Wejh; by Ali Bey Vadjeh and Wadjih; Wodjeh and Wosh by Burckhardt; and Wedge by Moresby.

by age and hard work. A wooden framework, pierced with circular apertures, supported a number of porous earthenware *gûllehs* full of cold sweet water; the charge for these was, as usual in El Hejaz, five paras a piece. Such was the furniture of the café, and the only relief to the barrenness of the view was a fine mellowing atmosphere composed of smoke, steam, flies, and gnats in about equal proportions. I have been diffuse in my description of this coffee-house, as it was a type of its class: from Alexandria to Aden the traveller will everywhere meet with buildings of the same kind.

Our happiness in this Paradise—for such it was to us after the "Golden Wire"—was nearly sacrificed by Saad the Devil, whose abominable temper led him at once into a quarrel with the master of the coffee-house. And the latter, an ill-looking, squint-eyed, low-browed, broad-shouldered fellow showed himself no wise unwilling to meet the Devil half way. The two worthies, after a brief bandying of bad words, seized each other's throats leisurely, so as to give the spectators time and encouragement to interfere. But when friends and acquaintances were hanging on to both heroes so firmly that they could not move hand or arm, their wrath, as usual, rose, till it was terrible to see. The little village resounded with the war, and many a sturdy knave rushed in, sword or cudgel in hand, so as not to lose the sport. During the heat of the fray, a pistol which was in Omar Effendi's hand went off—accidentally of course—and the ball passed so close to the tins containing the black and muddy mocha, that it drew the attention of all parties. As if by magic, the storm was lulled. A friend recognised Saad the Devil, and swore that he was no black slave, but a soldier at El Medinah —"no waiter, but a Knight Templar," —this caused him to be looked upon as rather a superior person, which he proved by insisting that his late enemy should dine with him, and when the other decorously hung back, by dragging him to dinner with loud cries.

My character that day was severely tried. Besides the Persian pilgrims, a number of non-descripts who came in the same vessel were hanging about the coffee-house, lying down, smoking, drinking water, bathing and correcting their teeth with their daggers. One inquisitive man was always at my side. He called himself a Pathan (Afghan settled in India); he could speak five or six languages, knew a number of people everywhere, and had travelled far and wide over central Asia. These men are always good detectors of an incognito. I avoided answering his question about my native place, and after telling him that I had no longer name or nation, being a Dervish, asked him, when he insisted upon my having been born somewhere, to guess for himself. To my joy he claimed me for a brother Pathan, and in course of conversation he declared himself to be the nephew of an Afghan merchant, a gallant old man who had been civil to me at Cairo. We then sat smoking together with "effusion." Becoming confidential, he complained that he, a Sunni or orthodox Moslem, had been abused, maltreated, and beaten by his fellow travellers, the heretical pilgrims. I naturally offered to arm my party, to take up our cudgels, and to revenge my compatriot. This thoroughly Afghan style of doing business could not fail to make him sure of his man. He declined, however, wisely remembering that he had nearly a fortnight of the Persians' society still to endure. But he promised himself the gratification, when he reached Meccah, of sheathing his charay * in the chief offender's heart.

* The terrible Afghan knife.

At 8 A.M. next morning we left Wijh, after passing a night tolerably comfortable, by contrast, in the coffee-house. We took with us the stores necessary, for though our Rais had promised to anchor under Jebel Hasan that evening no one believed him. We sailed among ledges of rock, golden sands, green weeds, and in some places through yellow lines of what appeared to me at a distance foam after a storm. All day a sailor sat upon the mast-head, looking at the water, which was transparent as blue glass, and shouting out the direction. This precaution was somewhat stultified by the roar of voices, which never failed to mingle with the warning, but we wore every half hour, and did not run aground. About mid-day we passed by Shaykh Hasan el Marábit's tomb. It is the usual domed and whitewashed building, surrounded by the hovels of its guardians, standing upon a low flat island of yellow rock, vividly reminding me of certain scenes in Sindh. Its dreary position attracts to it the attention of passing travellers; the dead saint has a prayer and a Fát-hah for the good of his soul, and the live sinner wends his way with religious refreshment.

Near sunset the wind came on to blow freshly,

and we cast anchor together with the Persian pilgrims upon a rock. This was one of the celebrated coral reefs of the Red Sea, and the sight justified Forskal's emphatic description of it—*luxus lususque naturæ.* It was a huge ledge or platform rising but little above the level of the deep; the water-side was perpendicular as the wall of a fort, and whilst a frigate might have floated within a yard of it, every ripple dashed over the reef, replenishing the little basins and hollows in the surface. The colour of the waves near it was a vivid amethyst. In the distance the eye rested upon what appeared to be meadows of brilliant flowers resembling those of earth, only brighter far and more lovely. Nor was this land of the sea wholly desolate. Gulls and terns here swam the tide, there, seated upon the coral, devoured their prey. In the air, troops of birds contended noisily for a dead flying fish *, and in the deep water they

* These the Arabs, in the vulgar tongue, call Jerad el Bahr, "sea locusts;" as they term the shrimp Burghút el Bahr, or the sea-flea. Such compound words, palpably derived from land objects, prove the present Ichthyophagi and the Bedouins living on the coast to be a race originally from the interior. Pure and ancient Arabs still have at least one uncompounded word to express every object familiar to them, and it is in this point that the genius of the language chiefly shows itself.

chased a shoal, which, in their fright and hurry to escape the pursuers, veiled the surface with spray and foam. And as night came on the scene shifted, displaying fresh beauties. Shadows clothed the background, whose features, dimly revealed, allowed full scope to the imagination. In the forepart of the picture lay the sea, shining under the rays of the moon with a metallic lustre, while its border, where the wavelets dashed upon the reef, was lit by what the Arabs call the "jewels of the deep" * — brilliant flashes of phosphoric light giving an idea of splendour which art would strive in vain to imitate. Altogether it was a bit of fairy land, a spot for nymphs and sea-gods to disport upon: you might have heard, without astonishment, old Proteus calling his flocks with the writhed horn; and Aphrodite seated in her conch would have been only a fit and proper climax of its loveliness.

But — as philosophically remarked by Sir Cauline the Knyghte—

> "Every whyte must have its blacke,
> And every sweete its soure—"

* The Arab superstition is, that these flashes of light are jewels made to adorn the necks and hair of the mermaids and mermen. When removed from their native elements the gems fade and disappear. If I remember right, there is some idea similar to this among the Scotch, and other northern people.

this charming coral reef was nearly being the scene of an ugly accident. The breeze from seaward slowly but steadily drove us towards the reef, a fact of which we soon became conscious. Our anchor was not dragging; it had not rope enough to touch the bottom, and vainly we sought for more. In fact the "Golden Wire" was as disgracefully deficient in all the appliances of safety, as any English merchantman in the nineteenth century, —a circumstance which accounts for the shipwrecks and the terrible loss of life perpetually occurring about the pilgrimage season in these seas. Had she struck upon the razor-like edges of the coral reef, she would have melted away like a sugar-plum in the ripple, for the tide was rising at the time. Having nothing better to do, we began to make as much noise as possible. Fortunately for us the Rais commanding the Persian's boat was an Arab from Jeddah, and more than once we had treated him with great civility. Guessing the cause of our distress, he sent two sailors overboard with a rope; they swam gallantly up to us; and in a few minutes we were safely moored to the stern of our useful neighbour. Which done, we applied ourselves to the grateful task of beating our Rais, and richly had he deserved it. Before noon, when the wind was shifting, he had not given himself the trouble to wear once; and when the breeze fell he preferred dosing to taking advantage of what little wind remained: with energy we might have been moored that night comfortably under the side of Mount Hasan, instead of floating about on an unquiet sea with a lee-shore of coral reef within a few yards of our counter.

At dawn next day we started; we made Jebel Hasan * about noon, and an hour or so before sunset we glided into Marsa Maliar. Our resting-place resembled Marsa Damghah at an humble distance; the sides of the cove, however, were bolder and more precipitous. The limestone rocks presented a peculiar appearance in some places the base and walls had crumbled away, leaving a coping to project like a canopy; in others the wind and rain had cut deep holes, and pierced the friable material with caverns that looked like the work of art. There was a pretty opening of backwood at the bottom of the

* The word Jebel will frequently occur in these pages. It is applied by the Arabs to any rising ground or heap of rocks, and, therefore, must not always be translated "mountain." In the latter sense, it has found its way into some of the Mediterranean dialects. Gibraltar is Jebel el Tarik, and "Mt. Ethne that men clepen Mounte Gybelle" is "Monte Gibello," —*the* mountain, par excellence.

cove, and palm trees in the blue distance gladdened our eyes, which pined for the sight of something green. The Rais, as usual, would have terrified us with a description of the Hutazmi tribe that holds these parts, and I knew from Welsted and Moresby that it is a troublesome race. But forty-eight hours of cramps on board-ship would make a man think lightly of a much more imminent danger.

Wading on shore we cut our feet with the sharp rocks. I remember to have felt the acute pain of something running into my toe, but after looking at the place and extracting what appeared to be a bit of thorn *, I dismissed the subject, little guessing the trouble it was to give me. Having scaled the rocky side of the cove, we found some half naked Arabs lying in the shade; they were unarmed, and had nothing about them except their villanous countenances wherewith to terrify the most timid. These men still live in caves, like the Shamud tribe of tradition; they are still Ichthyophagi, existing without any other subsistence but

* It was most probably a prickle of the "egg-fruit," or *Echinus*, so common in these seas, generally supposed to be poisonous. I found it impossible to cure my foot in El Hejaz, and every remedy seemed to make it worse. This was as much the effect of the climate of Arabia, as of the hardships and privations of a pilgrimage. After my return to Egypt in the autumn, the wound healed readily without medical treatment.

what the sea affords. They were unable to provide us with dates or milk, but they sold us a kind of fish called Bui, which, boiled upon the embers, proved delicious.

After we had eaten and drunk and smoked, we began to make merry; and the Persians, who, fearing to come on shore, had kept to their conveyance, appeared proper butts for the wit of some of our party: one of whom stood up and pronounced the orthodox call to prayer, after which the rest joined in a polemical hymn, exalting the virtues and dignity of the three first Caliphs.† Then, as general on such occasions, the matter was made personal by informing the Persians in a kind of rhyme sung by the Meccan *gamins*, that they were the "slippers of Ali and the dogs of Omar." But as they were too frightened to reply, my companions gathered up their cooking utensils, and returned to the "Golden Wire," melancholy, like disappointed candidates for the honours of Donnybrook.

Our next day was a silent and a weary one, for we were all heartily sick of being on board-ship. We should have made Yambu in the evening but for

* Abubekr, Omar, and Osman.

the laziness of the Rais. Having duly beaten him, we anchored on the open coast, insufficiently protected by a reef, and almost in sight of our destination. In the distance rose Jebel Radhwah or Radhwa *, one of the "Mountains of Paradise" † in which honoured Arabia abounds. It is celebrated by poetry as well as by piety.

> "Were Radwah to strive to support my woes,
> Radwah itself would be crushed by the weight."

says Antar.‡ It supplies El Medinah with hones. I heard much of its valleys and fruits and bubbling springs, but afterwards learned to rank these tales with the superstitious legends which are attached to it. Gazing at its bare and ghastly heights, one of our party, whose wit was soured by the want of fresh bread, surlily remarked that such a heap of ugliness deserved ejection from heaven, — an irreverence which was too public to escape

* I have found both these forms of writing the word in books; Moresby, or rather Mr. Rassam, erroneously spells it "Ridwah."

† In a future chapter, when describing a visit to Mt. Shoa, near El Medinah, I shall enter into some details about these "Mountains of Paradise."

‡ The translator, however, erroneously informs us, in a footnote, that Radwah is a mountain near Meccah.

general denunciation. He waded on shore, cooked there and passed the night; we were short of fresh water, which, combined with other grievances, made us as surly as bears. Saad the Devil was especially vicious; his eyes gazed fixedly on the ground, his lips protruded till you might have held his face by them, his mouth was garnished with bad wrinkles, and he never opened it but he grumbled out a wicked word. He solaced himself that evening by crawling slowly on all fours over the boy Mohammed, taking scrupulous care to place one knee upon the sleeper's face. The youth awoke in a fiery rage; we all roared with laughter, and the sulky Negro, after savouring the success of his spite, grimly, as but half satisfied, rolled himself into a ball like a hedgehog, and, resolving to be offensive even in his forgetfulness, snored violently all night.

We slept upon the sands and arose before dawn, determined to make the Rais start in time that day. A slip of land separated us from our haven, but the wind was foul, and by reason of rocks and shoals, we had to make a considerable *detour*.

It was about noon on the 12th day after our departure from Suez, when, after slowly beating up the narrow creek leading to Yambu harbour, we sprang into a shore boat and felt new life, when bidding an eternal adieu to the "Golden Wire."

I might have escaped much of this hardship and suffering by hiring a vessel to myself. There would then have been a cabin to retire into at night, and shade from the sun; moreover the voyage would have lasted five, not twelve days. But I wished to witness the scenes on board a pilgrim ship,—scenes so much talked of by the Moslem palmer home returned. Moreover the hire was exorbitant, ranging from 40*l.* to 50*l.*, and it would have led to a greater expenditure, as the man who can afford to take a boat must pay in proportion during his land journey. In these countries you perforce go on as you begin: to "break one's expenditure," that is to say, to retrench expenses, is considered all but impossible; the prudent traveller therefore will begin as he intends to go on.

CHAP. XII.

THE HALT AT YAMBU.

The heat of the sun, the heavy dews, and the frequent washings of the waves, had so affected my foot, that on landing at Yambu, I could scarcely place it upon the ground. But traveller's duty was to be done; so, leaning upon my "slave's" shoulder, I started at once to see the town, whilst Shaykh Hamid and the others of our party proceeded to the custom-house.

Yanbu el Bahr, Yambu of the sea*, the Iambia village of Ptolemy, is a place of considerable importance, and shares with others the title of "Gate of the Holy City." It is the third quarter of the caravan road† from Cairo to Meccah; and

* Yanbua "in Arabic is a fountain." Yanbua of the sea "is so called to distinguish it from Yanbua of the palm-grounds," a village at the foot of the mountains, about 18 or 20 miles distant from the sea-port. Ali Bey places it one day's journey E.¼ N.E. from Yanbua el Bahr, and describes it as a pleasant place in a fertile valley.

† The first quarter of the Cairo caravan is Akabah; the second is the Manhal Salmah (Salmah's place for watering camels); the third is Yambu; and the fourth Meccah.

here, as well as at El Bedr, pilgrims frequently leave behind them in hired warehouses goods too heavy to be transported in haste, or too valuable to risk in dangerous times. Yambu being the port of El Medinah, as Jeddah is of Meccah, is supported by a considerable transport trade and extensive imports from the harbour on the western coasts of the Red Sea. Here the Sultan's dominion is supposed to begin, whilst the authority of the Pacha of Egypt ceases; there is no Nizám, however, in the town*, and the governor is a Sheríf or Arab chief. I met him in the great bazaar; he is a fine young man of light complexion and the usual high profile, handsomely dressed, with a Cashmere turban, armed to the extent of sword and dagger, and followed by two large fierce-looking Negro slaves leaning upon enormous nebúts.

The town itself is in no wise remarkable. Built on the edge of a barren plain that extends between the mountains and the sea, it fronts the northern

* The Nizam, as Europeans now know, is the regular Turkish infantry. In El Hejaz, these troops are not stationed in small towns like Yambu. At such places a party of irregular horse, for the purpose of escorting travellers, is deemed sufficient. The Yambu police seems to consist of the Sheríf's sturdy negroes. In Ali Bey's time, Yambu belonged to the Sheríf of Meccah, and was garrisoned by him.

extremity of a narrow winding creek. Viewed from the harbour, it is a long line of buildings, whose painful whiteness is set off by a sky like cobalt and a sea like indigo; behind it lies the flat, here of a bistre-brown, there of a lively tawny; whilst the background is formed by dismal Radhwah,

"Barren and bare, unsightly, unadorned."

Outside the walls are a few little domes and tombs, which by no means merit attention. Inside, the streets are wide and each habitation is placed at an unsociable distance from its neighbour, except near the port and the bazaars, where ground is valuable. The houses are roughly built of limestone and coralline, and their walls full of fossils crumble like almond cake; they have huge hanging windows, and look mean after those in the Moslem quarters of Cairo. There is a large "Suk," or market-place in the usual form, a long narrow lane darkened by a covering of palm leaves, with little shops let into the walls of the houses on both sides. The cafés, which abound here, have already been described in the last chapter; they are rendered dirty in the extreme by travellers, and it is impossible to sit in them without a fan to drive away the flies. The custom-house fronts the landing place upon the harbour; it is managed by Turkish officials,—men dressed in tarbooshes, who repose the live-long day upon the divans near the windows. In the case of us travellers they had a very simple way of doing business, charging each person of the party three piastres for each large box, but by no means troubling themselves to meddle with the contents.* Yambu also boasts of a Hammam or hot bath, a mere date leaf shed, tenanted by an old Turk, who, with his surly Albanian assistant, lives by "cleaning" pilgrims and travellers. Some white-washed mosques and minarets of exceedingly simple form, a Wakálah or two for the reception of merchants, and a saint's tomb, complete the list of public buildings.

In one point Yambu claims superiority over most other towns in this part of El Hejaz. Those who can afford the luxury drink sweet rain water, collected amongst the hills in tanks and cisterns, and brought on camel back to the town two

* This, as far as I could learn, is the only tax which the Sultan's government derives from the northern Hejaz; the people declare it to be, as one might expect at this distance from the capital, liable to gross peculation. When the Wakhabis held Yambu, they taxed it, like all other places; for which reason their name is held in the liveliest abhorrence.

sources are especially praised, the Ayn el Birkat, and the Ayn Ali, which suffice to supply the whole population; but the brackish water of the wells is confined to coarser purposes. Some of the old people here, as at Suez, are said to prefer the drink to which years of habit have accustomed them, and it is a standing joke that, arrived at Cairo, they salt the water of the Nile to make it palatable.

The population of Yambu,—one of the most bigoted and quarrelsome races in El Hejaz—strikes the eye after arriving from Egypt, as decidedly a new feature. The Shaykh or gentleman of Yambu is over-armed and over-dressed as Fashion, the tyrant of the desert as well as of the court, dictates to a person of his consequence. The civilised traveller from El Medinah sticks in his waist-shawl a loaded pistol *, garnished with crimson silk cord, but he partially conceals the butt end under the flap of his jacket. The irregular soldier struts down the street a small armoury

* Civilians usually stick one pistol in the belt; soldiers and fighting-men two, or more, with all the necessary concomitants of pouches, turn-screws, and long iron ramrods, which, opening with a screw, disclose a long thin pair of pincers, wherewith fire is put upon the chibouque.

of weapons: one look at the man's countenance suffices to tell you what he is. Here and there stalk grim Bedouins, wild as their native wastes, and in all the dignity of pride and dirt; they also are armed to the teeth, and even the presence of the policeman's quarter staff* cannot keep their swords in their scabbards: what we should call the peaceful part of the population never leave the house without a "nebút" over the right shoulder, and the larger, the longer, and the heavier the weapon is, the more gallantry does the bearer claim. The people of Yambu practise the use of this implement diligently; they become expert in delivering a head blow so violent as to break through any guard, and with it they always decide their trivial quarrels.† The dress of the women differs

* The weapons with which nations are to be managed form a curious consideration. The Englishman tamely endures a staff, which would make a Frenchman mad with anger; and a Frenchman respects a sabre, which would fill an Englishman's bosom with civilian spleen. You order the Egyptian to strip and be flogged; he makes no objection to seeing his blood flow in this way; but were a cutting weapon used, his friends would stop at nothing in their fury.

† In Arabia, generally, the wound is less considered by justice and revenge, than the instrument with which it was inflicted. Sticks and stones are held to be venial weapons: guns and pistols, swords and daggers, are felonious.

but little from that of the Egyptians, except in the face veil *, which is generally white. There is an independent bearing about the people, strange in the East; they are proud without insolence, and look manly without blustering. Their walk partakes somewhat of the nature of a strut, owing, perhaps, to the shape of the sandals, not a little assisted by the self-esteem of the wearer, but there is nothing offensive in it; moreover, the population has a healthy appearance, and, fresh from Egypt, I could not help noticing their freedom from ophthalmic disease. The children, too, appear vigorous, nor are they here kept in that state of filth to which fear of the Evil Eye devotes them in the valley of the Nile.

My companion found me in a coffee-house, where I had sat down to rest from the fatigue of halting on my wounded foot through the town. They had

* Europeans inveigh against this article,—which represents the "loup" of Louis XIV.'s time,—for hideousness and jealous concealment of charms made to be looked at. It is, on the contrary, the most coquettish article of woman's attire, excepting, perhaps, the *Lisam* of Constantinople. It conceals coarse skins, fleshy noses, wide mouths, and vanishing chins, whilst it sets off to best advantage what in these lands is almost always lustrous and liquid—the eye. Who has not remarked this at a masquerade ball?

passed their boxes through the custom-house, and were now inquiring "Where's the Effendi?" in all directions. After sitting for half an hour, we rose to depart, when an old Arab merchant whom I had met at Suez, politely insisted upon paying for my coffee, still a mark of attention in Arabia as it was whilome in France; we then went to a Wakálah, near the bazaar, in which my companions had secured an airy upper room on the terrace opposite the sea, and tolerably free from Yambu's plague, the flies. It had been tenanted by a party of travellers, who were introduced to me as Omar Effendi's brothers; he had by accident met them in the streets the day before their start for Constantinople, where they were travelling to receive the Ikran.* The family was, as I have said before, from Daghistan (Circassia), and the male members still showed unequivocal signs of a northern origin, in light yellowish skins, grey eyes fringed with dark lashes, red lips, and a very scant beard. They were broad-shouldered, large-limbed men, distinguished in look only by a peculiar surliness of countenance; perhaps their expression was the result of their

* A certain stipend allowed by the Sultan to citizens of the *Haramani* (Meccah and El Medinah). It will be treated of at length in a future chapter.

suspecting me; for I observed them watching every movement narrowly during *Wuzûe* and prayers. There was a good opportunity for displaying the perfect *nonchalance* of a true believer, and my efforts were, I believe, successful, for afterwards they seemed to treat me as a mere stranger, from whom they could expect nothing, and who therefore was hardly worth their notice.

On the afternoon of the day of our arrival we sent for a *Mukharrij**, and began to treat for camels. One Amm Jemal, a respectable native of El Medinah who was on his way home, undertook to be the spokesman: after a long palaver, (for the Shaykh of the camels and his attendant Bedouins were men that fought for farthings, and we were not far inferior to them,) a bargain was struck. We agreed to pay three dollars for each camel, half in ready money, the other half after reaching our destination, and to start on the evening of the next day with a grain-caravan, guarded by an escort of irregular cavalry. I hired two animals,

* The Shaykh, or agent of the camels, without whose assistance it would be difficult to hire beasts. He brings the Bedouins with him, talks them over to fair terms, sees the "arbún," or earnest-money, delivered to them, and is answerable for their not failing in their engagement.

one for my luggage and servant, the other for the boy Mohammed and myself, expressly stipulating, that we were to ride the better, and that if it broke down on the road, its place should be supplied by another as good. My friends could not dissemble their uneasiness, when informed by the *Mukharrij*, that the Hazimi tribe was "out," and that travellers had to fight every day. The Daghistanis also contributed to their alarm. "We met," said they, "between 200 and 300 devils on a Razzia near El Medinah; we gave them the Salam, but they would not reply, although we were all on dromedaries. Then they asked us if we were men of El Medinah, and we replied 'Yes,' and lastly, they wanted to know the end of our journey; so we said Bir Abbas."* The Bedouins who had accompanied the Daghistanis belonged to some tribe unconnected

* The not returning "Salam" was a sign on the part of the Bedouins that they were out to fight, and not to make friends; and the dromedary riders, who generally travel without much to rob, thought this behaviour a declaration of desperate designs. The Bedouins asked if they were El Medinah men; because the former do not like, unless when absolutely necessary, to plunder the people of the Holy city. And the Daghistanis said their destination was Bir Abbas, a neighbouring, instead of Yambu, a distant post, because those who travel on a long journey, being supposed to have more funds with them, are more likely to be molested.

with the Hazimi: the spokesman rolled his head, as much as to say "Allah has preserved us!" And a young Indian of the party, —I shrewdly suspect him of having stolen my pen-knife that night,— displayed the cowardice of a "*Miyan* *," by looking aghast at the memory of his imminent and deadly risk. "Sir," said Shaykh Nur to me, "we must wait till all this is over." I told him to hold his tongue, and sharply reproved the boy Mohammed, upon whose manner the effect of finding himself suddenly in a fresh country had wrought a change for the worse. "Why ye were lions at Cairo —and here, at Yambu, you are cats—hens!" † It was not long, however, before the youth's impudence returned upon him with increased violence.

We sat through the afternoon in the little room on the terrace, whose reflected heat, together with

* "*Miyan*," the Hindostani word for "Sir," is known to the Bedouins all over El Hejaz; they always address Indian Moslems with this word, which has become contemptuous, on account of the low esteem in which the race is held.

† That is to say, sneaks and cowards. I was astonished to see our Maghrabi fellow-passengers in the bazaar at Yambu cringing and bowing to us, more like courtiers than Bedouins. Such, however, is the effect of a strange place upon Orientals generally. In the Persians such humility was excusable; in no part of El Hejaz are they for a moment safe from abuse and blows.

the fiery winds from the wilderness, seemed to incommode even my companions. After sunset we dined in the open air, a body of twenty: master, servants, children and strangers. All the procurable rugs and pillows had been seized to make a divan, and we all squatted round a large cauldron of boiled rice, containing square masses of mutton, the whole covered with clarified butter. Saad the Devil was now in his glory. With what anecdotes the occasion supplied him!—his tongue seemed to wag with a perpetual motion—for each man he had a boisterous greeting, and to judge from his whisperings he must have been in every one's privacy and confidence. Conversation over pipes and coffee was prolonged to 10 P.M.—a late hour in these lands; then we prayed the Ishah *, and, spreading our mats upon the terrace, slept in the open air.

The forenoon of the next day was occupied in making sundry small purchases. We laid in seven days' provisions for the journey, repacked our boxes, polished and loaded our arms, and attired ourselves appropriately for the road. By the advice of Amm Jemal † I dressed as an Arab,

* The night prayer.

† "Amm" means literally a paternal uncle. In the Hejaz

in order to avoid paying the *Jizyat*, a capitation tax*, which upon this road the settled tribes extort from stranger travellers; and he warned me not to speak any language but Arabic, even to my slave, in the vicinity of a village. I bought for my own conveyance a *shugduf* or litter † for

it is prefixed to the names of respectable men, who may also be addressed "Ya Amm Jemal!" (O Uncle Jemal!) To say "Ya Ammi!" (O my Uncle!) is more familiar, and would generally be used by a superior addressing an inferior.

* Jizyat properly means the capitation tax levied on infidels; in this land of intense pride, the Bedouins, and even the town-chiefs, apply the opprobrious term to black mail extorted from travellers, even of their own creed.

† The shugduf of El Hejaz differs greatly from that used in Syria and other countries. It is composed of two corded cots 5 feet long, slung horizontally, and parallel with the camel's sides, about half-way down. These cots have short legs, and at the halt may be used as bedsteads; the two are connected together by loose ropes, attached to the inner long sides of the framework, and these are thrown over the camel's packsaddle. Thick twigs inserted in the ends and the outer long sides of the framework, are bent over the top, bower-fashion, to support matting, carpets, and any other protection against the sun. There is an opening in this kind of wicker-work in front (towards the camel's head), through which you creep, and a similar one behind creates a draught of wind. Outside, towards the camel's tail, are pockets containing *gûllehs*, or earthenware bottles, of cooled water. Inside, attached to the wicker-work, are large provision pouches, similar

which I paid two dollars. It is a vehicle appropriated to women and children, fathers of families, married men, "Shelebis *," and generally to those who are too effeminate to ride. My reason for choosing it was that notes are more easily taken in it than on a dromedary's back; the excuse of lameness prevented it detracting from my manhood, and I wás careful when entering any populous place to borrow or hire a saddled beast.

Our party dined early that day, for the camels had been sitting at the gate since noon. We had the usual trouble in loading them: the owners of the animals vociferating about the unconscionable

to those used in old-fashioned travelling chariots. At the bottom are spread the two beds.

The greatest disadvantage of the shugduf is the difficulty of keeping balance. Two men ride in it, and their weights must be made to tally. Moreover, it is liable to be caught and torn by thorn trees, to be blown off in a gale of wind; and its awkwardness causes the camel repeated falls, which are most likely to smash it. Yet it is not necessarily an uncomfortable machine. Those for sale in the bazaar are of course worthless, being made of badly seasoned wood. But private litters are sometimes pleasant vehicles, with turned and painted framework, silk cordage, and valuable carpets. The often described Mahmal is nothing but a Syrian shugduf, royally ornamented.

* "Exquisites."

HANHART LITH.

AN ARAB SHAYK.

IN HIS TRAVELLING DRESS.

weight, the owners of the goods swearing that such weight a child could carry, while the beasts, taking part with their proprietors, moaned piteously, roared, made vicious attempts to bite, and started up with an agility that threw the half secured boxes or sacks headlong to the ground. About 3 P.M all was ready — the camels formed into Indian file, and were placed standing in the streets — but, as usual with Oriental travellers, all the men dispersed about the town, so we did not mount before it was late in the afternoon.

I must now take the liberty of presenting to the reader an Arab Shaykh fully equipped for travelling.* Nothing can be more picturesque than the costume, and it is with regret that we see it exchanged in the towns and more civilised parts for any other. The long locks or the shaven scalps are surmounted by a white cotton skull-cap, over which is a kufiyah — a large square kerchief of silk and cotton mixed, and generally of a dull red colour with a bright yellow border,

* It is the same rule with the Arab, on the road as at home; the more he is dressed the greater is his respectability. For this reason, you see Sherifs and other men of high family, riding or walking in their warm camel's hair robes on the hottest days. Another superstition of the Arabs is this, that thick clothes avert the evil effects of the sun's beams.

from which depend crimson silk twist ending in little tassels that reach the wearer's waist. Doubled into a triangle, and bound with an *Aakal** or fillet of rope, a skein of yarn or a twist of wool, the kerchief fits the head closely behind: it projects over the forehead, shading the eyes, and thus gives a fierce look to the countenance. On certain occasions one end is brought round the lower part of the face, and is fastened behind the head, leaving only the eyes visible. This veiling the features is technically called *Lisam:* the chiefs generally fight so, and it is the usual disguise when a man fears the avenger of blood, or a woman starts to take her *Sar.*† In hot weather it is supposed to keep the Simoom, in cold weather the catarrh, from the lungs.

* Sherifs and other great men sometimes bind a white turban or a Cashmere shawl round the kerchief, to keep it in its place. The Aakal varies in every part of the country. Here it is a twist of dyed wool, there a bit of common rope, three or four feet long. Some of the Arab tribes use a circlet of wood, composed of little round pieces, the size of a shilling, joined side by side, and inlaid with mother-of-pearl. The Eastern Arabs wear a large circle of brown wool, almost a turban in itself. In Barbary, they twist bright-coloured cloth round a rope, and adorn it with thick golden thread.

† Generally written "*Thar,*" the blood-revenge.

The body dress is simply a *Kamís* or cotton shirt; tight sleeved, opening in front, and adorned round the waist and collar, and down the breast, with embroidery like net-work, it extends from neck to foot. Some wear wide trousers, but the Bedouins consider such things effeminate, and they have not yet fallen into the folly of socks and stockings. Over the Kamís is thrown a long skirted and short-sleeved cloak of camel's hair, called an Aba. It is made in many patterns, and of all materials from pure silk to coarse sheep's wool; some prefer it brown, others white, others striped: in El Hejaz the favourite Aba is a white one, embroidered with gold *, tinsel, or yellow thread in two large triangles, capped with broad bands and other figures running down the shoulders and sides of the back. It is lined inside the shoulders and breast with handsome stuffs of silk and cotton mixed, and is tied in front by elaborate strings, and tassels or acorns of silk and gold. A sash confines the Kamís at the waist, and supports the silver-hilted *Jambíyah* †

* Gold, however, as well as silk, I may be excused for repeating, is a forbidden article of ornament to the Moslem.

† The silver-hilted dagger is a sign of dignity: "I would silver my dagger," in idiomatic Hejazi, means, "I would raise myself in the world."

or crooked dagger, and the picturesque Arab sandal*, complete the costume. Finally, the Shaykh's arms are a matchlock slung behind his back, and a sword; in his right hand he carries a light crooked stick about two feet and a half long, called a *Mas-hab*†, used for guiding camels, or a short javelin.‡

* Niebuhr has accurately described this article. It is still worn in the Madras army, though long discarded from the other presidencies; the main difference between the Indian and the Arab sandal is, that the former has a ring, into which the big toe is inserted, and the latter a thong, which is clasped between the big toe and its neighbour. Both of them are equally uncomfortable, and equally injurious to soldiers, whose legs fight as much as do their arms. They abrade the skin wherever the straps touch, expose the feet to the sun, wind, and rain, and admit thorns and flints to the toes and toe-nails.

In Arabia, the traveller may wear, if he pleases, slippers, but they are considered townsman-like and effeminate. They must be of the usual colours, red or yellow. Black shoes, though almost universally worn by the Turks at Cairo and Constantinople, would most probably excite suspicion in El Hejaz.

† The Mas-hab is of almond, generally brought from Syria; at the thick end is a kind of crook, formed by cutting off a bit of the larger branch from which the stick grows. This crook is afterwards cut into the shape useful to seize a camel's nose-ring, or a horse's bridle. Arabs of all degrees are fond of carrying these sticks. [It is also called *Máhgin.*]

‡ The *Mizrák,* as it is called, is peculiar to certain tribes, as

The poorer class of Arabs twist round their waist, next to the skin, a long plait of greasy leather, to support the back, and they gird the shirt at the middle merely with a cord, or with a coarse sash. The dagger is stuck in the sash, and, a bandoleer slung

the Karaghi and the Lahyami, and some, like the Hindayli near Meccah, make very pretty as well as very useful darts. The head is 15 or 16 inches long, nowhere broader than an inch, and tapering gradually to a fine point; its shape is two shallow prisms joined at their bases, and its socket, round like that of all lances, measures a little less than 2 inches. The lower third of the blade only is adorned with bars, lozenges, and cones of brass let into the iron in zig-zag and other figures. The shaft is of hard pliant wood—I do not know of what tree—well seasoned with grease and use; it is 23 inches long, and strengthened and adorned at distances of half an inch apart by bands of fine brass wire, about one inch and a half long. The heel of the weapon is a blunt spike, 14 inches long, used to stick it in the ground, and this, as well as the lower third of the blade, are ornamented with brass work. Being well balanced, the Mizrak is a highly efficient weapon for throwing in hunting, and by its handsome appearance adds not a little to the bearer's dignity.

But the stranger must be careful how he so arms himself. Unless he be undistinguishable from a Bedouin, by carrying a weapon peculiar to certain clans, he will expose himself to suspicion, or to laughter. And to offend an Arab of El Hejaz mortally, you have only to say bluntly, "Sell me thy spear." The proper style of address to the man whose necessities compel him to break through one of his "points d'honneur," is to say, "Give me that javelin, and I will satisfy thee;" after which he will haggle for each copper piece as though you were cheapening a sheep.

over the shoulders carries their cartridge-case, powder-flask, flint and steel, priming-horn, and other necessaries. With the traveller, the waist is an elaborate affair. Below all is worn the money pouch, concealed by the Kamís; the latter is girt with a waist shawl, over which is strapped a leathern belt * for carrying arms. The latter article should always be well garnished with a pair of long-barrelled and silver-mounted flint pistols †, a large and a small dagger, and an iron

* This article is composed of several oblong pieces of leather cut out to fit the front part of the body; between each fold there is room enough to stick a weapon; a substantial strap fastens it round the waist, and it serves to defend the sash or the shirt from iron mould, and the stains of gunpowder. It is made of all kinds of material, from plain Morocco leather to the richest velvet embroidered with gold.

† It is as well to have a good pair of Turkish barrels and stocks, fitted up with locks of European manufacture; those made by natives of these countries can never be depended upon. The same will apply to the gun or rifle. Upon the whole, it is more prudent to have flint locks. Copper caps are now sold in the bazaars of Meccah and El Medinah, where a Colt's "six-shooter" might excite attention for a day; but were the owner in a position to despise notoriety, he might display it everywhere without danger. One of our guards, who was killed on the road, had a double-barrelled English fowling-piece. Still, when doubts must not be aroused, the traveller will do well to avoid, even in the civilised Hejaz, suspicious appearances in his weapons. I carried in a secret

ramrod with pincers inside; a little leathern pouch fastened to the waist strap on the right side contains cartridge, wadding, and a flask of priming powder. The sword hangs over the shoulder with crimson silk cords and huge tassels*: well-dressed men apply the same showy ornaments to their pistols. In the hand may be carried a bell-mouthed blunderbuss, or, better still, a long single-barrel gun with an ounce bore. All these weapons must shine like silver,

pocket a small pistol with a spring dagger, upon which dependence could be placed, and I was careful never to show it, discharging it and loading it always in the dark.

Some men wear a little dagger strapped round the leg, below the knee. Its use is this: when the enemy gets you under, he can prevent you bringing your hand up to the weapon in your waist-belt; but before he cuts your throat, you may slip your fingers down to the knee, and persuade him to stop by a stab in the perineum. This knee dagger is required only in very dangerous places. The article I chiefly accused myself of forgetting was a stout English clasp-knife, with a large handle, a blade like an "Arkansas toothpick," and possessing the other useful appliances of picker, fleam, tweezers, lancet, and punch.

* Called "Habak:" these cords are made in great quantities at Cairo, which possesses a special bazaar for them, and are exported to all the neighbouring countries, where their price considerably increases. A handsome pistol-cord, with its tassels, costs about 12 shillings in Egypt; at Meccah, or El Medinah, the same would fetch upwards of a pound sterling.

if you wish to be respected; for attention to arms is here a sign of manliness.

Pilgrims, especially those from Turkey, carry a "Hamail," to denote their holy errand. This is a pocket Koran, in a handsome gold embroidered crimson velvet or red morocco case, slung by red silk cords over the left shoulder. It must hang down by the right side, and should never for respect depend below the waist-belt. For this I substituted a most useful article. To all appearance a "Hamail," it had inside three compartments, one for my watch and compass, the second for ready money, and the third contained penknife, pencils, and slips of paper, which I could hold concealed in the hollow of my hand. These were for writing and drawing: opportunities of making a "fair copy" into the diary-book*,

* My diary-book was made up for me by a Cairene; it was a long thin volume fitting into a breast-pocket, where it could be carried without being seen. I began by writing notes in the Arabic character, but as no risk appeared, my journal was afterwards kept in English. More than once, by way of experiment, I showed the writing on a loose slip of paper to my companions, and astonished them with the strange character derived from Solomon and Alexander, the Lord of the two Horns, which we Afghans still use.

For a short trip a pencil suffices; on long journeys ink is

are never wanting to the acute traveller. He must, however, beware of sketching before the Bedouins, who would certainly proceed to extreme measures, suspecting him to be a spy or a sorcerer.*

necessary; the latter article should be English, not Eastern, which is washed out clean the first time your luggage is thoroughly soaked with rain. The traveller may use either the Persian or the brass Egyptian ink-stand; the latter, however, is preferable, being stronger and less likely to break. But, unless he be capable of writing and reading a letter correctly, it would be unadvisable to stick such an article in the waist-belt, as this gives out publicly that he is a scribe.

When sketching, the pencil is the best, because the simplest and shortest mode of operation is required. Important lines should afterwards be marked with ink, as "fixing" is impossible on such journeys. For prudence sake, when my sketches were made, I cut up the paper into square pieces, numbered them for future reference, and hid them in the tin canisters that contained my medicines.

* An accident of this kind happened not long ago to a German traveller in Hadramaut, who shall be nameless. He had the mortification to see his sketch-book, the labour of months, summarily appropriated and destroyed by the Arabs. I was told by a Hadramaut man at Cairo, and by several at Aden, that the gentleman had at the time a narrow escape with his life; the Bedouins wished to put him to death as a spy, sent by the Frank to *ensorceler* their country, but the Shaykhs forbade bloodshed, and merely deported the offender. Travellers caught sketching are not often treated with such forbearance.

Nothing so effectually puzzles these people as our habit of putting every thing on paper; their imaginations are set at work, and then the worst may be expected from them. The only safe way of writing in presence of a Bedouin would be when drawing out a horoscope or preparing a charm; he also objects not, if you can warm his heart upon the subject, to seeing you take notes in a book of genealogies. You might begin with, "And you, men of Harb, on which origin do you pride yourselves?" And while the listeners become fluent upon the, to them, all interesting theme, you could put down whatever you please upon the margin. The towns-people are more liberal, and years ago the holy shrines have been drawn, and even lithographed, by Eastern artists: still, if you wish to avoid all suspicion, you must rarely be seen with pen or with pencil in hand.

At 6 P.M. descending the stairs of our Wakálat, we found the camels standing loaded in the street and shifting their ground in token of impatience.*

* All Arabs assert that it pains the loaded camel's feet to stand still, and, certainly, the "fidgettiness" of the animal to start, looks as if he had some reason to prefer walking.

My shugduf, perched upon the back of a tall strong animal, nodded and swayed about with his every motion, impressing me with the idea that the first step would throw it over the shoulders or the crupper. The camel-men told me I must climb up the animal's neck, and so creep into the vehicle. But my foot disabling me from such exertion, I insisted upon their bringing the beast to squat, which they did grumblingly.* We took leave of Omar Effendi's brothers and their dependents, who insisted upon paying us the compliment of accompanying us to the gate. Then we mounted and started, which was a signal for all our party to disperse once more. Some heard the report of a vessel having arrived from Suez, with Mahommed Shiklibah and other friends on board; these hurried down to the harbour for a parting word. Others, declaring they had forgotten some necessaries for the way, ran off to the bazaar to spend one last hour in gossip at the coffee-house. Then the sun

* It often strains the camel to rise with a full shugduf on his back, besides which the motion is certain to destroy the vehicle in a few days. Those who are unable to climb up the camel's neck usually carry with them a short ladder.

set, and prayers must be said. The brief twilight had almost faded away before all had mounted. With loud cries of "Wassat, ya hú!" and "Jannib, y'al Jammál!" * we threaded our way through long, dusty, narrow streets, flanked with white-washed habitations at considerable intervals, and large heaps of rubbish, sometimes higher than the houses. We were stopped at the gate to ascertain if we were strangers, in which case, the guard would have done his best to extract a few piastres before allowing our luggage to pass; but he soon perceived by my companions' accent, that they were sons of the Holy City, consequently, that the case was hopeless. While standing here, Shaykh Hamid vaunted the strong walls and turrets of Yambu, which he said were superior to those of Jeddah †: they kept Saud, the Wahhabi, at bay in A.D. 1802, but would scarcely, I should say, resist

* Wassit means, "go, in the middle of the road;" Jannib, "keep clear of the sides." These words are fair specimens of how much may be said by two Arabic syllables. Ya hu (O, he) is an address common in Arabia as in Egypt, and Y'al Jammal (O camel-man) is perhaps a little more civil.

† The rivalry between the sons of the two Holy cities extends even to these parts: the Madanis contending for Yambu, the Meccans for Jeddah.

a field battery in A.D. 1853. The moon rose fair and clear, dazzling us with light as we emerged from the shadowy streets, and when we launched into the Desert the sweet air delightfully contrasted with the close offensive atmosphere of the town. My companions, as Arabs will do on such occasions, began to sing.

CHAP. XIII.

FROM YAMBU TO BIR ABBAS.

On the 18th July, about 7 P.M., we passed through the gate of Yambu, and took a due easterly course. Our route lay over the plain between the mountains of Radhawh on the left, and the sea on the right hand; the land was desert, that is to say, a hard level plain, strewed with rounded lumps of granite and greenstone schist, with here and there a dwarf acacia, and a tuft of rank camel grass. By the light of a glorious moon, nearly at the full, I was able to see the country tolerably well.

Our little party consisted of twelve camels, and we travelled in Indian file, head tied to tail, with but one outrider, Omar Effendi, whose rank required him to mount a dromedary with showy trappings. Immediately in front of me was Amm Jemal, whom I had to reprove for asking the boy Mahommed "Where have you picked up that Hindi, (Indian)?" "Are we, the Afghans, the Indian slayers*, become Indians?" I vociferated with indignation,

* Alluding to the celebrated mountain, the "Hindu-kush," whence the Afghans sallied forth to lay waste India.

and brought the thing home to his feelings, by asking him how he, an Arab, would like to be called an Egyptian,—a Fellah? The rest of the party was behind, sitting or dozing upon the rough platforms made by the lids of the two huge boxes slung to the sides of their camels. Only one old woman, El Sitt Maryam (the lady Mary), returning to El Medinah, her adopted country, after a visit to a sister at Cairo, allowed herself the luxury of a half dollar Shibriyah or cot, fastened cross-wise over the animal's load. Moreover, all the party, except Omar Effendi, in token of poverty, were dressed in the coarsest and dirtiest of clothes,—the general suit consisting of a shirt torn in divers places and a bit of rag wrapped round the head. They carried short chibouques without mouth-pieces, and tobacco-pouches of greasy leather. Though the country hereabouts is perfectly safe, all had their arms in readiness, and the unusual silence that succeeded to the singing, (even Saad the Devil held his tongue,) was sufficient to show how much they feared for themselves and their property. After a slow march of two hours facing the moon, we turned somewhat towards the N.E., and began to pass over undulating ground, in which a steady rise was perceptible. We arrived at the halting-place at three in the morning after a short march of about eight hours, during which we could not have passed over more than sixteen miles.* The camels were *nakh'd* †; the boxes were taken off and piled together as a precaution against invisible robbers; my little tent, the only one in the party, was pitched; we then spread our rugs upon the ground and lay down to sleep.

We arose at about 9 A. M., and after congratulating one another upon being once more in the "dear Desert," we proceeded in exhilarated mood to light the fire for pipes and breakfast. The meal, a biscuit, a little rice, and a cup of milkless tea, was soon dispatched, after which I proceeded to inspect our position.

About a mile to the westward lay the little village of Musahlah‡, a group of miserable clay hovels. On the south was a strip of bright blue

* Throughout this work I have estimated the pace of a Hejazi camel, laden and walking in caravan line, under ordinary circumstances, at two miles an hour. A sandy plain or a rocky pass might make a difference of half a mile each way, but not more.

† See Chap. VIII.

‡ The reader must be warned that these little villages in Arabia, as in Sindh and Belochistan, are continually changing their names, whilst the larger settlements always retain the same. The traveller, too, must beware of writing down the first answer he receives; in one of our maps a village on the Euphrates is gravely named "M'adri," ("Don't know").

sea, and all around, an iron plain producing naught but stones and grass-hoppers, bounded northward by a grisly wall of blackish rock. Here and there a shrub fit only for fuel, or a tuft of coarse grass, crisp with heat, met the eye. All was sun-parched; the furious heat from above was drying up the sap and juice of the land, as the shivering and quivering atmosphere showed; moreover the heavy dews of these regions, forming in large drops upon the plants and stones, concentrate the morning rays upon them like a system of burning-glasses. After making these few observations I followed the example of my companions, and went to sleep.

At 2 P.M. we were roused to a dinner as simple as the breakfast had been. Boiled rice with an abundance of clarified butter*, in which Easterns delight, some fragments of *Kahk*†, and stale bread‡ and a handful of stoned and pressed date-paste,

* Here called Samn, the Indian ghee.

† The "Kahk" in this country is a light and pleasant bread made of ground wheat, kneaded with milk, leavened with sour bean flour, and finally baked in an oven, not, as usual in the East, upon an iron plate. The Kahk of Egypt is a kind of cake.

‡ Stale unleavened bread is much relished by Easterns, who say that keeping it on journeys makes it sweet. To prevent its becoming mouldy, they cut it up into little bits, and, at the risk of hardening it to the consistence of wood, they dry it by exposure to the air.

called Ajwah, formed the *menu.* Our potations began before dinner with a vile-tasted but wholesome drink called Akit *; at the meal we drank leather-flavoured water, and ended with a large cup-ful of scalding tea. Enormous quantities of liquid were consumed, for the sun seemed to have got into our throats, and the perspiration trickled from us as after a shower of rain. Whilst we were eating, a Bedouin woman passed close by the tent, leading a flock of sheep and goats, seeing which I expressed a desire to drink milk. My companions sent by one of the camel-men a bit of bread, and asked in exchange for a cup-ful of "laban." † Thus I learned that the Arabs, even

* This Akit has different names in all parts of Arabia; even in El Hejaz it is known by the name of Mazir, as well as "Igt," (the corruption of Akit). When very sour, it is called "Saríbah," and when dried, without boiling, "Jamídah."

The Arabs make it by evaporating the serous part of the milk; the remainder is then formed into cakes or lumps with the hand, and spread upon hair cloth to dry. They eat it with clarified butter, and drink it melted in water. It is considered a cooling and refreshing beverage, but boasts few attractions to the stranger.

The Belochis and wild tribes of Sindhians call this preparation of milk "Krút," and make it in the same way as the Bedouins do.

† In Arabic and Hebrew milk; the Maltese give the word a very different signification, and the Egyptians confine their

in this corrupt region, still adhere to the meaningless custom of their ancestors, who chose to make the term "labbán" (milk-seller)* an opprobrium and a disgrace. Possibly the origin of the prejudice might be the recognising of a traveller's guest-right to call for milk gratis. However this may be, no one will in the present day sell this article of consumption, even at civilised Meccah, except Egyptians, a people supposed to be utterly without honour. As a general rule in the Hejaz, milk abounds in the spring, but at all other times of the year it is difficult to be procured. The Bedouin woman managed, however, to send me back a cup-ful.

At 3 P.M. we were ready to start, and all saw, with unspeakable gratification, a huge black

use of it to sour milk or curds—calling sweet milk "laban halíb," or simply "halíb."

* In a previous work (History of Sindh), I have remarked that there exists some curious similarity in language and customs between the Arabs and the various races occupying the broad ranges of hills that separate India from Persia. Amongst these must be numbered the prejudice alluded to above. Dr. Stocks, of Bombay, who travelled amongst and observed the Brahui and the Belochi nomads in the Peshin valley, informed me that, though they will give milk in exchange for other commodities, yet they consider it a disgrace to make money by it. This, methinks, is too conventional a point of honour to have sprung up spontaneously in two countries so distant, and apparently so unconnected.

nimbus rise from the shoulder of Mount Radhwah, and range itself, like a good genius, between us and our terrible foe, the sun. We hoped that it contained rain, but presently a blast of hot wind, like the breath of a volcano, blew over the plain, and the air was filled with particles of sand. This is the "dry storm" of Arabia; it appears to depend upon some electrical phenomena which it would be desirable to investigate.* When we had loaded and mounted, my coachmen, two in number, came up to the shugduf and demanded "bakhshish," which, it appears, they are now in the habit of doing each time the traveller starts. I was at first surprised to find the word here, but after a few days of Bedouin society, my wonder diminished. The men were Beni-Harb of the great Hejazi tribe, which has kept its blood pure for the last thirteen centuries,—how much more we know not,—but they had been corrupted by intercourse with pilgrims, retaining none of their ancestral qualities but greed of gain, revengefulness, pugnacity, and a frantic kind of bravery, displayed on rare occasions. Their nobility, however, did not prevent my quoting the Prophet's saying, "Of a

* At Aden, as well as in Sindh, these dry storms abound, and there the work of meteorological investigation would be easier than in El Hejaz.

truth, the worst names among the Arabs are the Beni-Kalb and the Beni-Harb *," whilst I taunted them severely with their resemblance to the Fellahs of Egypt. They would have resented this with asperity, had it proceeded from their own people, but the Turkish pilgrim — the character in which they knew me, despite my Arab dress — is a privileged person. Their outer man was contemptible; small chocolate-coloured beings, stunted and thin, with mops of coarse bushy hair burned brown by the sun, straggling beards, vicious eyes, frowning brows, screaming voices, and well-made, but attenuated, limbs. On their heads were *kufiyahs* (kerchiefs) in the last stage of wear; a tattered shirt, indigo-dyed, and girt with a bit of common rope, composed their brief clothing; and their feet were protected from the stones by soles of thick leather, kept in place by narrow thongs tied to the ancle. Both were armed, one with a matchlock, and a *Shintiyan* † in a leathern scabbard, slung over the

* "Beni-Kalb," (or Juhaynah, Chap. X.), would mean the "dogs'-sons"—"Beni-Harb," the "sons of fight."

† The Shintiyan is the common sword-blade of the Bedouins; in Western Arabia, it is called Majar (from the Magyars?), and is said to be of German manufacture. Good old weapons of the proper curve, marked like Andrew Feraras with a certain number of lines down their length, will fetch, even in Arabia, from 7*l.* to 8*l.* The modern and cheap ones cost about 10*s.*

shoulder, the other with a *nebút*, and both showed at the waist the Arab's invariable companion, the *Jambiyah* (dagger). These ragged fellows, however, had their pride. They would eat with me, and not disdain, like certain self-styled Caballeros, to ask for more, but of work they would do none. No promise of "bakhshish," potent as the spell of that word is, would induce them to assist in pitching my tent; they even expected Shaykh Nur to cook for them, and I had almost to use violence, for even the just excuse of a sore foot was insufficient to procure the privilege of mounting the shugduf, while the camel was sitting. It was, they said, the custom of the country from time immemorial to use a ladder when legs would not act. I agreed with them, but objected that I had no ladder. At last, wearied with their thickheadedness, I snatched the camel's string, and by main force made him kneel.

Our party was now a strong one. We had

Excellent weapons abound in this country, the reason being, that there is a perpetual demand for them, and when once purchased, they become heir-looms in the family. I have heard that when the Beni Bu Ali tribe, near Ras el Khaymah, was defeated with slaughter by Sir Lionel Smith's expedition, the victors found many valuable old European blades in the hands of the slain.

about 200 camels carrying grain, attended by their proprietors, truculent looking as the contrabandists of the Pyrenees. The escort was composed of seven Irregular Turkish cavalry, tolerably mounted, and supplied each with an armoury in epitome. They were privily derided by our party, who, being Arabs, had a sneaking fondness for the Bedouins, however loth they might be to see them amongst the boxes.

For three hours we travelled in a south-easterly direction upon a hard plain and a sandy flat, on which several waters from the highlands find a passage to the sea westward. Gradually we were siding towards the mountains, and at sunset I observed that we had sensibly neared them. We dismounted for a short halt, and, strangers being present, my companions said their prayers before sitting down to smoke—a pious exercise in which they did not engage for three days afterwards, when they met certain acquaintances at El Hamra. As evening came on, we emerged from a scent of acacias and tamarisk and turned due east, traversing an open country with a perceptible rise. Scarcely was it dark before the cry of "Harámi" (thieves) rose loud in the rear, causing such confusion as one may see in a boat in the Bay of Naples when suddenly neared by a water-spout. All the camel-men brandished their huge staves, and rushed back vociferating in the direction of the robbers. They were followed by all the horsemen, and truly, had the thieves possessed the usual acuteness of the profession, they might have driven off the camels in our van with safety and convenience.* But these contemptible beings were only half a dozen in number, and they had lighted their matchlocks, which drew a bullet or two in their direction, whereupon they ran away. This incident aroused no inconsiderable excitement, for it seemed ominous of worse things about to happen to us when entangled in the hills, and the faces of my companions, perfect barometers of fair and foul tidings, fell to zero. For nine hours we journeyed through a brilliant moonlight, and as the first grey streak appeared in the Eastern sky we entered a scanty "*misyal*,"† or *fiumara*, strewed with pebbles

* The way of carrying off a camel in this country is to loosen him, and then to hang on heavily to his tail, which causes him to start at full gallop.

† The Arabic misyal, masyal, masil, or masilah, is the Indian nullah and the Sicilian "fiumara," a hill water-course, which rolls a torrent during and after rain, and is either partially or wholly dry at other seasons,—the stream flowing slowly underground. In England wo want the feature, and

and rounded stones, about half a mile in breadth, and flanked by almost perpendicular hills of primitive formation. I began by asking the names of peaks and other remarkable spots, when I found that a folio volume would not contain a three months' collection*: every hill and dale, flat, valley, and water-course here has its proper name or rather names. The ingenuity shown by the Bedouins in distinguishing between localities the most similar, is the result of a high organisation of the perceptive faculties, perfected by the practice of observing a recurrence of landscape features few in number and varying but little amongst themselves. After travelling two hours up this torrent bed, winding in an easterly direction, and crossing some "*Harrah*," or ridges of rock, and "*Ria*,"

therefore there is no single word to express it. Our "river" is an imperfect way of conveying the idea.

* Generalisation is not the forte of the Arabic language. "El Kulzum" (the Red Sea), for instance, will be unintelligible to the native of Jeddah; call it the Sea of Jeddah, and you at once explain yourself; so the Bedouins will have names for each separate part, but no single one to express the whole. This might be explained by their ignorance of any thing but details. The same thing is observable, however, in the writings of the Arabian geographers when they come to treat of the objects near home.

steep descents*, we found ourselves at 8 A. M., after a march of about thirty four miles, at Bir Said (Said's well), our destination.

I had been led to expect a pastoral scene, wild flowers, flocks and flowing waters at the "well;" so I looked with a jaundiced eye upon a deep hole full of slightly brackish water dug in a tamped hollow—a kind of punch-bowl with granite walls, upon whose grim surface a few thorns of passing hardihood braved the sun for a season. Not a house was in sight—it was as barren and desolate a spot as the sun ever "viewed in his wide career." But this is what the Arabian traveller must expect. He is to traverse, for instance, the Wady El Ward—the vale of flowers; he indulges in sweet recollections of Indian lakes beautiful with the lotus, and Persian plains upon which narcissus is the meanest of grasses; he sees a plain like tamp-work, where knobs of granite act daisies, and at every fifty yards some hapless bud or blossom dying of inanition among the stones.

The sun scorched our feet as we planted the

* About the classic "Harrah," I shall have more to say at a future time. The word "Ria" in literal and in vulgar Arabic is almost synonymous with Akabah, a steep descent, a path between hills or a mountain road.

tent, and, after drinking our breakfast, we passed the usual day of perspiration and semi-lethargy. In discomfort man naturally hails a change, even though it be one from bad to worse. When our enemy began slanting towards the west, we felt ready enough to proceed on our journey. The camels were laden shortly after 3 P.M., and we started with water jars in our hands through a storm of simoom.

We travelled five hours in a north-easterly course up a diagonal valley *, through a country fantastic in its desolation—a mass of huge hills, barren plains, and desert vales. Even the sturdy acacias here failed, and in some places the camel grass could not find earth enough to take root in. The road wound among mountains, rocks and hills of granite, over broken ground, flanked by huge blocks and boulders, piled up as if man's art had aided nature to disfigure herself. Vast clefts seamed like scars the hideous face of earth; here they widened into dark caves, there they were choked up with

* Valleys may be divided into three kinds. 1. Longitudinal, *i. e.* parallel to the axis of their ridges; 2. Transversal or perpendicular to the same; and, 3. Diagonal, which form an acute or an obtuse angle with the main chain of mountains.

glistening drift sand. Not a bird or a beast was to be seen or heard; their presence would have argued the vicinity of water, and though my companions opined that Bedouins were lurking among the rocks, I decided that these Bedouins were the creatures of their fears. Above, a sky like polished blue steel with a tremendous blaze of yellow light glared upon us without the thinnest veil of mist cloud. The distant prospect, indeed, was more attractive than the near view, because it borrowed a bright azure tinge from the intervening atmosphere; but the jagged peaks and the perpendicular streaks of shadow down the flanks of the mountainous background showed that no change for the better was yet in store for us.

Between 10 and 11 P.M., we reached human habitations—a phenomenon unseen since we left Musahhal — in the long straggling village called El Hamra, from the redness of the sands near which it is built, or El Wasitah, the "half-way" village, because it is the middle station between Yambu and El Medinah. It is therefore considerably out of place in Burckhardt's map, and those who copy from him make it about half-way nearer the sea-port than it really is. We wandered about nearly an hour in search of an encamping place, for the surly villagers ordered us off every flatter bit of ground, without, however, deigning to show us where our jaded beasts might rest. At last, after much wrangling, we found the usual spot; the camels were unloaded, the boxes and baggage were disposed in a circle for greater security against the petty pilferers in which this part of the road abounds, and my companions spread their rugs so as to sleep upon their valuables. I was invited to follow the general example, but I absolutely declined the vicinity of so many steaming and snoring fellow-travellers Some wonder was excited by the Afghan Haji's obstinacy and recklessness; but resistance to these people is sometimes *bien placé*, and a man from Cabool is allowed to say and to do strange things. In answer to their warnings of nightly peril I placed a drawn sword by my side* and a cocked pistol under my pillow; the saddle-bag, a carpet spread upon the cool loose sand, formed by no means an uncomfortable couch, and upon it I enjoyed a sound sleep till day-break.

* This act, by the bye, I afterwards learned to be a greater act of imprudence than the sleeping alone. Nothing renders the Arab thief so active as the chance of stealing a good weapon.

Rising at dawn, I proceeded to visit the village. It is built upon a narrow shelf at the top of a precipitous hill to the North, and on the South runs a sandy Fiumara about half a mile broad. On all sides are rocks and mountains rough and stony; so you find yourself in another of those punch-bowls which the Arabs seem to consider choice sites for settlements.* The fiumara, which hereabouts is very winding, threads the high grounds all the way down from the plateau of El Medinah, and during the rainy season it becomes a raging torrent, carrying westwards to the Red Sea the drainage of a hundred hills. Water of good quality is readily found in it by digging a few feet below the surface at the angles where the stream as it runs forms the deepest hollows, and in some places the stony sides give out bubbling springs.†

El Hamra itself is a collection of stunted houses

* Probably, because water is usually found in such places. In the wild parts of the country, wells are generally protected by some fortified building, for men consider themselves safe from an enemy until their supply of water is cut off.

† Near El Hamra, at the base of the southern hills, within fire of the forts, there is a fine spring of sweet water. All such fountains are much prized by the people, who call them "rock-water," and attribute to them tonic and digestive virtues.

or rather hovels, made of unbaked brick and mud, roofed over with palm leaves, and pierced with air-holes, which occasionally boast a bit of plank for a shutter. It appears thickly populated in the parts where the walls are standing, but, like all settlements in El Hejaz *, it abounds in ruins. It is well supplied with provisions, which are here cheaper than at El Medinah,—a circumstance that induced Saad the Devil to overload his hapless camel with a sack of wheat. In the village are a few shops where grain, huge plantains, ready-made bread, rice, clarified butter, and other edibles are to be purchased. Palm orchards of considerable extent supply it with dates. The bazaar is, like the generality of such places in Eastern villages, a long lane, here covered with matting, there open to the sun, and the streets—if they may be so called—though narrow are full of dust and glare. Near the en-

* As far as I could discover, the reason of the ruinous state of the country at present is the effect of the old Wahhabi and Egyptian wars in the early part of the present century, and the misrule of the Turks. In Arabia the depopulation of a village or a district is not to be remedied, as in other countries, by an influx of strangers; the land still belongs to the survivors of the tribe, and trespass would be visited with a bloody revenge.

camping ground of caravans is a fort for the officer commanding a troop of Albanian cavalry, whose duty it is to defend the village*, to hold the country, and to escort merchant travellers. The building consists of an outer wall of hewn stone, loopholed for musketry, and surmounted by "*Shararif*," "*remparts coquets*," about as useful against artillery as the sugar gallery round a twelfth-cake. Nothing would be easier than to take the place: a false attack would draw off the attention of the defenders, who in these latitudes know nothing of sentry-duty, whilst scaling-ladders or a bag full of powder would command a ready entrance into the other side. Around the El Hamra fort are clusters of palm-leaf huts, where the soldiery lounge and smoke, and near it the usual coffee-house, a shed kept by an Albanian. These places are frequented probably on account of the intense heat inside the fort.

We passed a comfortless day at the "Red village." Large flocks of sheep and goats were

* Without these forts the Turks, at least so said my companions, could never hold the country against the Bedouins. There is a little *amour propre* in the assertion, but upon the whole it is true. There are no Mohammed Alis, Jezzárs, and Ibrahim Pachas in these days.

being driven in and out of the place, but their surly shepherds would give no milk, even in exchange for bread and meat. The morning was spent in watching certain Bedouins, who, matchlock in hand, had climbed the hills in pursuit of a troop of cranes — not one bird was hit of the many fired at — a circumstance which did not say much for the vaunted marksmanship of the savages. Before breakfast I bought a moderately sized sheep for a dollar. Shaykh Hamid "*halâled*" * it, according to rule, and my companions soon prepared a feast of boiled mutton. But that sheep proved a "bone of contention." The boy Mohammed had, in a fit of economy, sold its head to a Bedouin for three piastres, and the others, disappointed in their anticipations of haggis, lost temper. With the "Devil's" voluble tongue and impudent countenance in the van, they opened such a volley of raillery and sarcasm upon the young "tripe-seller," that he in his turn became excited — furious; I had some difficulty to keep the peace, for it did not suit my interests that they should quarrel. But to do

* To "*halál*" is to kill an animal according to Moslem rites: a word is wanted to express the act, and we cannot do better than to borrow it from the people to whom the practice belongs.

the Arabs justice, nothing is easier for a man who knows them than to work upon their good feelings. "He is a stranger in your country—a guest!" acted as a charm; they listened patiently to Mohammed's gross abuse, only promising to answer him when in *his* land, that is to say, near Meccah. But what especially soured our day was the report that Saad, the great robber-chief, and his brother were in the field; consequently that our march would be delayed for some time: every half-hour some fresh tattle from the camp or the coffee-house added fuel to the fire of our impatience.

A few particulars about this Schinderhannes of El Hejaz may not be unacceptable. He is the chief of the Sumaydat and the Mahamid, two influential sub-families of the Hamidah, the principal family of the Beni-Harb tribe of Bedouins. He therefore aspired to rule all the Hamidah, and through them the Beni-Harb, in which case he would have been, *de facto*, monarch of the Holy Land. But the Sherif of Meccah, and Ahmed Pacha, the Turkish governor of the chief city, for some political reason degraded him, and raised up a rival in the person of Shaykh Fahd, another ruffian of a similar stamp, who calls himself chief of the Beni-

Amr, the third sub-family of the Hanidah family. Hence all kinds of confusion. Saad's people, who number it is said 5000, resent, with Arab asperity, the insult offered to their chief, and beat Fahd's, who do not amount to 800. Fahd supported by the government cuts off Saad's supplies. Both are equally wild and reckless, and nowhere doth the glorious goddess, Liberty, show a more brazen face than in this Eastern

> "Inviolate land of the brave and the free:"

both seize the opportunity of shooting troopers, of plundering travellers, and of closing the roads. This state of things continued till I left the Hejaz, when the Sherif of Meccah proposed, it was said, to take the field in person against the arch-robber. And, as will afterwards be seen in these pages, Saad, because the Pachas of El Medinah and of the Damascus caravan would not guarantee his restitution to his former dignity, had the audacity to turn back the Sultan's Mahmal—the ensign of Imperial power,—and to shut the road against its *cortège.* That such vermin is allowed to exist proves the imbecility of the Turkish government. The Sultan pays pensions in corn and cloth to the very chiefs who arm their varlets against him, and the Pachas, after purloining all they can, hand over to their enemies the means of resistance. It is more than probable, that Abdul Mejid has never heard a word of truth concerning El Hejaz, and that fulsome courtiers persuade him that men there tremble at his name. His government, however, is desirous, if report speaks truth, of thrusting El Hejaz upon the Egyptian, who on his side would willingly pay a large sum to avert such a calamity. The Holy Land drains off Turkish gold and blood in abundance, and the lords of the country hold in it a contemptible position. If they catch a thief, they dare not hang him. They must pay black mail, and yet be shot at in every pass. They affect superiority over the Arabs, hate them, and are despised by them. Such in El Hejaz are the effects of the charter of Gulhaneh, a panacea like Holloway's pills for all the evils to which Turkish, Arab, Syrian, Greek, Egyptian, Persian, Armenian, Kurd, and Albanian flesh is heir to. Such the results of the Tanzimat, the silliest copy of Europe's folly — bureaucracy and centralisation — that the pen of empirical statecraft ever traced.* Under a strong handed and

* The greatest of all its errors was that of appointing to the provinces, instead of the single Pacha of the olden time, three

strong-hearted despotism, like Mohammed Ali's, El Hejaz, in one generation, might be purged of its pests. By a proper use of the blood feud, by vigorously supporting the weaker against the stronger classes, by regularly defeating every Bedouin who earned a name for himself, and, above all, by the exercise of unsparing, unflinching, justice*, the few thousands of half-naked bandits, who now make the land a fighting field, would soon sink into utter insignificance. But to effect such end, the Turks require the old stratocracy, which, bloody as it was, worked with far less

different governors, civil, military, and fiscal, all depending upon the supreme council at Constantinople. Thus, each province has three plunderings instead of one, and its affairs are referred to a body that can take no interest in it.

* Ziyad ben Abihi was sent by El Muáwiah, the caliph, to reform Basrah, a den of thieves; he made a speech, noticed that he meant to rule with the sword, and advised all offenders to leave the city. The inhabitants were forbidden under pain of death to appear in the streets after evening prayers, and dispositions were made to secure the execution of the penalty. Two hundred persons were put to death by the patrol during the first night, only five during the second, and not a drop of blood was shed afterwards.

By similar severity, the French put an end to assassination at Naples, and the Austrians at Leghorn. We may deplore the necessity of having recourse to such means, but it is a silly practice to salve the wound which requires the knife.

misery than the charter and the new code. What Milton calls

> "The solid rule of civil government"

has done wonders for the race that nurtured and brought to perfection an idea spontaneous to their organisation. But the world has yet to learn that the admirable exotic will thrive amongst the country gentlemen of Monamotapa or the ragged nobility of El Hejaz. And it requires no prophetic eye to foresee the day when the Wahhabis or the Bedouins, rising *en masse*, will rid the land of its feeble conquerors.*

Saad, the old man of the mountains, was described to me as a little brown Bedouin, contemptible in appearance, but remarkable for courage and ready wit. He has a keen scent for treachery, and requires to keep it in exercise. A blood feud with Abdul Muttaleb, the present sherif of Meccah, who

* A weak monarch, a degenerate government, a state whose corruption is evidenced by moral decay, a revenue bolstered up by a system of treasury paper, which even the public offices discount at from three to six per cent., an army accustomed to be beaten, and disorganised provinces; these, together with the proceedings of a ruthless and advancing enemy, form the points of comparison between the Constantinople of the present day and the Byzantine metropolis 800 years ago. Fate has marked upon the Ottoman Empire in Europe "*delenda est:*" we are now witnessing the efforts of human energy and ingenuity to avert or to evade the fiat.

slew his nephew, and the hostility of several Sultans has rendered his life an eventful one. He lost all his teeth by poison, which would have killed him, had he not in mistake, after swallowing the potion, corrected it by drinking off a large pot full of clarified butter. Since that time he has lived entirely upon fruits, which he gathers for himself, and coffee which he prepares with his own hand. In Sultan Mohammed's time he received from Constantinople a gorgeous purse, which he was told to open himself, as it contained something for his private inspection. Suspecting treachery, he gave it for this purpose to a slave, bidding him carry it to some distance; the bearer was shot by a pistol cunningly fixed, like Rob Roy's, in the folds of the bag. But whether this well-known story be "true or only well found," it is certain that Shaykh Saad now fears the Turks, even "when they bring gifts." The Sultan sends, or is supposed to send him presents of fine horses, robes of honour, and a large quantity of grain. But the Shaykh, trusting to his hills rather than to steeds, sells them; he gives away the dresses to his slaves, and distributes the grain amongst his clansmen. Of his character men tell two tales; some praise his charity, and call him the friend of the poor, as certainly as he is a foe to the rich. Others on the contrary describe him as cruel, cold-blooded, and notably, even among Arabs, revengeful and avaricious. The truth probably lies between these two extremes, but I observed that those of my companions who spoke most highly of the robber chief when at a distance seemed to be in the *sudori freddi* whilst under the shadow of his hills.

El Hamra is the third station from El Medinah in the Darb Sultani—"Sultan's" or "High Road," the westerly line leading to Meccah along the sea coast. When the robbers permit, the pilgrims prefer this route to all others on account of its superior climate, the facility of procuring water and supplies, the vicinity of the sea, and the circumstance of its passing through "Bedr," the scene of the Prophet's principal military exploits. After mid-day, (on the 21st July,) when we had made up our minds that fate had determined we should halt at El Hamra, a caravan arrived from Meccah, and the new travellers had interest to procure an escort, and permission to proceed towards El Medinah without delay. The good news filled us with joy. A little after 4 P. M. we urged our panting camels over the fiery sands to join the Meccans, who were standing ready for the march, on the other side of the torrent bed, and at 5 we started in an easterly direction.

My companions had found friends and relations in the Meccan caravan,—the boy Mohammed's elder brother, about whom more anon, was of the number;—they were full of news and excitement. At sunset they prayed with unction: even Saad and Hamid had not the face to sit their camels during the halt, when all around were washing, sanding themselves *, and busy with their devotions. We then ate our suppers, remounted, and started once more. Shortly after night set in, we came to a sudden halt. A dozen different reports arose to account for this circumstance, which was occasioned by a band of Bedouins, who had manned a gorge, and sent forward a "parliamentary" ordering us forthwith to stop. They at first demanded money to let us pass; but at last, hearing that we were sons of the Holy cities, they granted us transit on the sole condition that the military,— whom they, like Irish peasants, hate

* When water cannot be obtained for ablution before prayers, Moslems clap the palms of their hand upon the sand, and draw them down the face and both fore-arms. This operation, which is performed once or twice—it varies in different schools—is called Tayammum.

and fear,—should return to whence they came. Upon this, our escort, 200 men, wheeled their horses round and galloped back to their barracks. We moved onwards, without, however, seeing any robbers; my camel-man pointed out their haunts, and showed me a small bird hovering over a place where he supposed water trickled from the rock. The fellow had attempted a sneer at my expense when the fray was impending. "Why don't you load your pistols, Effendi," he cried, "and get out of your litter, and show fight?" "Because," I replied as loudly, "in my country, when dogs run at us, we thrash them with sticks." This stopped Mansúr's mouth for a time, but he and I were never friends. Like the lowest orders of Orientals he required to be ill-treated; gentleness and condescension he seemed to consider a proof of cowardice or of imbecility. I began with kindness, but was soon compelled to use hard words at first, and then threats, which, though he heard them with frowns and mutterings, produced manifest symptoms of improvement.

> "Oignez vilain, il vous poindra!
> "Poignez vilain, il vous oindra!"

says the old French proverb, and the axiom is more valuable in the East even than in the West.

Our night's journey had no other incident. We travelled over rising ground with the moon full in our faces, and about midnight passed through another long straggling line of villages, called Jadaydeh*, or El Khayf.† The principal part of it lies on the left of the road going to El Medinah; it has a fort like that of El Hamra, springs of tolerable drinking water, a Nakhil or date ground, and a celebrated (dead) saint, Abd el Rahim el Burai. A little beyond it lies the Bughaz‡, or defile, where in A.D. 1811 Tussun Bey and his 8000 Turks were totally defeated by 25,000 Harbi Bedouins and Wahhabis.§ This is a famous attacking point of

* I write this word as my companions pronounced it. Burckhardt similarly gives it "Djedeyde," and Ali Bey "Djideïda." Giovanni Finati wrongly calls the place "Jedeed Bughaz," which Mr. Bankes, his editor, rightly translates the "new opening or pass."

† El Khayf is a common name for places in this part of Arabia. The word literally means a declivity or a place built upon a declivity.

‡ Bughaz means in Turkish the fauces, the throat, and signifies also here a gorge, or a mountain pass. It is the word now commonly used in El Hejaz for the classical "nakb," or "mazik." Vincent (Periplus) errs in deriving the word from the Italian "Bocca."

§ Giovanni Finati, who was present at this hard-fought and disastrous field as a soldier in Tussun's army, gives a lively description of it in vol. i. of his work.

the Beni Harb. In former times both Jezzar Pacha, the celebrated "butcher" of Syria, and Abdullah Pacha of Damascus, were baffled at the gorge of Jadaydeh*; and this year the commander of the Syrian caravan, afraid of risking an attack at a place so ill-omened, avoided it by marching upon Meccah by the desert of Nejd. At 4 A.M., having travelled about twenty-four miles due east, we encamped at Bir Abbas.

* This Abdullah, Pacha of Damascus, led the caravan in A.D. 1756. When the Shaykhs of the Harb tribe came to receive their black-mail, he cut off their heads, and sent the trophies to Stamboul. During the next season the Harb were paralysed by the blow, but in the third year they levied 80,000 men, attacked the caravan, pillaged it, and slew every Turk that fell into their hands.

END OF THE FIRST VOLUME.

LONDON:
A. and G. A. SPOTTISWOODE,
New-street-Square.

CPSIA information can be obtained at www.ICGtesting.com
Printed in the USA
BVOW081548111012

302716BV00001B/1/P

9 781108 041980